Praise for *Building the Agile Business through Digital Transformation*

'Whatever your business, the prospect of staying ahead in digital transformation is daunting. Neil Perkin and Peter Abraham have created an outstandingly researched guide that anyone can use to lead their own transformation.' **Bruce Daisley, VP EMEA, Twitter**

'Packed full of insights, actionable ideas and other people's experiences, a toolkit to build on no matter where you sit in an organization or the stage of change you're at.' **Sean Cornwell, Chief Digital Officer, Travelex**

'This is the handbook that I wish I had written. A must-read for organizations going through digital transformation... It cuts through the hype and buzzwords into simple, practical insights that all of us can learn from and apply.' **Marco Ryan, Chief Digital Officer, Wärtsilä Corporation**

'A fantastic guide to conquering the challenges of continuous and accelerating change in today's digital world. Neil Perkin and Peter Abraham are masters of agile business transformation, and they've bottled their experience and wisdom into a highly actionable book. A must-read for modern leadership.' **Scott Brinker, Author, *Hacking Marketing***

'An essential and comprehensive guide for those leading digital transformation in their business or wanting to truly understand the impact of digital on modern leadership practice.' **Louise Howells, Global Head of Leadership Development, TUI**

'Neil Perkin and Peter Abraham are one of the best choices to help anyone respond to the challenges of digital transformation – and their book is a veritable gold mine as they share dozens of bottom lines and powerful stories with the reader. Read this book to not just innovate but to transform your business!' **Gerd Leonhard, Futurist, and Author, *Technology vs Humanity***

'Reads like a field guide for digital transformation. Full of actionable insights, frameworks and practical advice for any organization preparing for a digital-empowered world.' **Ben Malbon, Senior Director, Google**

'*Building the Agile Business through Digital Transformation* is the definitive guide for every executive and intrapreneur looking to navigate the exponential changes that every company must deal with or succumb to... A practical how-to you will refer to again and again, it is expansive but not exhausting. With meticulously researched ideas and insights that provide frameworks for understanding why change is both necessary and hard, it's the handbook you need to help you create the company you always wished you worked at.' **Faris Yakob, Founder, Genius Steals, and Author, *Paid Attention***

'This is an important book. A lot has been written about various aspects of agile, but nowhere else have I seen the thinking and practice brought to light so intelligently and comprehensively as here.' **Ashley Friedlein, Founder, Econsultancy**

'In times of rapid change, evolving with the new rules of consumer engagement and leveraging digital channels is now a must for every business in every sector. This book clearly distils key insights, strategies, examples and advice – providing the tools for anyone wanting to grow, advance and transform their business.' **Jeremy Willmott, Director, Group Consumer Engagement**

'Pragmatic, yet ruthlessly visionary, this fast-paced book is a wide-ranging and generously referenced handbook. Ideal both as a c-suite primer and as a ready-reference for practitioners, this is a triumph of distillation by two of our sector's pioneers.' **Ian Jindal, Leadership and Transformation in Multichannel Retail and Ecommerce**

'Disruption is all about mindset. Dealing with uncertainty is a challenge leaders need to integrate into their modus operandi. *Building the Agile Business through Digital Transformation* will help you unlock a treasure.' **Arjen van Berkum, Chief Disruption Officer and Entrepreneur**

Building the Agile Business through Digital Transformation

Neil Perkin

Peter Abraham

First published in Great Britain and the United States in 2017 by Kogan Page Limited

2nd Floor, 45 Gee Street
London
EC1V 3RS
United Kingdom

c/o Martin P Hill Consulting
122 W 27th St, 10th Floor
New York, NY 10001
USA

4737/23 Ansari Road
Daryaganj
New Delhi 110002
India

www.koganpage.com

ISBN 978 0 7494 8039 4
E-ISBN 978 0 7494 8040 0

British Library Cataloguing-in-Publication Data

A CIP record for this book is available from the British Library.

Library of Congress Cataloging-in-Publication Data

Names: Perkin, Neil, author. | Abraham, Peter, 1960- author.
Title: Building the agile business through digital transformation / Neil Perkin, Peter Abraham.
Description: 1st Edition. | New York : Kogan Page Ltd, [2017] | Includes bibliographical references and index.
Identifiers: LCCN 2017000808 (print) | LCCN 2017009073 (ebook) | ISBN 9780749480394 (alk. paper) | ISBN 9780749480400 (ebook)
Subjects: LCSH: Business enterprises–Technological innovations. | Strategic planning. | Creative ability in business.
Classification: LCC HD45 .P4177 2017 (print) | LCC HD45 (ebook) | DDC 658.4/06–dc23

Typeset by Integra Software Services, Pondicherry
Print production managed by Jellyfish
Printed and bound by CPI Group (UK) Ltd, Croydon, CR0 4YY

CONTENTS

ACKNOWLEDGEMENTS

This book would not have been possible without the support, understanding and patience of our contributors, interviewees, co-conspirators, and publishers. We are particularly grateful to Russell Davies, Faris Yakob, Gareth Kay, Marco Ryan, Duncan Hammond, Eva Appelbaum, Gerd Leonhard, John Coleman for contributing insight from their personal experience directly to the book. We owe a big thanks to all those who provided inspiration and insight through sharing their thinking in interviews or via their writing, blogs and social media, most notably: John Willshire, Tim Kastelle, Kevin Kelly, Mark Raheja, Tracey Follows, Bud Caddell, Mel Exon, Ben Malbon, Tim Malbon, Simon Wardley, Aaron Dignan, David Carr, Adam Morgan, Tom Goodwin, Antony Mayfield, Toby Barnes, Scott Brinker, Anjali Ramachandran, Mike Bracken, Dave Snowden, Victor Newman, Matt Edgar, Paul Graham, Brian Solis, Martin Bailie, John Battelle, Emily Webber, Tom Loosemore, Noah Brier, Scott Gallacher, Gemma Greaves, Charles Leadbetter, Michael Sahota, Jason Fried, Ben Thompson, Steven Anderson, Jonathan Lovatt-Young, James Haycock, John Kotter, Stewart Brand, Charles Duhigg, Rita Gunther MacGrath, Marc Andreesen, Clay Christensen, Ray Kurzweil, Charles Handy, Robert Coram, Steven Johnson, Atul Gawande, Eric Ries, Jim Collins, Carol Dweck, Steve Blank, Dave McClure, Roger Martin, Richard Rumelt, Sir Laurence Freedman, Amy Edmonson, Dan Pink, Ben Horowitz, Simon Sinek, Laszlo Bock, Caroline Webb, Ashley Friedlein, Tim Harford, Ben Salmon, Seth Godin, BJ Gallagher Hateley, Warren H Schmidt, Michael Crowe, David Armano, Mirage Islam, Chip Heath, Dan Heath, Ben Pask, Nir Eyal, Frederic Lloux. We thank Kogan Page for providing the opportunity to publish what we've learnt in the hope others will gain some additional insight. We thank our families for allowing us the time and providing their patience. We know we have missed a few people out along the way and we hope they accept our apology for that here.

PART ONE
The digital-native organization

In this introductory Part we set the context for digital transformation, define the key characteristics of a digital-native organization, make the case for why these characteristics are necessary, and discuss some of the key barriers to change, particularly within large organizations.

INTRODUCTION

Change is the process by which the future invades our lives.

Alvin Toffler[1]

In the contemporary business environment, the ability to be a genuinely agile company, and one that is native to the digitally empowered world in which we all live and operate has become not only a driver of competitive advantage and success, but critical for business survival.

It was researcher Marc Prensky who, in 2001, originated the term 'digital native' (Prensky, 2001)[2] as a way to describe people who were born after 1980 and whose lives have been characterized by access to networked digital technologies having grown up never knowing a way of life other than one mediated by digital.

Digital immigrants on the other hand, may be quite sophisticated in their use of such technologies but grew up in an analog world and so their experience is typically characterized by less familiarity with the digital environment.

In a similar way, the digital native organization might be considered to be one that has grown up in, and has been very much shaped by, a digitally empowered world. As such, their view on the world is not tainted by legacy technologies, thinking, culture, strategies, or approaches. While some organizations have proved to be very adept at transforming for the radically different environment in which they find themselves, this distinction is an important one since just about every area of every business (including customer interactions and expectations, operational efficiency and productivity, marketing and communications, sales, logistics and distribution) has been significantly changed by the impact of digital technologies.

Digital-native organizations may have originated more naturally from the technology sector, but they now stretch across the widest range of industries from retail to logistics to marketing to automotive. Yet what they hold in common is a natural, inherent ability to take a different view on the world and the competitive markets in which they operate, to take an often contrasting approach to traditional ways of solving problems, and even to have a different 'feel' to the values and organizational culture that they embrace. These are capabilities, approaches, processes and cultures that are informed by the networked, technology-centric world in which we live, but it is also a shift in mindset. It is as much about the behaviours of individuals and members of the team as it is the technology or digital solutions they are providing.

In the same way as people's early experience helps shape them for the rest of their lives, so companies that are digital immigrants are required to unravel a lot of outmoded assumptions, ways of doing things, and organizational habits in order to rebuild to become not only native speakers in the digital world, but native do-ers. We call it digital transformation, not digital adaptation because the change it requires impacts how things get done, how people work, the way in which the company is structured, and how people *feel* when they walk through the door in the morning. In other words the very fabric of how a company operates, behaves and does business.

This book is about transforming business to be fit for purpose in a digitally empowered world. Alongside our own insights, we have incorporated into the text some 'stories from the frontline' – contributions from other experienced practitioners of digital transformation bringing to life their observations about how to do it well. Our book seeks to capture, distill and define the key lessons that might be learned in order to help companies on their journey of transformation towards becoming true digital-native businesses.

Notes

1 Alvin Toffler, *Future Shock*, Introduction, Bantam Books (1990), ISBN-10: 0553277375, ISBN-13: 978-0553277371

2 Prensky, M (2001) Digital Natives, Digital Immigrants, [Online] http://www.marcprensky.com/writing/Prensky%20-%20Digital%20Natives,%20Digital%20Immigrants%20-%20Part1.pdf [last accessed 16 October 2016]

The key forces for change 01

There can surely be very few businesses that do not feel the vivid and urgent need to acquire a heightened level of agility in order to deliver against evolving customer expectation and in response to the challenges and opportunities brought by digital technologies. Technologies that are impacting right across the business from marketing and sales, to HR, finance and operations. Technologies that show little respect for existing business models, competitive advantage or established best practice. Technologies that are actively rewiring the way in which entire markets operate with unprecedented speed and comprehensiveness.

Processing capability has increased exponentially (an Apple iPhone 5 has almost three times the processing power of the 1985 Cray-2 supercomputer)[1] meaning that everyone has a supercomputer in their pocket with access to virtually universal information. And yet, while these changes may be driven by technology, they are very far from just being *about* technology. If we want to understand the real impact we need to consider the behaviours that surround the technology. Similarly, if we want to understand how best to respond to these challenges, we need to consider not only strategies but our approaches, thinking, mindset and behaviours.

In fact, in this book we are deliberately *not* focusing on technology. Our observation before writing it was that there were many discourses on the need for organizations to change in response the impact of digital, but very few that gave practical advice, models or methodologies for understanding what we need to actually *do* in response to this rapidly shifting environment. Consequently, we will focus on the 'how' of digital transformation rather than the 'why'. On the far reaching and comprehensive change that is needed in the very fabric of how we run our organizations. But it is also focused on the practical steps that organizations can take to embark on their own journey towards digital maturity.

But let us begin by summarizing some early context around the key driving forces that are shaping this urgent requirement. Organizations are currently sat at the centre of a perfect storm characterized by accelerating change, and rapidly shifting competitive, consumer and company contexts (Figure 1.1).

Figure 1.1 Characteristics of change

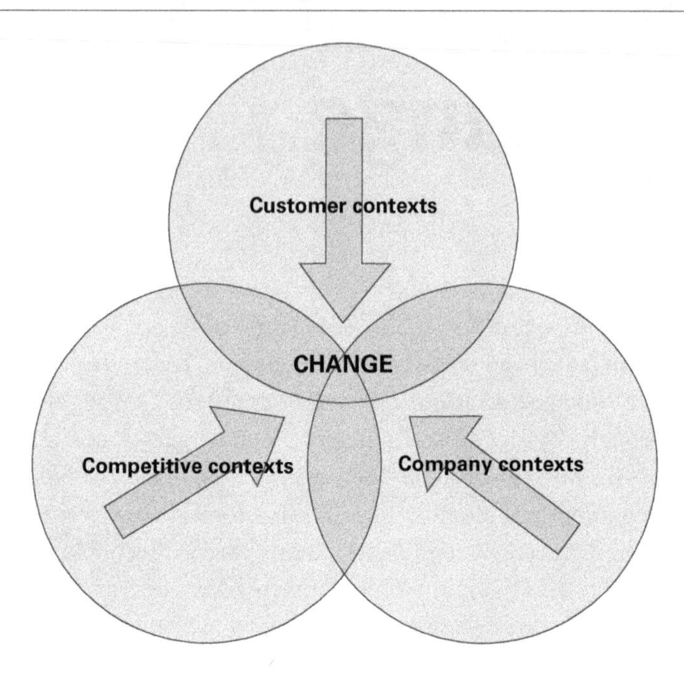

Relentless, accelerating change

In 2006 the world's most valuable companies by market capitalization were Exxon Mobile (oil), General Electric (conglomerate), Microsoft (tech), Citigroup (financial services), BP (oil), Royal Dutch Shell (oil). A decade later in 2016, that list is dominated by technology businesses, comprising Apple, Alphabet (the holding company that owns Google), Microsoft, Amazon, Exxon Mobile (the only non-tech company in the top six) and Facebook.

Change is not new. Progress has always been with us. Advancement is a given. But what digital has brought to just about every sector, industry and business is a transformed scale, scope and *pace* of change. Meaning that the required organizational response is not only wide, but deep and fundamental.

'Adapt or die' goes the mantra. The need to transform businesses to become more native for a digitally empowered world is not only urgent, but essential and inevitable. Those that are slow to transform will be left behind, disrupted and disintermediated.

As far back as 1938, Buckminster Fuller was talking about 'Ephemeralization', describing the trend for how technological advancement means doing *'more and more with less and less until eventually you can do everything with nothing'* (Fuller, 1973).[2] Joseph Schumpeter, the economist who taught at Harvard in the 1930s, described capitalism as an evolutionary process involving a 'gale of creative destruction' that sees new companies and industries continually emerge to remove or replace the old. But technology has brought a new urgency to this process.

Ray Kurzweil's renowned 2001 essay 'The Law of Accelerating Returns'[3] famously argues that technological change and therefore progress, evidenced by historical trajectory, is exponential rather than linear, and that breakthroughs spawned by technology will be increasingly common.

Research by Professor Richard Foster of Yale University found that the average lifespan of a company in the S&P 500 index has decreased from 61 years in 1958 to around 15 years today.[4] His estimation is that by 2027, more than three-quarters of the S&P 500 will be companies that we have not yet heard of.

Yet the picture is perhaps more nuanced than this headline finding suggests. Analysis done by Boston Consulting Group (Reeves and Pueschel, 2015)[5] that looked at the patterns of entry, growth and exit for 35,000 publicly listed companies in the United States since 1950 showed that over the long term company lifespans have indeed decreased (and mortality risk increased) yet in the more recent past they have plateaued. Research from the Santa Fe Institute ('The mortality of companies')[6] using a database of 25,000 American companies from 1950 to 2009 for example, pegged the typical half-life of a publicly traded company at around 10 years but found that the most common reason for a company to disappear is merger or acquisition.

So while mortality risk for businesses has increased over the long term, the true picture about the impact of accelerating change on businesses is more nuanced. High-profile examples of businesses that have failed to innovate successfully in the face of digital disruption (Kodak, Blockbuster, Nokia) encourage us to think of the impact of digital and accelerating technological change in terms of corporate fatality.

Yet while these examples represent perhaps the most acute result of this phenomenon, for most organizations the impact of accelerating change is likely to be reflected in multiple scenarios and challenges that the company will need to deal with, and all with multiple potential consequences. For example, by creating a significantly more volatile environment in which the company operates, unexpected new entrants to the sector, growing competition from all sides, rapid shifts in customer expectation, fundamental changes in operating relationships with customers, suppliers and partners, and accelerated changes in product or service propositions and lifecycles.

In response to relentless, accelerating change, a new heightened level of agility is not only desirable, but critical to survival. It has never been more important to determine a defined organizational response to the shifts in our three crucial contexts: competitive, consumer and company.

Transformed competitive contexts

With barriers to entry in just about every sector dramatically reducing through ever-cheaper, easier, more flexible and scalable access to cloud-based support and infrastructure services and markets, the threat from new, potentially disruptive entrants is concurrently increasing. And it is happening at an ever-faster pace.

Digital technologies have served to disrupt the power balance in markets between consumers and organizations. Digital and social platforms have brought with them the connected and empowered consumer, reducing the control that businesses have over their brand perception, and creating new ways to empower discovery, trial and adoption. Greater transparency in pricing has brought new downwards pressure on pricing towards commoditization of products and services. The integration of digital into operations and supply chain brings significant potential advantage in timescales, efficiencies or costs. The challenges for senior corporate leaders are not only numerous but varied, emergent and rapidly evolving.

Horizontal innovation (competition from anywhere)

IBM's 2015 global C-suite study[7] interviewed over 5,000 business leaders from more than 70 countries and from 21 industries. One of the most interesting findings focuses on so-called 'horizontal innovation' – the idea that where once it was comparatively easier for senior leaders to be able to anticipate where competition will come from, there is now a much greater risk from competition that is invisible until it is too late.

As new digitally empowered businesses scale rapidly in one sector, rewiring the value chain in a particular market through software, they are then able to more easily move horizontally into other sectors by reapplying their capability and expertise in new ways. The net effect is increasingly blurred boundaries between industries as sectors are brought together and potentially redefined. When the IBM survey asked senior leaders about the developments that they expect the next 'wave' to consist of, this industry convergence eclipsed other trends including rising cyber risk, the 'anywhere' workplace and the sharing economy.

As we will go on to discuss, digital is, of course, exceptionally adept at rewriting the rules of competitive advantage but when the potential is high for rapid disruption to come from anywhere, and disintermediation (the switching of, or reduction in, intermediaries between producers and consumers) is happening at pace, we need to reimagine our response and reorientate our organizations towards a new and consistently higher level of organizational agility.

The 'full stack startup'

Competitive threats from horizontal innovation may originate from anywhere of course, but one of the unique dynamics that digital has enabled is the increasing potential for disruption from a new breed of ambitious startups that have in their sights not just incumbent businesses but entire industries.

These are startups empowered through digital technology to operate at global scale, access the best talent, reduce communication costs and reach far broader audiences than was once possible.

Hal Varian, Google Chief Economist, talks of micro-multinational companies:

> *If the late 20th Century was the age of the multinational company, the early 21st will be the age of the micro-multinational: small companies that operate globally.*
>
> (Varian, 2011)[8]

Varian believes that just as in the 19th century (where the elements were standardized mechanical parts like wheels and gears) and the 20th century (internal combustion engines, electronics and, eventually, microchips) we live now in another era of combinatorial innovation.

Today, a large proportion of software development and innovation on the web involves connecting standardized components (including open source operating systems, servers, database management systems and languages such as Linux, Apache, MySQL, Python) in new ways. Not only are the building blocks of innovation readily accessible, but the barriers to entry have reduced dramatically through improved accessibility to support infrastructure and systems such as cloud computing, data, business, communication and content services.

As a consequence the pace of innovation has increased. The smallest company can access the kind of infrastructure, much of it accessible from a device in your hand, that was barely available to even the largest companies 15 years ago, compete for best people, work with global talent around the clock, capitalize on global variation in knowledge, skills and wages:

> *Innovation has always been stimulated by international trade, and now trade in knowledge and skills can take place far more easily than ever before.*
>
> (Varian, 2011)[9]

Renowned writer, technologist and the founding executive editor of *Wired*, Kevin Kelly talks about how it may feel as though many of the most significant digital innovations have already been developed over the past 30 years, yet we have barely begun:

> *... from our perspective now, the greatest online things of the first half of this century are all before us. All these miraculous inventions are waiting for that crazy, no-one-told-me-it-was-impossible visionary to start grabbing the low-hanging fruit.*
>
> (Kelly, 2014)[10]

With the kind of standardized component and infrastructure access that Hal Varian talked about, the potential for entrepreneurs, says Kelly, has never been greater. He describes how there has never been a better time 'in the whole history of the world' to invent something, to start something new. How there has never been a time:

> *... with more opportunities, more openings, lower barriers, higher benefit/risk ratios, better returns, greater upside, than now. Right now, this minute. This is the time that folks in the future will look back at and say, 'Oh to have been alive and well back then!'*
>
> (Kelly, 2014)

The phrase 'unicorns' has become a label (derived from the investment and VC community) used to denote startup businesses that are in rapid growth and that have acquired a valuation in excess of US$1 billion. A better descriptor perhaps is the 'full stack startup',[11] originated by internet entrepreneur and venture capitalist Chris Dixon to describe the new breed of company that is setting out to disrupt and rewire entire markets. Except the real disruptors might better be termed 'full stack stay-ups' rather than 'startups' owing to their innate ability to generate sustainable growth through continuous but rapid innovation.

Dixon believes that we are in what he calls the 'deployment phase' of the internet. Technological revolutions, he says, happen in two main phases: the installation phase and the deployment phase. The early stages of each revolution are typically characterized by a financial bubble that drives the installation of the new technology at an irrationally fast rate. The crash that inevitably follows is, in turn, followed by a recovery and then a protracted period of productive growth that 'deploys' the technology much more broadly throughout other industries and society as a whole.

If a company develops a new technology that is valuable to an industry, says Dixon, where once the expectation would be to license or sell the technology to existing companies in that industry, the new approach is to build a complete, end-to-end product or service (a 'full stack' approach) that bypasses existing companies:

> *The most interesting tech companies aren't trying to sell software to other companies. They are trying to reshape industries from top to bottom.*
>
> (Dixon, 2015)

So Buzzfeed is a media company in the same way that Netflix is a streaming movie company, or Uber a taxi company, or Tesla a car company. These are companies that have technology at their core. They can deliver improved product experience, circumvent cultural resistance to new technologies and capture a greater portion of the economic benefits.

It is a potent combination. With big ideas, grand ambitions, exceptional talent, unprecedented access to global markets and lower barriers to entry than ever before, the potential for disruption and horizontal innovation is writ large. A rolling survey conducted by CB Insights[12] was tracking 169 unicorn companies at time of writing, across sectors as diverse as hardware, retail, data, fintech, social, transportation, healthcare and media.

But while more renowned unicorns like AirBnB and Uber are visibly rewiring entire markets, a perhaps less immediately conspicuous but no less present danger comes from large corporates with broad product and service portfolios coming under attack from multiple startups. New competitive threats from young, early stage businesses that utilize disruptive business models and are empowered by digital to attack individual product areas or service offerings, threatening to 'unbundle'[13] incumbent businesses.

The shifting nature of advantage

Just about every organization is finding that navigating the ever-changing environment in which they find themselves is like riding a surfboard on a choppy sea of uncertainty. Yet for many, their approach to strategy has not changed.

We need a new kind of strategy for a new world. A strategy that is far more adaptive than the fixed, inflexible forms of strategy that are still prevalent in many businesses. A 'digitally native' strategy that is more suited to the fast-changing, technologically empowered markets that we now operate in.

Columbia Business School professor Rita Gunther McGrath (in *The End of Competitive Advantage*)[14] frames this as a change in the purpose of strategy from trying to secure sustainable competitive advantage to exploiting a series of transient competitive advantages that in themselves combine to form long-term advantage. McGrath based this assertion on research that looked at companies which had a market cap of over US$1 billion and that had, over the period 2000–09, sustained a net income growth of 5 per cent above global GDP. There were only 10 of these companies, but she looked in detail at the lessons from their strategies.

Drawn from that, McGrath developed a useful framework for a more agile organizational strategy that echoes many of the themes discussed in this book:

- **Continuous reconfiguration:** moving on from extreme restructuring programmes to a process of 'continuous morphing' that combines core stability in essentials like corporate vision, while enabling dynamism in operations, structures and execution. This is empowered through fluidity in the allocation of talent rather than narrowly defined roles.
- **Healthy disengagement:** rather than defending an advantage to the end, taking a more systematic, frequent, formal approach to disengagement, and feeding the learnings back into the business.
- **Resource allocation that supports agility:** key resources are managed under central control and not held hostage by local business units, resources are organized around opportunity rather than opportunities being squeezed into existing structures, access to assets and leveraging external capability being key, not necessarily needing to own or build everything yourself.

- **Innovation proficiency:** moving from episodic to continuous and systematic innovation, protected through governance and budgeting being separate from business as usual, dedicated resourcing, and a balanced approach of resource investment across core, growth and entirely new initiatives. Higher levels of experimentation and learning from failure encouraged.
- **Leadership:** promoting continual shifts with broader constituencies involved in the strategy process, talent directed towards seizing opportunity, and rather than seeking perfection, accepting of fast and roughly right.

We are at a watershed moment for organizational strategy. One where attachment to traditional, deeply ingrained approaches that seek to extract maximum value from sustainable competitive advantage for as long as possible, even when that competitive advantage is in decline, is becoming a significant barrier to progress. One where outmoded, inflexible, slow-moving systems, strategies and processes that are optimized over time around sustainable advantages are becoming a liability.

Much of this is not only about enabling companies to be more agile and flexible, but about moving away from a number of the things that create a great deal of demoralizing frustration among employees – the inflexible pursuit of legacy models, an episodic approach to innovation, narrow job roles, rigid planning processes, post strategic-review downsizing and so on. Instead, the continuous pursuit of new markets, new technologies, innovation and improved capability around a focused vision has the potential to be hugely energizing, motivating and inspiring for employees.

If navigating the current business and consumer environment is like riding a surfboard on a choppy sea of uncertainty, we need to learn how to surf the waves of opportunity. McGrath talks about how strategy and innovation have historically been thought of as two separate disciplines:

> *Strategy was all about finding a favorable position in a well-defined industry and then exploiting a long-term competitive advantage. Innovation was about creating new businesses and was seen as something separate from the business's core set of activities.*

The disparate fields of organizational change, strategy and innovation are all coming together, driven by the need for far greater adaptability in order to win in a world of transient competitive advantage. Every company now needs to think more like a startup. Today's digitally native organizations, for example, are making huge efforts to retain the culture and agility of a startup as they scale.

So what does this really mean in terms of organizational strategy? In June 2014, Boston Consulting Group revisited their classic growth share matrix. The matrix, originated by BCG founder Bruce Henderson 40 years ago, famously plots a product portfolio on a 2 × 2 against growth rate and market share, giving us categorizations like 'stars', 'problem child' (or 'question marks'), 'dogs' and 'cash cows', and is a key part of business school teaching on strategy.

Many large organizations have used its principles of mapping company competitiveness (share) against market attractiveness (growth) as the basis for investment and resourcing decisions. High share could result in sustainably superior returns and eventually cost-efficiencies driven by scale and experience, high growth indicated markets with the greatest leadership potential.

In the face of rapid change and uncertainty driven by (among other factors) technological impact, BCG now say that companies need to 'constantly renew their advantage, increasing the speed at which they shift resources among products and business units'. In addition, market share is no longer a direct predictor of sustained performance, with competitive advantage increasingly coming from other factors such as adaptability.

Their research, which mapped every US listed company to a quadrant on the matrix, found that companies circulated through the matrix quadrants faster than in previous years (comparing a five-year period 2008–12 to one from 1988–92). In fact, looking at some of the largest conglomerates, the average time any business unit spent in a quadrant was less than two years in 2012 (with only a few exceptionally stable industries seeing fewer disruptions).

There were also changes in the distribution of companies across the matrix, and a breakdown in the relationship between relative market share and sustained competitiveness. Cash cows generated a smaller share of total profits (25 per cent lower than in 1982), and were proportionately fewer, with the lifespan of this stage declining (by some 55 per cent in industries that saw faster matrix circulation).

Unsurprisingly, BCG go on to say that the matrix is still relevant, but needs to be applied with greater agility and a focus on 'strategic experimentation' to allow greater adaptability. This is likely to mean more experimentation in the question marks quadrant, run more quickly, economically and systematically in order to identify promising ones that can grow into stars. It is also likely to mean faster response to cashing out stars, retiring cows and maximizing what value they can from dogs.

Transformed consumer contexts

The power shift from organizations to consumers, and the greater transparency and democratization in product and service creation, development, marketing, sales and operation that has been fuelled by technological empowerment has brought new and challenging consumer contexts to many businesses.

As digital empowers ever-richer and more seamless interaction, customer expectations are dramatically increasing. As soon as we are spoiled by a seamlessly intuitive, smartly designed, on-demand customer experience like Amazon one-click or Prime, we want and expect everything to be like that. In their book *A Beautiful Constraint*,[15] Adam Morgan and Mark Barden neatly describe this phenomenon and the rise in 'unreasonable' levels of consumer expectation as 'Uber's Children'.

As more products become services, impatience with even the tiniest annoyances becomes a brand differentiator and the most exceptional (even if not directly related) customer experience the benchmark by which everything else is judged. If I can renew my car tax online so easily, why is it so cumbersome to change a standing order online with my bank? If I can see real-time how far my taxi driver is away from me, why am I waiting in at home not knowing when my package will arrive? If I can navigate seamlessly to immediately stream on-demand almost any piece of music that I want, why can't I do that with all forms of content?

So while service design has become a real differentiator and driver of advantage, the competitive context for brands has also become far broader, consumer expectations far more challenging to address, and the advantage of continually innovating around customer need never greater.

As Adam Morgan has pointed out, the unreasonable consumer is, in effect, asking businesses questions that challenge and propel brands and companies to greater heights and changing the face of entire categories in the process:

> *... if we don't ask propelling questions of ourselves, someone is going to ask them of us, someone with authority and legitimacy. It may be our largest or most influential customer, or our noisiest challenger, but if we don't anticipate this, by the time we hear them we will already be behind the curve. This is the corollary of the new.*
>
> (Morgan, 2015)[16]

As advantage increasingly resides in customer experience and usability, those businesses that have long been schooled in great service design and that can adapt rapidly to shifting consumer contexts will increasingly show the way. And as wave after wave of innovation hits customer interfaces (once desktop, and then mobile, now increasingly those mediated by artificial intelligence), this, and the market-beating competitive advantage that will be derived from investment in the smart application of new technologies, will increasingly separate the great from the simply good.

The 'gateway principle' and the customer interface battle

As technology exponentially advances, so the interfaces that we have with that technology advances and evolves with it. Ever-more sophisticated user interfaces enable the potential for more progressive user interaction and seamless user experience. Put simply, the way in which humans are interacting with technology, and the expectations that we have in terms of convenience, capability and ease of use, is shifting at pace alongside the development of that technology.

So text and keyboards are augmented with touch screens, voice activation, artificial intelligence, and eventually virtual and augmented reality. As this advances, it becomes essential for businesses to understand where the value lies, and how to best optimize for not only rapidly shifting customer interactions and expectations, but also behaviours. Underlying customer needs may change less than we think, but the behaviours that surround them and how we choose to fulfil those needs *do* change, and is ultimately a very real source of advantage or disadvantage. So while technology is important, understanding the underlying behaviours that surround it and how they change is even more so. As Henry Jenkins (Professor of Communication, Journalism and Cinematic Arts, University of Southern California) once said: 'Our focus should be not on emerging technologies but on emerging cultural practices'.[17]

Yet alongside the shifts in customer interfaces (and the rapidity of those shifts) there is another key dynamic which has become more important over time: who *owns* that customer interface or at least the data that comes from customer interaction. While it remains important to optimize for shifting customer touchpoints the dangers of digital disintermediation are never far away. Aggregators (like MoneySupermarket or ComparetheMarket) enable consumers to compare prices more easily but also then become the primary gateway for that market. Rather than go to multiple insurance providers for example, it is far easier and more convenient to use a comparison service, but as a consequence that service becomes the funnel through which customers are channelled to providers.

Similarly, ubiquitous digital services such as Google, Apple, Facebook and Amazon (so-called 'GAFA') are building ecosystems of digital touchpoints around users through which we are able to perform all manner of tasks. Leave a comment on a website? Easily login with Facebook. Find a restaurant nearby? Voice search on Google. Need a recipe? Ask Siri. Need that recipe to be read out to you as you cook? Ask Amazon's Alexa assistant via their Echo speaker.

The power in being the primary gateway, of course, is more customer data, which can in turn be leveraged to create more personalized digital experiences and generate revenue. The customer relationship with the service provider is now mediated through multiple service 'layers', all battling to be the customer interface.

As our use of smartphones matures, an increasing amount of interaction happens not direct with apps (where brands can own more of the interaction), but via search and the notifications layer, at the operating system level (where Apple or Google own more of the interaction). As GAFA invest more in AI-driven automation and services like Facebook M (in Messenger), Google Now, Apple Siri and Amazon Alexa, and these services are embedded and integrated into an increasing number of third-party applications, service providers become ever-more mediated.

It is, as Tom Goodwin, memorably describes it, like the 'thin internet': a 'more seamless, more pervasive, personal and even predictive' (Goodwin, 2014)[18] blanket spread thinner in more context specific layers across more devices. The battle is increasingly for the customer interface,[19] with the balance of power increasingly tilting towards a new breed of company that derives enormous value from software-driven services that are the gateway, and mediate between large (more often not owned) supply systems and consumers. Digital disintermediation is a continuous, ever-shifting danger.

Transformed company contexts

The Data Explosion

The exponential increase in the amount of data generated by the ever-growing volume of connected devices and services is not new news. Most organizations are awash with data. In 2010, Eric Schmidt famously described (at Google's Atmosphere Convention) how:

> *There were 5 Exabytes of information created between the dawn of civilization through 2003, but that much information is now created every 2 days.*[20]

EMC's Digital Universe Study in 2014[21] (using research conducted by IDC) predicted that with the ever-increasing number of connected people (believed to be almost 3.5 billion, or 46 per cent of the world population, at time of writing),[22] connected and increasingly smart devices and 'things', the 'digital universe' will grow by 40 per cent a year into the next decade, increasing from 4.4 zetabytes in 2013 to 44 zetabytes in 2020. In 2005, the digital universe was estimated to comprise 'only' 132 exabytes of data.

But the challenge of deriving value from it all remains very real. For all the talk of 'Big Data', most companies are struggling to handle, analyse and extract potentially valuable insights from the (comparatively small) amount of data they already have access to. An oft quoted finding from the 2012 EMC/IDC Digital Universe study revealed that less than 1 per cent of the world's data is actually analysed.[23]

Data may well be the new oil, but as one of the interviewees for this book said: 'Data is the new oil because it's toxic unless you refine it', a reference to the widely acknowledged originator of the metaphor Clive Humby (Founder and Chairman of well-known customer science business Dunnhumby) who described (to the Association of National Advertisers in 2006, written up by Michael Palmer)[24] how:

> *Data is the new oil. It's valuable, but if unrefined it cannot really be used. It has to be changed into gas, plastic, chemicals, etc to create a valuable entity that drives profitable activity; so must data be broken down, analyzed for it to have value.*

Gartner's model for maturity in data analytics[25] sees a progression of value (and also difficulty) that begins with the basic descriptive analytics (what happened), moves to diagnostic analytics (in which we understand why it happened), to predictive analytics (where we can predict what *will* happen), and eventually to prescriptive analytics (understanding how we can actually *make* it happen).

As simple information moves towards optimization, the opportunity for greater operational efficiency and benefit increases dramatically.

Everything becoming a service, and software 'eating the world'

As the internet becomes ever-more pervasive and is integrated into an increasing number of not just devices but also objects, an increasing number of products are morphing into services. As more things become connected, so the potential to augment product experience through service becomes much greater. So we have the connected car that enables voice-controlled access to a whole range of new services, the smart thermostat that I can access and control remotely via my smartphone, the album that is updated multiple times by the artist even after release.[26]

Where once products were released into the world and subsequent improvements would only come from new versions of that same product, now continuous augmentation, fixes and enhancements can happen in the same way that our smartphone operating system is continually updated.

As more products become services, the operational requirements on a business change significantly. Ubiquitous, always-on connection creates opportunities (and demands) for ongoing improvements and updates. Ongoing customer interaction generates the potential for enhanced service delivery through data collection, visualization, personalization and recommendation. Real-time data acquisition and aggregation allows for near real-time response, adjustment and adaptation. The product sits at the centre of a connected ecosystem of touchpoints and interactions, glued together by data and the single customer view, and blurring real-world with virtual world experiences.

Writing about the launch of a new Nike+ app, for example, Toby Barnes (Product Strategy Director at AKQA in Portland) has described[27] how transformative the app is not just to Nike's customer and product proposition, but to the business itself:

> *The app is a sharp point to a service. A service that involves physical stores, runs clubs, events, knitted products that are created as consumers design them, content strategies based on physical activities, non linear story telling and breaking org charts into atoms and networks.*
>
> (Barnes, 2016)

The proliferation of services in turn means that service design, adept collection, analysis and application of data, and seamless, exceptional customer experience become real product differentiators and sources of advantage. As that advantage increases, so does the importance, potential and power of software across just about every product category.

In a prophetic *Wall Street Journal* article authored in 2011, Marc Andreesen wrote about how more and more business problems start to look like software problems and why 'software is eating the world'.[28] As an increasing number of product areas become surrounded by service propositions, and an ever-growing number of industries, from travel to logistics, banking to healthcare, education to consumer packaged goods are remodelled by software, Marc Andreesen's prognosis is fast becoming reality.

As seamless integration of software with hardware and other physical and real-world product experience becomes ever-more critical to customer perception and advantage, many businesses across a broad range of sectors are needing to not only redesign product experiences, technology and support infrastructure, and operations, but learn a raft of new skills to equip themselves for a very different world.

From linear to networked dynamics

The digital age has brought with it an unprecedented level of connectedness at both an individual and an organizational level creating far greater opportunity for value to be derived less from linear, one-way relationships and increasingly from networked systems of customers, suppliers and partners, involving two-way value exchanges.

An increasing number of digital-native businesses are creating platforms that connect, facilitate and enable value creation and exchange that involve all parties. Think business models built on peer-to-peer. Or the so-called 'sharing economy' in which customers 'rent' usage of products rather than own them, facilitated through digitally enabled communities. Think open source models and ecosystems of external developers that create value for themselves but also the business, accessing data through APIs.

Think of networked approaches to supply chain management that now enable a move away from linear flows of information along the supply chain to a far more connected system and communication flow between key suppliers, secondary suppliers, manufacturing, distribution centres and retail, enabling better decisioning, a heightened level of responsiveness to change, and real-time visibility to demand, thereby reducing wastage and latency.

And also think of networks of external or remotely based talent or services that can be tapped into at short notice. When Nobel economist Ronald Coase wrote about why companies exist in 'The Nature of the Firm' in his classic 1937 economics article,[29] he described it as being to make it easier to coordinate, and lower the cost of, producing goods and services. Yet digital technologies are unbundling traditional aggregations of value, enabling a far more distributed approach to sourcing and accessing value, and reducing the transaction costs of utilizing flexible and scalable talent and services.

In the same way that technology has rebalanced the power relationship between companies and their customers, so the advent of ever-more accessible and more loosely coupled architectures of micro-services (cloud-based services accessed often through APIs or Application Programming Interfaces that enable remote access to data and services) is driving a move away from monolithic software to services that are far more flexible, agile and scalable. Hugely powerful software and services that were once expensive, complex and the domain of only those businesses that could invest heavily, are now accessible to the smallest startup. Powerful data sources that were once locked behind firewalls can now be accessed to drive new insights and power new services.

The transition from linear value chains to dynamic, networked ecosystems where data, information and value more readily flows between all parties in the system is one of the key business shifts of our time. Yet networked dynamics require new approaches, new partnerships and new levels of openness.

If we are to truly capitalize on this trend we need to change our understanding of how businesses can create and retain value in a digitally empowered world.

The heightened impact of talent

While having the best staff has always been central to business success, the whirlwind impact of technology has brought with it a stark amplification in the importance of talent. The potential for performance divergence between those companies that can attract and retain the best digital talent and those that can't has never been greater. Put simply, it has never been more critical to have the best people.

Digital technologies have shifted power towards individuals and small teams within companies who can create dramatic change through the origination *and* execution of exceptional ideas. The difference between the great and the merely good in digital talent increasingly makes the difference between the outstanding and the also-rans in business.

And yet, as the demand for great digital talent expands, shortages in talent pools from which businesses can draw have left companies fighting to fulfill shifting skills requirements. Worse still, acute shortages in specific areas (notably developers, data and analytics, and content) have generated intense competition in which the winners win big, and the losers get very little.

At the same time, the competitive context for digital talent has shifted rapidly. If you are a large multinational with a stuffy, traditional corporate headquarters in the suburbs, you are not only up against other large multinationals but the cool, funky startup in the trendy part of town. The best people can be choosy about where they work, the environment in which they work and learn, and whom they work with and learn from. Increasing transparency in employer practice and brand means there is nowhere to hide. The culture and environment into which those people arrive become critical determining factors for whether you will be able to keep them for any length of time or attract them to work for you in the first place.

Changing employee expectations means that talented individuals at all levels, the kind that can really make a difference to wider business performance and advantage, will only work in the kind of culture and environment that truly gives them greater freedom and flexibility, a sense of purpose and empowerment, one that enables them to thrive alongside like-minded people, and one where they can learn from the best in the industry.

The agile context model

We have created a practical tool for understanding the key questions that sit at the intersection of the key contexts (competitive, customer, company) and the attributes of agility (velocity, focus, flexibility). Workshop these questions, using the canvas in Table 1.1 as a way to identify key areas of challenge and opportunity:

Table 1.1 Questions to workshop

	Velocity	Focus	Flexibility
Competitive	What are the market factors that prevent you from moving quickly?	How does your vision and strategy compare to your competitors?	Are there cultural aspects to the industry that create inertia?
Customer	How well does your organization understand shifting customer need?	How well is your strategy and innovation linked to your customer need?	How quickly are you able to respond to shifting customer need?
Company	What are the key forces for inertia in your organization?	How well is organizational execution linked to a compelling vision?	How well does your culture support agility?

The key challenge: rates of change

When we begin to consider our response to these not insignificant shifts, we first need to appreciate the fundamental challenge that sits at the heart of digital transformation – the variance between the rate of change within organizations and that which is characteristic of the external environments in which they operate. Put simply, change within businesses typically happens at a slower pace than the rate of change in technology and the consumer behaviour that surrounds it. Too often, companies are playing catch up with consumers.

Marketing technologist, author and blogger Scott Brinker frames this dilemma rather neatly (in his thinking around 'Martec's Law'),[30] describing this as the 'quintessential management challenge of the 21st Century'. Technological change happens exponentially, but organizational change is dependent on factors that transition far more slowly (attitudes, thinking, structures, behaviours, culture) and so is logarithmic (Figure 1.2).

The widening gap between these two curves is perhaps the key leadership, management and organizational challenge of our times. A company's ability to absorb, respond and adapt to and master accelerating technological change is critical to its success in the modern world yet most companies are simply too slow. Too slow in adapting processes. Too slow in making decisions. Too slow in reorganizing around opportunity. Too slow in identifying

Figure 1.2 Organizational change is logarithmic

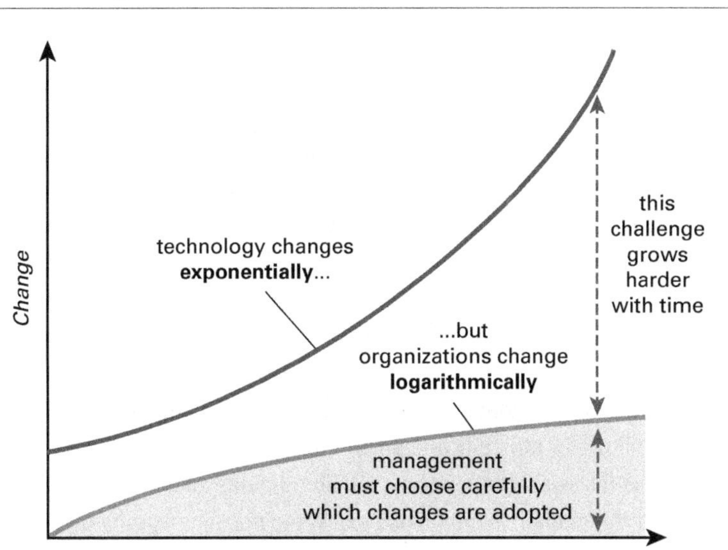

where value lies and innovating to capture that value. There is a paradigm shift required in the level of organizational agility that most companies are currently capable of and in the very fabric of how they work. If strategy is about linking execution and action with purposeful choices and direction, we need a new kind of corporate strategy. One that is altogether more suited to a digitally empowered world.

Yet before we even begin on our journey towards becoming a more agile business, we need to recognize some fundamental truths: to appreciate the way in which digital disrupts so that we might identify potential dangers and opportunity and respond before it is too late; to develop a common way of understanding what digital really means within the business so that we can execute against a clear vision and provide direction; and to be prepared to deal with the barriers and blockers that are contributing towards inertia and preventing change from happening.

Stories from the frontline

Gerd Leonhard, Futurist and Author: The Future of Digital Transformation

The term 'Digital Transformation' is well on its way to becoming overused, long before it even has a chance of becoming a reality. It has become an expression that implies a readiness for the future but which rarely indicates any profound change in thinking. The kind of changed thinking necessary to equip today's corporations for surviving the imminent transition awaiting humanity as technology becomes truly embodied. The shifts that this will bring, not only to the world of work but to education, retirement, our concepts of birth, life and death mean that we must not only digitally transform, we must transform digitization.

Transforming digitization means that we must reassume the lead narrative and change technology before it changes us utterly. Digitization must not become the vehicle to mass layoffs and unemployment, social contract erosion or cultural collapse and resource wars. Today, we already exist in a world where a shared economic narrative has almost disappeared and as humans on a planet with finite resources we must master technology in ways that we have not yet demonstrated, including socially, culturally, ethically and environmentally.

The time for treating ethics as a public relations exercise, a nice-to-have after the economic model has extracted maximum profit, is long gone. We are entering the age of digital ethics. Technology now enables economic sanctioning of any brand that oversteps the moral mark and as the world becomes ever-more networked, economic demonstrations of discontent will become increasingly common.

The talk about digital transformation needs to move beyond the focus on efficiency and towards wider human progress. We love to talk of exponential technologies rather than of exponential humanism. Technology is not just removing the intermediaries in every market, it's tearing down the walls between public and private life, between economic survival and moral thriving. The future is not nirvana, neither is it some kind of Hollywood dystopia. The future, I'm afraid, is all too human. It will look and feel like today, only much faster and hyper-connected. It will relentlessly punish any kind of outdated thinking.

Transformation means difference, not merely improvement. We need androrithms as much as algorithms – human values of creativity and empathy that transcend the merely mechanistic. We may be the last generation in history to live biologically organic lives. Before this bodily marriage with technology, we should use every remaining minute to evolve morally as much as we do economically. The next 20 years will change humanity more than the previous 300 years.

Notes

1. Processing Power Compared, [Online] http://pages.experts-exchange.com/processing-power-compared/ [last accessed 16 October 2016]
2. Buckminster Fuller, R (1938, 1973) *Nine Chains to the Moon*, Anchor Books, pp 252–59
3. Kurweil, R (2001) The Law of Accelerating Returns, [Online] http://www.kurzweilai.net/the-law-of-accelerating-returns [last accessed 16 October 2016]
4. Innosight (2012) Creative Destruction Whips Through Corporate America, [Online] http://www.innosight.com/innovation-resources/strategy-innovation/creative-destruction-whips-through-corporate-america.cfm [last accessed 16 October 2016]
5. Reeves and Pueschel (2015) BCG: Die Another Day: What Leaders Can Do About the Shrinking Life Expectancy of Corporations, [Online] https://www.bcgperspectives.com/content/articles/strategic-planning-growth-die-another-day/ [last accessed 16 October 2016]

6 Madeleine I G Daepp, Marcus J Hamilton, Geoffrey B West, Luís M A Bettencourt (2015), The mortality of companies, [Online] http://rsif.royalsocietypublishing.org/content/12/106/20150120 [last accessed 16 October 2016]

7 IBM Global C-Suite Study 2015, [Online] http://www-935.ibm.com/services/c-suite/study/study/ [last accessed 16 October 2016]

8 Hal Varian (2011), Micro-multinationals Will Run The World, [Online] http://foreignpolicy.com/2011/08/15/micromultinationals-will-run-the-world/ [last accessed 16 October 2016]

9 Hal Varian (2011), Micro-multinationals Will Run The World, [Online] http://foreignpolicy.com/2011/08/15/micromultinationals-will-run-the-world/ [last accessed 16 October 2016]

10 Kevin Kelly (2014), You Are Not Late, [Online] https://medium.com/message/you-are-not-late-b3d76f963142 [last accessed 16 October 2016]

11 Chris Dixon (2015), Full Stack Startups, [Online] http://cdixon.org/2014/03/15/full-stack-startups/ [last accessed 16 October 2016]

12 CB Insights: The Unicorn List, [Online] https://www.cbinsights.com/research-unicorn-companies [last accessed 16 October 2016]

13 CB Insights: Unbundling, [Online] https://www.cbinsights.com/blog/category/disrupting-unbundling/ [last accessed 16 October 2016]

14 Rita Gunther McGrath (2013), *The End of Competitive Advantage: How to keep your strategy moving as fast as your business*, Harvard Business Review Press

15 Adam Morgan, Mark Barden, (2015) *A Beautiful Constraint: How to transform your limitations into advantages, and why it's everyone's business*, Wiley

16 Adam Morgan (2015), The Rise of Unreasonableness, Marketing Society, [Online] https://www.marketingsociety.com/the-gym/rise-unreasonableness [last accessed 16 October 2016]

17 Jenkins, H (2006), Eight Traits of the New Media Landscape, [Online] http://henryjenkins.org/2006/11/eight_traits_of_the_new_media.html [last accessed 16 October 2016]

18 Tom Goodwin (November 2014), 6 Trends for 2017 and Beyond, LinkedIn, [Online] https://www.linkedin.com/pulse/20141119102703-6433797-6-trends-for-2017-and-beyond [last accessed 16 October 2016]

19 Tom Goodwin (March 2015), The Battle Is for the Customer Interface, Techcrunch, [Online] https://techcrunch.com/2015/03/03/in-the-age-of-disintermediation-the-battle-is-all-for-the-customer-interface/ [last accessed 16 October 2016]

20 Events@Google: Atmosphere, [Online] http://www.youtube.com/eventsatgoogle#p/u/5/qBaVyCcw47M [last accessed 16 October 2016]

21 EMC/IDC Digital Universe Study (2014), [Online] http://www.emc.com/leadership/digital-universe/2014iview/index.htm [last accessed 16 October 2016]

22 Global internet users, [Online] http://www.internetlivestats.com/internet-users/ [last accessed 16 October 2016]

23 Study: Less than 1% of the world's data is analysed, over 80% is unprotected, *The Guardian*, December 2012, [Online] https://www.theguardian.com/news/datablog/2012/dec/19/big-data-study-digital-universe-global-volume [last accessed 16 October 2016]

24 Data is the new oil, ANA Marketing Maestros, [Online] http://ana.blogs.com/maestros/2006/11/data_is_the_new.html [last accessed 16 October 2016]

25 Gartner, Predictive Analytics, [Online] http://www.gartner.com/it-glossary/predictive-analytics/ [last accessed 16 October 2016]

26 Evan Minsker, Pitchfork (March 2016), Kanye West Updates the Life of Pablo Again, [Online] http://pitchfork.com/news/64503-kanye-west-updates-the-life-of-pablo-again/ [last accessed 16 October 2016]

27 Toby Barnes (2016), On designing everything as a service, [Online] https://blog.prototypr.io/on-designing-everything-as-a-service-cbae99bd15a8#.ux5k3fth0 [last accessed 16 October 2016]

28 Marc Andreesen, (August 2011), Why Software Is Eating the World, *Wall Street Journal*, [Online] http://www.wsj.com/articles/SB10001424053111903480904576512250915629460 [last accessed 16 October 2016]

29 Ronald Coase, (9 December 1991), Lecture to the memory of Alfred Nobel, referencing *The Nature of the Firm*, (1937), [Online] http://www.nobelprize.org/nobel_prizes/economic-sciences/laureates/1991/coase-lecture.html [last accessed 16 October 2016]

30 Scott Brinker (June 2013), Martec's Law, [Online] http://chiefmartec.com/2013/06/martecs-law-technology-changes-exponentially-organizations-change-logarithmically/ [accessed 16 October 2016]

How digital disrupts

02

Perhaps it is the transformational role that data is starting to play in the healthcare industry. Or it is the revolutionizing of mapping and navigation through user generated input and augmented reality. Or it is the increasing sophistication of algorithms and different forms of curation in news and content discovery. Or it is the growing use of automation and artificial intelligence in customer service. Or it is the role that digitally enabled 3D printing will increasingly take in the manufacturing and construction industries. It seems that everywhere we look there is a different nuance to how digital is driving fundamental shifts in the propositions, revenue sources, costs and operations across many different industries.

Digital disruption is as broad as it is deep, impacting right across sectors and organizational functions. So just why and how have digital technologies disrupted so many businesses and markets so fundamentally?

It was strategy guru Michael Porter who, in his 1985 bestseller *Competitive Advantage: Creating and sustaining superior performance*[1] originated the concept of value chains to describe what businesses do – a value chain being a set of activities that a company performs in order to deliver value to market in the form of a product or service.

An organization is essentially a string of components forming a value chain welded together by transaction costs. Primary activities (inbound logistics, operations, outbound logistics, marketing and sales, service) are set out alongside supporting activities (infrastructure, people, technology, procurement). A business's competitive advantage is the sum or the average of its transaction costs. Companies usually wield large advantages in some components and are lagging in others, but they are founded on the idea of a sustainable competitive advantage, focused on continued improvement in efficiency and standardization as a main ingredient in order to lower transaction costs in particular components.

If competitive advantage is derived from cost leadership and/or differentiation, then digital can enable new sources for either or both.

As businesses grow, pressure to add in resource and cost and to deliver ongoing shareholder return may well result in the need to increase prices. This need may be justified through the optimization of goods and services. Yet a new digitally empowered competitor entering the market may only (to use Pareto's principle) deliver 80 per cent of the value but can do so at 20 per cent of the cost. When this is combined with a potentially sector-defining change in customer experience, this creates a significant disruptive threat.

In his TED talk on 'How Data Will Transform Business', Philip Evans, author and MD of the Boston Consulting Group, argues that with digitization it may become possible to achieve zero marginal cost in some components, meaning that the transactional costs plummet to a level where there is less or nothing to economize on.

Evans argues that when certain components in the value chain plummet it can change the rules of the game for an entire industry – because it breaks up both the welding and usually (but not always) the entire value chain and allows for new competitive advantages and new value chains to take root – especially if the component that did plummet has been protecting the industry from outside competition.

> *... what used to be vertically integrated, oligopolistic competition among essentially similar kinds of competitors is evolving... from a vertical structure to a horizontal one... The plummeting of transaction costs weakens the glue that holds value chains together, and allows them to separate.*
>
> (Evans, 2013)[2]

This is comparable to the theory of disruption where Clayton Christensen argues that an industry is ripe for disruption when its core technology (or the component in the value chain that is essential to the nature, protection or capitalization of the industry) is 'stretchable'.[3]

Christensen uses the example of education. A teacher is a technology, and was not stretchable in 2000, and therefore not ripe for disruption, but with MOOCs (Massive Online Open Courses), a plethora of digital learning resources available and even Stanford University making course material available for digital consumption, the shape of education is morphing into a very different future.

As a succession of markets succumb to digital disintermediation where incumbent mediators in sectors (media or content businesses, retailers, brokers to name a few) are challenged, usurped and even replaced or removed altogether, the scope of digital disruption simply gets wider.

The lifecycle of a technology

Invention is a lot like surfing; you have to catch the wave at the right time.

Ray Kurzweil

Renowned futurologist (and Google's Head of Engineering) Ray Kurzweil has described the lifecycle of a technology (or an invention based on a new technology) as being shaped as an 'S-curve'. Kurzweil noted back in 2004 that the pace of innovation is doubling every decade and so he said that inventions should be aimed at the world of the future, not the world that exists when your R&D project is launched, since so many contexts change so rapidly.[4] So if technologies follow an S-curve over time (slow, then rapid adoption and development, before plateauing into maturity) in order to time an invention properly you need to be aware of the entire lifecycle (Figure 2.1).

Kurzweil describes seven key stages in the evolution of a technology:

1. Precursor: the enabling factors for the new technology are in place (and visionaries may even be able to describe its goals or its operation), but it has yet to become a reality.
2. Invention: for which determination and timing are often key.
3. Development: the refining of the invention, which has likely entered the world as 'an ungainly and impractical device'.

Figure 2.1 Lifecycle of an invention

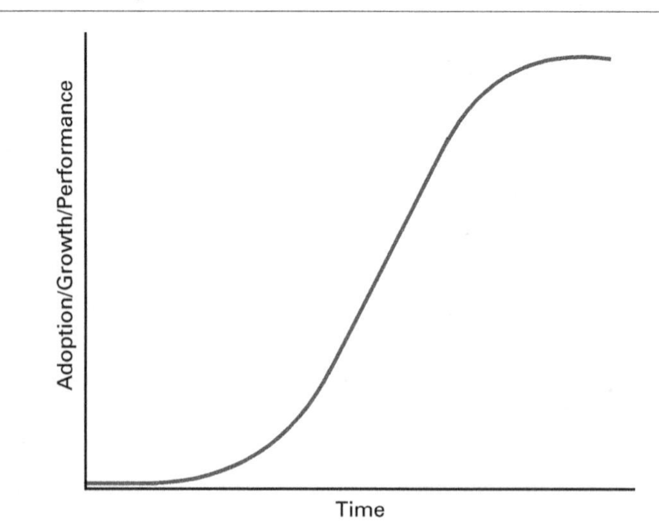

4 Maturity: this stage often comprises the bulk of a technology's lifespan. It has become an integral part of everyday life and probably seems as though it will never be replaced.
5 False pretenders: assaults on the now established technology from potentially disruptive newcomers that claim to be in a position to replace it, and indeed might be better in some ways, but are invariably lacking in salient, critical features. The failure of the newcomer(s) only leads to a stronger conviction that the existing technology will survive indefinitely.
6 Obsolescence: further newcomers master the absent qualities, pushing the older technology into obsolescence.
7 Antiquity: the final resting place.

Kurzweil says that in order to be successful, an invention needs to move through each phase (precursor, invention, development and maturity), which reminds us of the Schumpeter definition of the process of technological change which is divided into three key stages: 1) Invention (ideas); 2) Innovation (the development of new ideas into marketable products and processes, or commercialization); 3) Diffusion (scaling or adoption).[5] There are, of course, challenges at each of these stages which are often forgotten about but worth considering at an organizational level, since we need to be good at all three of them.

Why businesses get disrupted: the ambiguity zone

While Ray Kurzweil applied the S-curve to describe the lifecycle of a technology, it was Charles Handy who (in *The Empty Raincoat*)[6] originally described how the S-curve is a way of understanding the trajectory of many successful systems, demonstrating the need for significant and regular reinvention and change, and how disruption can often happen just when an existing technology looks like it is performing the best that it ever has. The duration of specific curves may vary but each one typically begins with an initial period of learning through trial and error, followed by rapid growth, and then a plateauing and ultimately decline in performance.

The overlapping of S-curves, caused by the introduction of new technologies or models into a market is what creates both challenge and opportunity (Figure 2.2). Many organizations will avoid significant change until crisis is

Figure 2.2 Overlapping S-curves

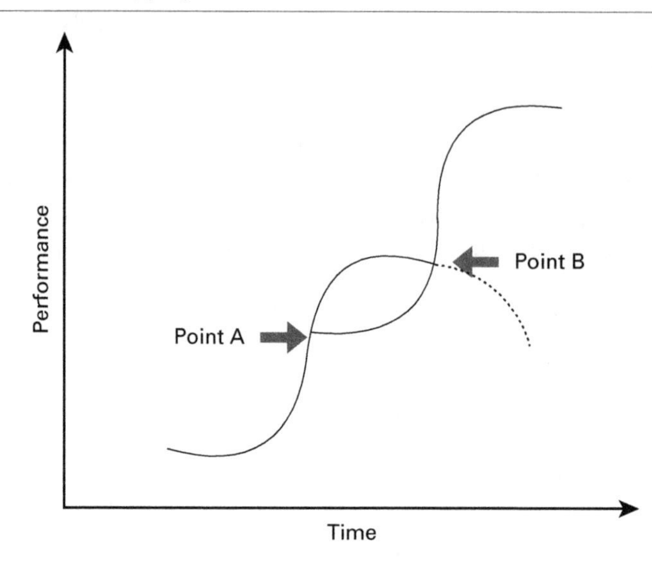

reached or disruption is obvious (Point B), which is often too late. By then, resources may well already be depleted, competitive position already weakened, leadership credibility already damaged, and energy for new or creative thinking drained. Starting the change earlier, at Point A, brings challenges in terms of initiating a period of transition, continuing to optimize the old while building the new, and managing different and potentially competing business models, ways of working and/or cultures concurrently. But change needs to start here. As Charles Handy put it, when you are standing at Point A you might look back along the curve and see success and growth, but you can also look forwards over the horizon and see the fall to Point B, so the trick is look openly at where the trends will lead you, what Point B is telling you, and use that to help navigate the right path on from Point A and on to the next curve. So continual reinvention, even when things are seemingly going well, is the name of the game.

There are two metaphors that are valuable in relation to this. The first comes from Dave Snowden, who describes the delicate balancing act of understanding when it is right to focus on the new and stop clinging to the old as akin to knowing when the moment is right to get in the water:

> *... it is easier to get in just as the tide turns, you don't want to be stranded on the beach, but you want to minimise the energy required to get into the blue ocean.*
>
> (Snowden, 2016)[7]

The second comes from Clay Christensen who frames the all-too-frequent slow organizational response to the need for innovation in this way:

> *If a company has ignored investing in new businesses until it needs those new sources of revenue and profits, it's already too late. It's like planting saplings when you decide you need more shade. It's just not possible for those trees to grow large enough to create shade overnight. It takes years of patient nurturing to have any chance of the trees growing tall enough to provide it.*
>
> (Christensen, 2012)[8]

There are not only companies but possibly entire industries that have been guilty of this. It is one of the key innovation challenges for just about every business. But as they say in endurance sports, we need to eat before we are hungry and drink before we are thirsty.

Defining digital

In this context of rapid disruption empowered by digital technologies, it has never been more important to develop a common language within an organization for what digital really means.

In fact, this is as good a starting point as any for digital transformation. Ask a hundred people to define what digital is and you will get a hundred different responses. Developing a commonly understood definition enables the business to align around just that – a common understanding. Yet so few businesses actually do this. Since digital is so broad, touching so many areas of what we do, and since it blurs traditional boundaries between roles, functions, departments, categorizations, having a common understanding forms the basis for not only a shared vision and an inherently more aligned approach, but also the foundation from which to create change.

Many definitions often focus on aspects such as content, video, mobile, interaction, scale, ubiquity – in other words on what digital *does* rather than what digital *is*. Yet the simplest possible definition is to characterize digital in terms of binary code (ones and zeros). A method of getting information from one place to another that is not analog.

In one sense this is helps us to get past the idea that digital is a mysterious, amorphous, ever-changing thing that is impossible to grasp, and instead frames it in the context of taking common needs, wants, actions and delivering to them or applying them in a new way. Digital technologies are radically shifting behaviours and reinventing entire markets, but that does not mean that we should forget everything we know about great companies, great products and great brands.

Yet if we are to form a useful, instructive definition we should take account of more than the technical aspects of digital. It is often the case that within organizations there is a disproportionate focus on the technology itself (new technology for the sake of new technology), over all the enablers that surround the technology, really bring it to life, and fully realize its capability (people, behaviours, processes, skills, culture).

When the team that drove the initial digital transformation of service delivery for the UK Government moved to do the same thing at the Co-Op, they originated a definition that recognized that when done well, digital means more than fundamentally redesigning services; it also means changing the way in which we work:

> *Applying the culture, practices, processes and technologies of the Internet era to respond to people's raised expectations.*
>
> (Bracken, 2016)[9]

Creating a single sentence definition for what digital means to your business creates the platform from which change can be actioned.

Notes

1 Michael E Porter (2008) *Competitive Advantage: Creating and Sustaining Superior Performance*, Free Press; new Ed edition, ASIN: B003YCQ2O4

2 Philip Evans (November 2013) How Data Will Transform Business, TED @ BCG San Francisco, [Online] http://www.ted.com/talks/philip_evans_how_data_will_transform_business?language=en [accessed 16 October 2016]

3 Clay Christensen on Disruptive Innovation, Clarendon Lectures 10 June 2013, [Online] https://www.youtube.com/watch?v=rpkoCZ4vBSI [accessed 3 November 2016]

4 Ray Kurzweil (2004) Kurzweil's Rules of Invention, MIT Technology Review, [Online] https://www.technologyreview.com/s/402705/kurzweils-rules-of-invention/ [accessed 16 October 2016]

5 Proven Models, invention innovation diffusion trilogy, [Online] http://www.provenmodels.com/14/invention-innovation-diffusion-trilogy/joseph-a.-schumpeter [accessed 16 October 2016]

6 Charles Handy (August 1995) *The Empty Raincoat, Making Sense of the Future*, Random House, ISBN-10: 0099301253

7 Dave Snowden (July 2016) Cognitive Edge, … taken at the flood, [Online] https://cognitive-edge.com/blog/taken-at-the-flood/ [accessed 16 October 2016]

8 Clay Christensen (May 2012) *How Will You Measure Your Life?*, HarperCollins, ISBN-10: 1633692566

9 Mike Bracken (June 2016) Co-op digital blog, What we mean when we say digital, [Online] https://digital.blogs.coop/2016/06/14/what-we-mean-when-we-say-digital/ [accessed 16 October 2016]

What's stopping you? 03

Slow by design

If we are to embark on the journey towards becoming a more agile business, it is worth pausing to consider some of the key forces for inertia within organizations and potential blockers to change.

The interviews conducted for this book surfaced a wide range of barriers to progress, the most commonly cited reflecting technology, strategy and people related reasons, including:

- **Technology and data:** outdated, inflexible systems, creaking IT infrastructure, difficulty in systems integration and joining up data.
- **Short-termism:** a focus on short-term targets and priorities, hampering the ability to progress with larger, longer-term projects or change.
- **Talent:** the challenge of attracting and retaining the best digital talent.
- **Legacy approaches:** entrenched behaviours, processes and decision-making that are inherently slow and problematic to unlearn.
- **Organizational silos:** the drag brake of internal politics, competing divisional agendas, siloed decision-making.
- **Prioritization:** challenges around understanding how best to allocate limited resources, often due to lack of knowledge or certainty of impact, and the ability to show identifiable, short-term gain or benefit.
- **Culture and structure:** the inhibiting effect of an organizational culture that rewards and entrenches behaviours that counteract change, or inflexible structures that slow progress. Comments included the need to change culture in order to work smarter and/or faster, or around how structures are inhibiting, or too much micro management.

Many of these barriers reflect fundamental aspects of organizational culture and practice. As Eric Schmidt and Jonathan Rosenberg describe it in *How Google Works*, most companies are run today to minimize risk, not maximize freedom and speed. Information is hoarded, not shared; decision-making power lies in the hands of the few:

> *Their design is a vestige of an era when failure was expensive, and deliberation was a virtue.*
>
> (Schmidt and Rosenberg, 2014)[1]

In other words, they are slow by design. If an organization has scaled and grown utilizing specific, established processes or ways of doing things, it creates inbuilt inertia that is very hard to counteract. As the company becomes larger and focus moves more towards efficiency and optimization rather than breakthrough innovation, the approaches become not only established but honed and embedded. As hierarchies flourish within the larger company, and grow up around embedded practices, the inward focus of the company increases as the outward focus declines. Inertia strengthens over time.

Why organizations become 'sticky'

Why do organizations and people become resistant to change? And why does change seem to become harder the larger the organization gets? One key reason is that organizational culture becomes entrenched and intransigent over time, resulting in what Professor Victor Newman describes (in his book *Power House: Strategic knowledge management*)[2] as the 'sticky organization'. If a culture grows up around the problem-solving experiences and processes associated with a particular kind of technology, then relationships between people and patterns of behaviour also grow up around that and can adapt to block change in an effort to maintain social stability.

The relationship capital, or the social capital that has been built up over time between teams and individuals through the accumulation of reputation, influence and positive impressions becomes a powerful blocker to change. As innovation specialist Matt Edgar has said, a startup spends much of its formative life making and breaking new relationships and links. These are unpredictable social conditions but ones in which innovation can flourish. A large organization on the other hand:

> *... is almost nothing but a massive knot of pre-existing relationships. Getting something done, even something new, often means following a well-trodden path to actors already known to each other.*
>
> (Edgar, 2013)[3]

In this case, the 'innovation pipeline' involves moving concepts from one predictable stage to another and the only way in which real innovation can happen in that environment is 'with the intervention of new actors and the reconfiguration of old ones'. In order to innovate, therefore, large companies are required to consciously remain open to new actors or to counter-intuitively disrupt existing relationships and force the formation of new ones.

In this common scenario, the idea of infallible uniqueness perpetuates ('we're different, so that wouldn't work here'), and there is a disinclination to admit failure. Specific 'craft' language, or terms and acronyms that have been developed inside the business as a shorthand way of describing specific technologies, properties or practices can reinforce the entrenchment of behaviours that may have become outdated. As Victor Newman says:

> *Strong cultures continually evolve new behaviours to block change, to maintain social stability and preserve power structures based upon existing patterns and accumulated reserves of mutual relationship capital. The greater the relationship capital in the network, the 'stickier' the organization and the stronger its defence of current structures and knowledge products embedded in the technology of the organization. The stickier an organization, the more pronounced its tendency to focus on the problems it can solve, rather than the problem it needs to solve.*
>
> (Newman, 2013)[4]

Relationship capital is a powerful potential barrier to change since if the underlying business or technology changes, it also changes the value of the relationships within the company, which is something that is resisted. The way in which teams are incentivized or remunerated can amplify this resistance. Take, for example, the executives who are unwilling to adopt new practices since they believe it will impact their quarterly bonus. Or the sales team who are wary of a new piece of technology since it will enable other teams to immediately see the status of a piece of business. Or the team that continue with outdated practices even when new technology is implemented because they feel comfortable with the old way of working.

Entrenched behaviours generate resistance to change, and therefore inertia, but can also create organizational habits that are often hidden and unacknowledged yet might be powerful drivers of response and action. Such habitual thinking and behaviours can not only go unrecognized, but can prove very difficult to change. The Roman poet Ovid said 'Nothing is stronger than a habit', and he could well be right. A study from Duke University estimated that habits, rather than conscious decision-making, shape up to 45 per cent of the choices we make every day.

Why good ideas become battles

Many of us have experienced the very real frustration of coming up with an exceptional idea that we believe self-evidently has great potential value for our business only to find that those around us do not share our vision, leaving us with an arduous struggle to build support, create momentum and garner enthusiasm. A compelling business case, however cogent and persuasive, may still not be enough to gain acceptance of an idea that seems to you to be utterly convincing in its attractiveness, simplicity or common sense.

In these situations maintaining confidence in your idea (particularly if it is a potentially disruptive one) and having the determination to pursue it in apparent adversity, can be a very real and personal challenge. To paraphrase Hugh MacLeod,[5] good ideas can disrupt the power balance of relationships within businesses and so are often resisted.

Conformity has its own hidden power. Loss aversion, or the strong preference most people have towards avoiding losses over acquiring gains (some studies have suggested that in some contexts losses can psychologically be up to twice as powerful as gains)[6] can be a powerful barrier to progress when people feel that change threatens existing constructs, relationships or systems into which they might have invested considerable effort over time. This results in a risk-averse culture and a biased assessment on potential gains against visible losses.

Some internal innovation schemes (often little more than idea generating competitions) can prove far more demotivating than they are galvanizing when good ideas are dismissed because of internal politics, or because the person who submitted the idea is perceived not to have the skills to lead the project, or due to poor feedback mechanisms. There are few more efficient ways to turn passion and enthusiasm into disappointment and disengagement than a mishandled idea generation process.

Trying to get a good idea off the starting block in an environment that feels like it is trying to put as many obstacles as possible in the way of that happening turns it into a campaign to gain consensus among key decision makers who were often not party to the origins of the idea and so feel no ownership of it. Working on new ideas may be additive to workloads, result in a higher demand on already tight resources, or require constant justification. As designer Adam Katz once said:[7] 'All of my good ideas are battles'.

But they are always worth it. Famously it took James Dyson five years and 5,127 prototypes to invent the world's first bagless vacuum cleaner.[8] Resilience propels real innovation. Without it ideas wither and die.

The arrogance of scale

As companies grow larger it becomes ever-more difficult for them to retain the right balance between ambition and humility, external curiosity and inward focus, restlessness and complacency.

Market dominance and scale can easily turn into corporate arrogance and lack of urgency. The pressures brought by demands for ever-greater scale and efficiency are a catalyst for internal politics, bureaucracy, managing upwards and internal focus. Hubris can cause poor listening and analysis, missed opportunities and kill the ability to reinvent.

The opposite, in other words, of the qualities of organizational longevity listed by Arie de Geus in his renowned book on *The Living Company*:[9] the ability to learn and adapt from being sensitive to their environment; to show tolerance for experimentation and different thinking; to retain a strong, cohesive sense of identity; to be adept at managing resources to enable flexibility.

A comprehensive study by the Telfer School of Management at the University of Ottawa[10] into the implosion of Canadian telecoms giant Nortel gives us some stark lessons. The researchers interviewed 48 per cent of all the Nortel executives who were in charge of the company from 1997 through to 2009 when it filed for bankruptcy, and spoke to executives at 53 different companies that were customers of Nortel in that time. In spite of the rapidity of Nortel's decline, they found that corporate failure is a long and complicated process dependent on multiple accumulating factors. When asked about Nortel's biggest management failure however, the study's lead author, Jonathan Calof, said:

> *There were three major factors that caused the failure. When Nortel was a market leader in the '70s, it developed an arrogant culture, which led to poor financial discipline. Then in the '90s, it focused so intensely on growth that it broke its ability to innovate and read the market. And after the tech bubble popped, it turned inward and cut costs to the point where it alienated customers.*
>
> (Calof, 2014)[11]

Arrogance, pursuing growth at all costs, efficiency at the expense of innovation. Many of these problems were seemingly originating from a culture that became baked into the company long before it was in trouble, and served to reinforce the kind of toxic assumptions we talk about in the next section. Assumptions that damaged the business and brought focus away from where it needed to be and created an internally facing company. Says Calof:

> *It escalated into hubris to the extent of making it especially difficult to absorb acquisitions, to quickly respond to market needs, and to accept and understand what customers wanted (largely as result of the delusion of 'we know better').*

As businesses become leaders in their market it is very easy for them to become blinded by conceit: for the language of leadership to slip into the language of arrogance. As they become overly focused on growth it is very easy for them to become parochial and lose sight of what really matters. As they pursue efficiency gain over forward thinking it is very easy for them to become internally focused, for informal reward systems (such senior management attention and recognition) to subtly put a premium on inward-looking management. The potential for rapid disruption that digital has brought to so many markets serves only to amplify the impact of such misaligned corporate culture.

Protecting against obsolete beliefs and 'toxic assumptions'

Legacy systems, processes, and approaches often have their own assumptions on which they were originally based that then become embedded in ways of working and thinking without us even acknowledging that they exist. They may be assumptions about competitive or partner context, resources, customer needs, channels, market size or positioning, but they are fundamental, hidden, ingrained.

Let's call them 'toxic assumptions'. They are the most dangerous kind of assumptions because despite being unnoticed, they become entrenched over time and they are powerful drivers of thinking and inertia. They will go unchallenged yet are typically based on a view of the world that relies on historical or existing market, model or competitive dynamics. As soon as those dynamics change, potentially in unforeseen ways, the business is underprepared and struggles to adapt. When people in the organization say things like 'that wouldn't work here', or 'we tried something like that a few years ago and it didn't work' or 'we've always done it like that', these are signals that you have some beliefs or assumptions that are potentially obsolete.

So how do we protect ourselves from toxic assumptions? The answer, of course, is that we need to be continually reassessing our beliefs and our view on the world in light of the ever-changing environment in which our companies operate. Paul Graham, essayist, VC, and founder of startup incubator Y Combinator, has written about how in order to respond well to a rapidly changing world, we need not only to have an explicit belief in change (in other words to be actively looking for change) but also to be 'aggressively open-minded'. In a static environment, the confidence we have in our beliefs increases over time as they survive more and increasingly varied experiences, and are therefore reinforced and less likely to change. The same is true of our opinions. But when it comes to things that continually change, we cannot trust our opinions in the same way. Beliefs become obsolete because the frame of reference on which they were based has changed:

> *When experts are wrong, it's often because they're experts on an earlier version of the world.*
>
> (Graham, 2014)[12]

So it is with inflexible, outdated thinking within organizations. Having an explicit belief in an ever-changing environment means that rather than regarding the world as static you start to actively look for change. Focusing on aspects of a market, customer interaction or situation that don't change (like human nature, our desire for convenience, and exceptional user experience) can be an important source for innovation, but it is just as important to understand when key dynamics are shifting and, as Graham says, meaningful change often originates from unforeseen places meaning that our view on the world can easily and quickly become outdated.

Until very recently the organization was moving faster than the consumer, the world was more predictable and consumers were informed and listened, but now the consumer is moving faster than the organization, they no longer wait to be told, but can make so many decisions on the fly about so many aspects of their life. Organizations consist of consumers but we rarely look at ourselves in this way. We go to work and the technology we use internally is often less advanced than the technology we use at home or on the way to work. Only recently has 'bring your own device' (BYOD) become more acceptable within organizations, reflecting the need for companies to become employee-centric as much as they are customer-centric, in order to maintain the connection with the real world outside.

So this means that we must be disciplined about not letting our working hypotheses or domain-expertise overly constrain our view on the future. Becoming an expert in a changing world means that it is essential to not just look for change, but to always be ready to flex your thinking in response to it, and avoid becoming imprisoned by your own proficiency. If knowledge is power, then change can easily threaten inflexible domain-expertise, leading to entrenched beliefs and even greater inflexibility. Being what Graham describes as 'aggressively open-minded' means always being ready to challenge our existing beliefs in response to new information or ideas:

> *Within Y Combinator, when an idea is described as crazy, it's a compliment – in fact, on average probably a higher compliment than when an idea is described as good.*
>
> (Graham, 2014)[13]

In a shifting environment we need to recognize that strength and growth in knowledge comes from adaptability. There is a final point that Graham makes, which is about people. When the future is hard to predict it becomes just as, if not more, important to focus on the people rather than the ideas as a way of protecting against obsolete beliefs. Great ideas come from enthusiastic, earnest, independent-minded people, so:

> *Surround yourself with the sort of people new ideas come from. If you want to notice quickly when your beliefs become obsolete, you can't do better than to be friends with the people whose discoveries will make them so.*
>
> (Graham, 2014)[14]

The tyranny of rigid planning

Later in the book we will discuss fundamentally more agile approaches to planning that take far more account of the rapidly changing (or as it is often called VUCA: Volatile, Uncertain, Complex, Ambiguous) environment in which businesses now operate. But it is worth remembering the restrictive, inhibiting power of traditional, rigid planning techniques.

A typical, linear, business planning process is not the most motivating of experiences, as marketer and cartoonist Tom Fishburne has neatly described:

> *Crafting an annual plan is like getting a bill through Congress. Behind the final numbers and strategies lie countless hours of spreadsheet crunching, hallway meetings, and waterfall charts. We debate assumptions, broker compromises, and eventually settle on a plan that is wrong the moment it's inked.*
>
> (Fishburne, 2013)[15]

There are some significant potential flaws that sit at its heart:

- **The predicted outcome will be wrong.** Let's face it, in the environment in which we now operate no one can predict what will happen in the next month let alone the next year, or five years. In their book, *Rework*,[16] Jason Fried and David Heinemeier Hansson talk about why we should start referring to plans as what they really are – guesses. Start referring to business plans as business guesses, financial plans as financial guesses and strategic plans as strategic guesses, and stuff becomes a whole lot simpler. Plans become objectives, so if your predicted outcome is wrong, your objective is already flawed.

- **The assumptions on which the plan is built are wrong.** Most plans use the previous year's numbers as the basis for the forecast of the following year's numbers (and often those beyond). Last year's numbers, which were the result of last year's competitive context, consumer demand and behaviour. All of which (you can guarantee) will be very different a year later. Planning is typically done part way through the year and so the numbers you finally finish the year on are inevitably different from those that formed the basis of your plan. So your year-on-year variable starts to look either gloriously easy or (more likely) increasingly unreachable and unrealistic as the year goes on. Either way, the basis for the plan is flawed.
- **Plans 'let the past drive the future'.** Business planning, as does much 'management thinking', favours inductive thinking (based on directly observable facts) and deductive thinking (logic and analysis, typically based on past evidence). It is how we are taught at business school, and often the basis of reward when we start in gainful employment. And it is the kind of thinking with which business process is most comfortable. Abductive thinking (of the kind emphasized in design, imagining what could be possible) on the other hand, is not. Many businesses are characterized by processes that are convergent (focused on making choices, closing down on a solution), rather than divergent (focused on creating choices, opening up options). Making big decisions based on contexts that are no longer relevant or information that will soon be out of date is flawed.
- **It perpetuates incremental thinking.** The context for most plans is the percentile variable from the previous year. Usually it is an increase of somewhere between 0 and 10 per cent. The criteria for success is set at doing-what-you-did-before-but-slightly-better. This focuses the mind on driving incremental gain through incremental benefit or efficiencies. When entire industries are being reinvented, this kind of approach in isolation breeds complacency and in complacency sits risk.
- **Detailed, rigid plans are the enemy of adaptability.** The more fixed and detailed your plan is, the harder you have to work to do something outside it.

> The harder it is to improvise; the higher the cost of change. The more difficult it is to budget to the pace of innovation, rather than innovate to the cycle of your budget. As circumstance changes (as it inevitably will), plans are revised, reworked, re-justified. Revisions and justifications are focused on the differential from the first plan (which was fundamentally flawed in the first place) making for an unhelpful comparison. Managers spend time generating reports and attending meetings to justify why the original plan (which was fundamentally flawed in the first place) is no longer relevant.

A not insignificant amount of management time is spent on over-complex and over-burdening planning processes. It kills morale and it kills time that could be spent on ideas that will genuinely move the business forward.

The legacy technology problem

Legacy technologies and the processes that surround them can be another powerful blocker to change. A good example of this was demonstrated relatively recently in the banking sector, an area where you would think that advanced modern technology infrastructure could not be more essential. In 2013 a systems outage meant that for three hours on one of the busiest online shopping days of the year, Royal Bank of Scotland (RBS) customers could not access their bank accounts. This followed catastrophic system problems in 2012, which for a number of days affected 16 million customers' ability to withdraw cash from ATMs, transactions on their accounts, handling of wages and direct debit payments. The RBS Chief Executive admitted at the time:[17] 'For decades, RBS failed to invest properly in its systems.'

Frances Coppola, a former RBS employee and an independent analyst, wrote an analysis[18] talking about the legacy systems problem that besets the banking sector. Technology investment, she says, has traditionally been focused on building front-end applications, meaning that the core systems that run the basic banking processes have not been upgraded. So in spite of the huge increase in processing power and storage capacity in modern IT systems, banks like RBS still had massive traditional mainframe computing systems at their heart.

The thing that prevents these old systems being replaced outright, she says, is their sheer size, complexity and criticality. Over time, the huge cost and risk involved in replacing them has meant that these organizations have adopted a system of 'wrapping' – effectively treating the core legacy system as a black box which remains largely untouched while a 'shell' of additional applications that create customer interfaces, point-of-sale functionality, settlement processing and even real-time updates are created around it. These newer applications rely heavily on the information contained within the core system but over time build complexity upon complexity as the 'shell' gets larger, issues of technological compatibility and connectivity have to be worked through, and customers rely on them more and more.

This means that there may well be divergence in the financial information presented to customers and that which appears to the bank (before reconciliation occurs), the potential for system errors and data corruption grows, and the risk of significant failure just increases over time:

> *The more fragmented your systems architecture, and the more it relies upon stable interconnections between different technologies, the riskier it becomes... the 'pasta rule' still applies: the more your systems architecture looks like spaghetti, the higher risk it will be.*
>
> (Coppola, 2013)[19]

A significant reason for consistent underinvestment, says Coppola, is that investment in infrastructure is likely to impact short-term profits and yet it is not the most interesting type of expenditure. So while balance sheet risk may have been reduced, operational risk hasn't. Banks that are focused instead on rapid expansion have the very real potential of building up a patchwork of incompatible technologies, and failing to invest in suitable time or resources for systems support or proper integration. As long as it keeps on running, as long as it is easier to patch it up or build a workaround, the longer it goes on, the more complex the interdependencies become, and the risk and the associated costs build.

In the case of huge banking systems the risks can elevate to levels that have implications for the whole economy, but this kind of legacy systems issue is not confined to the banking sector. It can often be regarded as one of the most significant barriers to making companies fit for purpose for the modern digital world. And it is not just about the technology, of course, but the policies, practices, skills and behaviours that surround it. The consequences of an overly short-term focus on profits may be far greater than is visible to those looking in from the outside.

Marginal thinking

> *The safest road to Hell is the gradual one – the gentle slope, soft underfoot, without sudden turnings, without milestones, without signposts.*
>
> C S Lewis

How do we avoid the trap of incremental approaches and mindsets? Or the danger of what Clay Christensen (in *How Will You Measure Your Life?*)[20] calls marginal thinking? An executive in an established company, says Christensen, will have two alternatives when making an investment decision – either to incur the full cost of setting up something completely new, or to leverage what already exists so that you only need to incur the marginal cost and revenue. The marginal-cost argument will almost always outweigh the full-cost one. But for a new entrant in the market the only choice is the full-cost alternative ('Because they are new to the scene, in fact, the full cost is the marginal cost').

The problem with marginal thinking however, is that it typically comes with lots of baggage. The established company is basing the investment decision on the perspective of its existing operations and may decide not to invest if the marginal upside is not worth the marginal cost of doing it. The trap with this, however, is that while it is easy to see immediate costs of investing, it is much harder to accurately see the costs of not investing. While the company still has a perfectly acceptable existing product, the upside of investment may well be considered too small, but this assumes things will remain as they are and fails to take into account a future in which someone else brings the new product to market. This can lead to a series of relatively minor investment decisions, the consequences of which may not become apparent for some time but which ultimately and in totality may doom the company to failure.

Culture and behaviour

As we mentioned earlier in the book, while technology is important, the behaviours that surround it are a fundamental component of change and agility. Successfully transitioning to an organizational state that is far more characterized by fluidity, adaptability and constant change depends heavily on the skills, attitudes and behaviours of the people in your business. Becoming a truly agile, digital-native business will mean adopting not just new technologies, but new customer-centric thinking and approaches. It will mean embracing and responding to new processes and expectations. And it may well mean adapting to new structures, incentives and responsibilities.

Change requires clarity and leadership to create the environment in which it can happen, to demonstrate why change is necessary and to direct and guide behaviour in the right direction, but culture and behaviour are inextricably linked. Just as culture helps determines behaviour, behaviour helps shape culture.

So just as entrenched culture and behaviour can be one of the most powerful barriers to progress, so an enabling culture and new practices and behaviours can be powerful forces of advancement towards a more agile business. Digital transformation is less about 'talking the talk', and more about 'walking the walk'. It is not about jargon, it is about action. As digital literacy grows at all levels of the organization, beyond the more tangible metrics and results it will be the expectations that are set, the questions that are asked, the questions that are not asked, and the visible behaviours of the senior leadership down, that will be critical indicators that progress is being made.

Stories from the frontline

Faris Yakob, co-founder, strategy and innovation consultancy Genius Steals, author of *Paid Attention*:[21] Everyone likes progress, no one likes change

The world pulses to an exponential beat, daring companies to keep up, as Jack Welch so famously feared. And rightly so, since most companies will fail to and will die.

That means more and more companies are failing to adapt to the exogenous changes that either power or destroy businesses.

Why? Why is corporate change so hard?

Some answers are obvious, the well worn territory of The Innovator's Dilemma, but others are less well explored and just as important. In our consulting work, we have uncovered the same barriers, again and again, at very different kinds of companies.

Formal

Legacy infrastructure, built in an industrial age, represents a massive cost base in labour, equipment which is being amortized, software, systems and so on. Public companies cannot abandon them and take the mark down, their Wall Street owners would never allow it. So they must simply continue, cutting costs, to prop up share prices. Processes, once codified, become orthodoxies instead of guidelines.

Worse, should the problem these companies solve melt away through new technologies, they will be forced to attempt the even more difficult task of halting progress at a political and cultural level.

The 'Shirky Principle': 'Institutions will try to preserve the problem to which they are the solution.'

Informal

Companies often hire 'change agents' to usher in new ideas, products and processes. This is a death sentence, for it sets up said harbingers of the future in opposition to every other employee. Implicit in naming change agents is the idea that change is needed and that no current employee is bringing it. This oppositional stance makes collaboration nigh impossible.

Perverse incentives are rife in corporations. At the board level there is a desperate appetite for growth, which often means change, but the way it's pushed through the system creates inverted incentives. Ridiculous sales targets turned Wells Fargo employees into criminals, destroying the bank's reputation. Both the targets and the employees have been removed.

I spent weeks working on a business and communication strategy for one of the world's largest telecoms companies. Our approach was to simplify the purchase process and migrate it online. Within the recommendation was a call to close many of the call centres taking sales calls (which the company had in every state in America) which would have saved millions of dollars by itself. The clients loved the work in the meeting – and subsequently killed it. Turned out one of the bosses' bonuses was based on call volume, as a proxy for leads.

Goodhart's Law (named after economist Charles Goodhart): 'When a measure becomes a target, it ceases to be a good measure.'

Conformal

Ideas can come from anywhere, says every CEO. At least in public. But there is a window of acceptable ideas that conform to expectations, and ideas that fall outside them are ignored.

Overton Window (also known as the 'Window of discourse'): the range of ideas the public will accept also operates inside companies, as a barrier to innovation.

The key to addressing barriers is correctly identifying them, which is usually impossible inside the system, since anyone working at the company is at the mercy of informal and conformal ones. Companies that can't work with partners are unlikely to see the end of the broken bridge until it's too late.

Notes

1. Eric Schmidt and Jonathan Rosenberg (September 2014) *How Google Works*, Grand Central Publishing, ISBN-10: 1455582344
2. Victor Newman (2013) *Power House: Strategic knowledge management*, [Online] http://www.blurb.co.uk/b/4278274-power-house
3. Matt Edgar (June 2013) Quora Answer, Why Don't Big Companies Innovate More? [Online] http://www.quora.com/Why-dont-big-companies-innovate-more/answer/Matt-Edgar?srid=pJZn&share=1 [accessed 16 October 2016]
4. Victor Newman (2013) *Power House: Strategic knowledge management*, [Online] http://www.blurb.co.uk/b/4278274-power-house [accessed 16 October 2016]
5. Hugh MacLeod (July 2004) Ignore Everybody, [Online] http://gapingvoid.com/2004/07/31/ignore-everybody/ [accessed 16 October 2016]
6. John Dawes 'Price changes and defection levels in a subscription-type market: can an estimation model really predict defection levels?', *Journal of Services Marketing*, (**18**:1)
7. Adam Katz (2011) Behance, All of my good ideas are battles, [Online] https://www.behance.net/gallery/905959/All-of-My-Good-Ideas-Are-Battles [accessed 16 October 2016]
8. About Dyson, [Online] http://www.dyson.co.uk/community/aboutdyson.aspx [accessed 16 October 2016]
9. Arie de Geus (1999) *The Living Company: Growth, learning and longevity in business*, Nicholas Brealey Publishing; New edition, ISBN-10: 1857881850
10. Nortel Study, University of Ottawa, Telfer School of Management (2014) Jonathan Calof, Greg Richards, Laurent Mirabeau, [Online] http://sites.telfer.uottawa.ca/nortelstudy/?_ga=1.151813053.549191806.1369078998 [accessed 16 October 2016]
11. Nortel Study, University of Ottawa, Telfer School of Management (2014) Jonathan Calof, Greg Richards, Laurent Mirabeau, [Online] http://sites.telfer.uottawa.ca/nortelstudy/?_ga=1.151813053.549191806.1369078998 [accessed 16 October 2016]
12. Paul Graham (December 2014) How to Be an Expert in a Changing World, [Online] http://paulgraham.com/ecw.html [accessed 16 October 2016]
13. Paul Graham (December 2014) How to Be an Expert in a Changing World, [Online] http://paulgraham.com/ecw.html [accessed 16 October 2016]

14 Paul Graham (December 2014) How to Be an Expert in a Changing World, [Online] http://paulgraham.com/ecw.html [accessed 16 October 2016]

15 Tom Fishburne (October 2010) Waterfall Planning, [Online] https://marketoonist.com/2010/10/waterfall-planning.html [accessed 16 October 2016]

16 Jason Fried and David Heinemeier Hansson (March 2010) *Rework*, Crown Business, ISBN-10: 0307463745

17 Steve Slater and Aashika Jain (December 2013) Reuters, RBS Admits Decades of IT Neglect, [Online] http://uk.reuters.com/article/2013/12/03/uk-rbs-technology-idUKBRE9B10YB20131203

18 Frances Coppola (March 2013) The Legacy Systems Problem, [Online] http://coppolacomment.blogspot.co.uk/2013/03/the-legacy-systems-problem.html [accessed 16 October 2016]

19 Frances Coppola (March 2013) The Legacy Systems Problem, [Online] http://coppolacomment.blogspot.co.uk/2013/03/the-legacy-systems-problem.html [accessed 16 October 2016]

20 Clay Christensen (10 May 2012) *How Will You Measure Your Life?*, HarperCollins ASIN: B006I1AE92

21 Faris Yakob (April 2015) *Paid Attention: Innovative advertising for a digital world*, Kogan Page, ISBN-10: 0749473606, ISBN-13: 978-0749473600

Defining digital transformation 04

So how might we best define exactly what digital transformation is? We must first acknowledge three foundational truths:

1. **Digital transformation is inevitable.** Change is happening whether you like it or not. You can either choose to respond or get left in its wake.
2. **Digital transformation is about more than technology.** As we will discuss at length in this book, it is also about strategy, process, culture, behaviours and people
3. **Digital transformation involves fundamental and comprehensive change.** It is the reinvention of the way in which a company operates. Clay Christensen has a useful way of framing an organization's capabilities (what it can and cannot do), defining three broad areas:[1] a) Resources (tangible ones like buildings and headcount, intangible ones like brands and IP); b) Priorities (the consensus on what's right to do, the values, and the strategy; c) Processes (the formal or informal way in which the work gets done). This is useful since, as Christensen says, these aspects are mutually exclusive in that a part of a business cannot fit into more than one of the categories, but are also collectively exhaustive (put together the three categories account for everything inside of the business). So digital transformation is fundamental in all three of these areas.

In 2014, digital and business consultancy Altimeter defined digital transformation as:[2]

> *the realignment of, or new investment in, technology and business models to more effectively engage digital customers at every touchpoint in the customer experience lifecycle.*

This definition acknowledges the shift required in not only technology but also business models and customer experience. Yet it perhaps does not emphasize enough the changes to processes, ways of working and culture.

So, bearing in mind Clay Christensen's way of summarizing the entire capabilities of an organization, this is our way of capturing a one sentence definition:

> *The transformation and reinvention of the resources, priorities and processes of a company in order to be fit for purpose in a digitally empowered world.*

What digital transformation is NOT

Digital transformation is not simply chasing shiny new technology. There is a salutary lesson contained in research conducted by Cap Gemini and MIT Sloan. The study (The Digital Advantage: How digital leaders outperform their peers in every industry)[3] looked at more than 400 large companies over a two-year period to assess the impact of digital technologies and how those companies were responding to those challenges.

The study found that while most companies were active with digital initiatives, only a few had positioned themselves to capture real business benefit. A combination of two separate but related dimensions combined to contribute toward digital maturity: digital intensity was defined as investment in technology enabled initiatives to change how the company operates (including customer engagements, internal operations, business models); transformation management intensity was about creating the leadership capabilities to drive digital transformation (including the vision, governance, engagement in the process of change, IT or business relationships to empower it). These two dimensions mapped out four different types of digital maturity on a two-by-two matrix:

1. **Beginners:** organizations that do very little with advanced digital capabilities, have a low awareness of opportunities.
2. **Conservatives:** companies that favour prudence over innovation, have a unified vision but are sceptical of the value of digital trends.
3. **Fashionistas:** follow digital trends and implement shiny new digital apps, but do not have a unified vision for the digital transformation of their business.
4. **Digirati:** those that truly understand how to drive value through the digital transformation of their business. In other words combining transformative vision and governance with investment, innovation and continuous improvement in people, process and technology.

These more digitally mature companies (or 'digirati') were able to combine a focus on change through new technology, with a concurrent focus on change management, people, process and culture. The study found that this latter group of companies were, on average, 26 per cent more profitable, had a 12 per cent higher market capitalization, and derived 9 per cent more revenue from existing assets.

This was an advantage that persisted across different industries. But what was also notable in the research was how companies that pursued shiny new technologies without the underlying strategies, processes, team structures and cultures to exploit it (the 'fashionistas') effectively damaged their business performance and were 11 per cent less profitable than the average.

The overarching lesson of the research is that digital transformation drives real advantage but pursuing shiny new technology ('the digital magpie syndrome') without focusing on all the supporting behaviours, skills, culture, vision and leadership is bad for business.

What good looks like: a maturity model for change

So that we might better represent and summarize many of the key shifts that we will be talking about in the coming chapters, we have developed a maturity model for what good looks like. This model describes three key stages of development:

1. **Legacy:** the state before a business has begun their journey toward digital transformation, wherein traditional thinking and approaches still dominate.
2. **Enabled:** the business is in the midst of the journey, and has likely adopted many of the foundational shifts in mindset, strategy, process, resources and culture, but there is still work to do to fully embed, extend and realize the full potential value of these new elements.
3. **Native:** the business is native to the fluid, rapidly changing environment in which it operates, and this is reflected right across the organization in the fabric of its culture and how it operates.

It is important to note that we are not describing a transition with a beginning, middle and an end. Rather, that the transition is one to an organization that is able to operate within a constant state of flux, continuously adapting to new challenges and opportunities that arise. In order to provide some structure to the model, we have delineated levels of maturity across multiple aspects including customers (orientation of the business), planning and processes, resources, strategy, vision and culture.

Customers

- **Legacy** – multichannel, not omnichannel, company orients around efficiency rather than customer need.
- **Enabled** – organization orients around customer need, joined up processes and data create coherent, consistent, high-quality customer experience.
- **Native** – seamless, rapid customer feedback loops inform strategies, tactics, innovation and continuous improvement.

Planning and processes

- **Legacy** – rigid waterfall processes, rigid approaches to planning, waterfall project management, infrequent release cycle, control centralized.
- **Enabled** – agile development, SCRUM, test and learn, deployment of rapid prototyping and build, operations empowered by digital, strong governance, measurement frameworks.
- **Native** – interdisciplinary agility, cross-functional, small, nimble teams, embracing of uncertainty, permission to fail, rapid test and learn embedded throughout, lean methodologies, embedded digital operations, data-driven and adaptive processes.

Resources

- **Legacy** – siloed data sources, basic analysis tools, descriptive analytics, technology restricts, legacy platforms, isolated knowledge, vertical skillsets, poor training, organizational structures oriented around functional siloes, rigid structures that do not adapt to opportunity.
- **Enabled** – software-as-a-service, integrated technology stack, flexible partnerships, joining up data, basic modelling, predictive analytics, digital centre of excellence, specialists and generalists, tech skills, more fluid structures, collaborative environment, integrated digital and online/offline.
- **Native** – structures and resourcing oriented around the customer, continuous reconfiguration of resourcing, flexible, adaptive structures, organizing around opportunity, joined-up data/tech, prescriptive analytics, empowered frontline staff, customized dashboards, scalability of the cloud, actionable modelling, real-time decisions, T-shaped, deep knowledge, human layer over tech, fluid flow of knowledge.

Strategy

- **Legacy** – digital capability development not central to organizational strategy/KPIs, clinging to legacy advantage, episodic innovation, short-term view.
- **Enabled** – systematically designed innovation process, more fluidity to strategy and planning, innovation accounting.
- **Native** – fully agile and adaptive strategy, systematic and embedded experimentation, healthy disengagement from legacy advantage, long-term view.

Vision

- **Legacy** – assumes retention of existing advantage, lack of clarity around organizational direction or purpose on the ground.
- **Enabled** – compelling vision and strategy, strong link between vision and organizational priorities/KPIs, rigid execution of vision.
- **Native** – clear organizational purpose and vision lived through leadership and operations, evident in explicit tactics and implicit behaviours, adaptive execution of vision.

Culture

- **Legacy** – precise, slow, controlling, restrictive, focused on efficiency, incremental improvement, highly discursive.
- **Enabled** – collaborative, customer-centric, data-driven, focus on talent, challenging norms, ownership mindset, greater autonomy, learning from failures as well as successes.
- **Native** – highly fluid/collaborative, agile culture, 'fast and roughly right', entrepreneurial, empowered teams, distributed authority, bias to action, 10X thinking, networked, embedded learning culture.

The agile formula

With comprehensive change requiring a comprehensive response, our definition of organizational agility incorporates three key foundational elements:

1. **Velocity:** heightened pace and progression through broad and proficient adoption and application of digital-native processes including design

thinking, agile and lean, continuous experimentation and a culture that supports constant testing and learning, coupled with an exhaustive, customer-centric innovation process that enables rapid origination, validation and commercialization of ideas.

2 **Focus:** building organizational momentum through an enabling, agile and adaptive strategy with strong links to execution, and aligned to a curious, outwardly looking perspective and a clear vision and purpose.
3 **Flexibility:** creating the culture, environment and structures to move fast through agile structures and small, multi-disciplinary teams, greater agility in decision-making and governance, productive and collaborative environments and an empowering and engaging culture characterized by autonomy, mastery and purpose.

Each of the elements is essential in becoming truly agile. Without velocity we lack momentum, without focus we lack direction and governance, without flexibility we lack the enabling environment necessary for success (Figure 4.1).

We will take each of these elements in turn in this book to help set out the structure and logic of our arguments. Since these foundational elements are not mutually exclusive, but are combinatorial in expounding the essential components of change, we can represent our formula for the agile business as:

$$\text{Agility} = (\text{Velocity} \times \text{Focus} \times \text{Flexibility})$$

Each Part of this book will incorporate a series of short discourses that build to form a blueprint for change, and in the final section we will bring these elements together to form a roadmap to becoming an agile business.

Figure 4.1 Elements of agility

	Focus	Flexibility	= Slow
Velocity		Flexibility	= Slapdash
Velocity	Focus		= Stifled
Velocity	Focus	Flexibility	= Success

Notes

1. Clay Christensen, Assessing Your Organization's Capabilities, [Online] http://cb.hbsp.harvard.edu/cbmp/product/607014-PDF-ENG
2. Altimeter, Brian Solis (2014) The State of Digital Transformation, 2014, [Online] http://www.altimetergroup.com/2014/07/the-2014-state-of-digital-transformation/ [accessed 16 October 2016]
3. CAP Gemini/MIT Sloan (November 2012) The Digital Advantage, [Online] http://www.capgemini.com/resources/the-digital-advantage-how-digital-leaders-outperform-their-peers-in-every-industry [accessed 16.10.16]

PART TWO
Velocity

In this Part, we focus on how to apply digital-native thinking and processes to build organizational velocity and momentum.

DEFINING VELOCITY

> **Velocity** – Rapidity of motion or operation; swiftness; speed; tempo; the rate with which something happens; action and reaction; heightened pace and progression towards a specific direction of change.

How should we think about velocity in the context of organizational agility? The best framework for understanding this comes not from a business consultant but from a military strategist. Colonel John Boyd was arguably not only one of the best fighter pilots that the United States Air Force has seen, but went on to became perhaps one of the best military strategists of all time. He was a maverick who fought multiple battles with Pentagon and military hierarchy in order to promote the application of his theories and ideas.

In the 1960s he worked with mathematician Thomas Christie to originate the Energy-Maneuverability (EM) theory of aerial combat which incorporated elements such as thrust, weight, drag and velocity into a formula that could be used to model the performance and combat capabilities of existing aircraft and even potential new fighter designs. The theory revolutionized how fighter aircraft were designed and evaluated. At the time, an ingrained design bias among the USAF hierarchy towards 'Bigger-Higher-Faster-Farther' meant that the US Air Force was consistently building larger, heavier, multifunctional fighter aircraft with significant technical complexity. Boyd was able to use his EM theory to show that US fighters faced the very real prospect of being convincingly outmanoeuvred in combat by Soviet MiGs. Instead, he and his collaborators (the so-called 'fighter mafia' who operated inside the Pentagon but challenged conventional thinking and therefore authority) championed a new lightweight fighter concept that would eventually become the renowned F16 jet fighter.

The impact of Boyd's prescient theories has reached far beyond military strategy, and his ideas now have a sharp resonance and relevance to the modern world of business. His maxim that technology must serve its larger purpose ('People, ideas, hardware – in that order.') has never been more true. When Boyd taught the Marines about his new form of warfare he preached that in battle there are always several ways to solve a problem so never to commit rigidly to just a single solution.

One of Boyd's most famous intellectual legacies is the OODA (Observation, Orientation, Decision, Action) loop, a decision-loop model designed to illustrate responses to an event.

In his biography of Boyd (*Boyd: The fighter pilot who changed the art of war*),[1] Robert Coram details how the maverick colonel, who served in the Korean War, was inspired by the success rate that American F86 Sabre fighters had achieved over the Russian built MiG15 jet in the skies over North Korea (some sources peg this as an overall 'kill ratio' of around 6 MiG-15s destroyed for every F86 lost). When Boyd looked into the reasons behind situations where F86s had performed in a superior way to the MiGs, he realized that rather than this advantage coming from the F86s being faster or more heavily armed than their opposition, it was derived from their ability to manoeuvre and respond more rapidly to swiftly changing battle conditions.

This insight, and his work on EM theory, led to Boyd developing ideas around how success and victory in rapidly changing environments (such as the battlefield) comes from the ability to make smart decisions in response to dynamic situations more quickly than your opponent. The OODA loop breaks down the decision cycle into four constituent parts:

1. **Observation** – through collection of data and information.
2. **Orientation** – forming a mental perspective using analysis and synthesis. The former breaks down data or information into components that allow for deductions that lead to understanding. The latter takes (sometimes unrelated) components and recombines them to form a new whole. Analysis, Boyd said, can lead to understanding but not to creativity.
3. **Decision** – based on your current mental perspective, the determination of a course of action.
4. **Action** – the resultant activity informed by the decisions.

Boyd believed that all intelligent organizations and organisms undergo a continuous cycle of interaction with their environment in this way, thereby enabling adaptation, but also that a key advantage can be derived not only through making smarter decisions, but by responding faster to changing situations. In describing the OODA loop, Harry Hillaker (who worked with Boyd as the Chief Designer of the lightweight F16 fighter) said:

> *Time is the dominant parameter. The pilot who goes through the OODA cycle in the shortest time prevails because his opponent is caught responding to situations that have already changed.*[2]

Boyd's thinking effectively became the intellectual kernel for a whole new approach to warfare for the American military that favoured greater agility over scale and sheer power. It enabled a move away from hundreds of years of linear, attritional warfare strategy, and it also came to be applied in multiple contexts to support business and learning objectives.

But the devil (and the true lesson for becoming an agile business) is in the detail. Rather than being thought of as a simple one-dimensional cycle where the advantage comes from being able to progress through the cycle at the fastest rate possible, the real power in the OODA loop comes from the ability to use the explicit *and* implicit knowledge and abilities of those on the frontline to create significant advantage through responsiveness, and to create confusion and disorientation among your opponent by using speed and agility to get into their decision cycle so that they are making decisions based on less up-to-date or relevant information. As Robert Coram describes it in the Boyd biography:

> *Thinking about operating at a quicker tempo – not just moving faster – than the adversary was a new concept in waging war. Generating a rapidly changing environment – that is, engaging in activity that is so quick it is disorienting and appears uncertain or ambiguous to the enemy – inhibits the adversary's ability to adapt and causes confusion and disorder that, in turn, causes an adversary to overreact or underreact.*
>
> (Coram, 2003)[3]

Thus, rather than being simply about speed, it is all about tempo and manoeuvrability. As the tempo increases the officers on the ground can bypass the explicit application of the 'Orientation' and 'Decision' parts of the loop to use more implicit and intuitive understanding of a changing environment to 'Observe' and 'Act' almost simultaneously. This adaptability compresses time, enables unexpected actions to be taken by the protagonist that in turn confuse the enemy, which then leads to even slower decision-making on their part, increasing the advantage even further.

One of the key notions that Boyd drew on to explain this came from the German concept of *Blitzkrieg* ('lightning war') warfare that involved the use of speed and surprise through concentrations of highly mobile, motorized, armoured units that could break through lines of defence and encircle potential larger enemy forces.

Blitzkrieg was all about a high operational tempo that was enabled not only through mechanized units but a form of command that empowered frontline commanders to respond faster, and was characterized by the concepts of *Schwerpunkt* and *Fingerspitzengefuhl*. *Schwerpunkt* (meaning the underlying goal, intent or focus of effort) gave the officers on the frontline focus, clarity of direction and objective. *Fingerspitzengefuhl* (meaning fingertip feel) enabled a level of flexibility within that for officers to make rapid, intuitive decisions on the ground in the face of fluid situations. A frontline officer would know the intent of his superior and understand the role of his unit in fulfilling that objective, but the executional detail could be far more fluid and responsive.

The reduced time needed to make decisions, improved communication and use of initiative by frontline officers, better exploitation of emerging opportunities, and a dramatically increased tempo through which tactics could be changed in response to new conditions, all combined with technology (highly mobile mechanized divisions and units) to powerful effect. Central to this new way of thinking was the idea that whoever is able to handle the quickest rate of change would win. Boyd stressed that once the process begins it should only accelerate. As Coram describes it:

> *Success is the greatest trap for the novice who properly implements the OODA Loop. He is so amazed at what he has done that he pauses and looks around and waits for reinforcements. But this is the time to exploit the confusion and to press on.*
>
> (Coram, 2003)[4]

Boyd's OODA loops point the way towards a new way of working for every business. Many of today's large organizations still subscribe to the 'Bigger-Higher-Faster-Farther' philosophy that was so ingrained in the US Air Force. Responses to significant challenges are often characterized by large, expensive, complex implementations of new technology that ignore the need to be more agile. All organizations want to move quicker but true agility is about more than just speed.

As Boyd's work shows us, in rapidly changing environments advantage comes from speed of response and manoeuvrability. And that's about people, process and culture – enabling technology to serve its wider purpose. As Boyd so succinctly expressed: 'People, ideas, hardware – in that order'. Instead of the context of responding faster to enemy action in war, our context is the need for every business to speed up response to changing customer behaviour and need, and competitive and market context. Just like Blitzkrieg, the key to this is how we balance a clear, overarching vision, direction and objective with the autonomy to enable more executionally oriented teams and managers to make and act on rapidly taken, data-driven but also intuitively led decisions in response to swiftly changing contexts. Velocity is important, but it is *the context in which it is important* that matters. Modern business advantage comes less and less from scale and more and more from manoeuvrability, or the ability to move quickly and seamlessly from one state to another.

Notes

1. Coram, R (15 April 2004) *Boyd: The fighter pilot who changed the art of war*, Back Bay Books, Reprint edition, ISBN-13: 978-0316796880
2. Ross Johnson (21 February 2013) *Antiterrorism and Threat Response, Planning and Implementation*, CRC Press, 1st edition, ISBN-10: 1466512903, ISBN-13: 978-1466512900
3. Coram, R (15 April 2004) *Boyd: The fighter pilot who changed the art of war*, Back Bay Books, Reprint edition, ISBN-13: 978-0316796880
4. Coram, R (15 April 2004) *Boyd: The fighter pilot who changed the art of war*, Back Bay Books, Reprint edition, ISBN-13: 978-0316796880

Operating in the 'ambiguity zone'

05

In Part One of this book, we discussed Charles Handy's S-curves as a model for understanding how digital disrupts markets and businesses.

The overlapping S-curves (Figure 5.1) create points at which a new technology or model enters the market (Point A), but it is also the point at which the incumbent technology or model is well optimized and potentially performing the best that it ever has, giving the incumbent business little apparent reason to disrupt its own model. Yet this is, of course, also the point of opportunity. Investment in experimentation, testing and learning, and innovation position the company well to generate new, distinctive and potentially disruptive ideas and therefore capitalize on a second curve.

Many organizations will only do this when they have reached point B, and are faced with a crisis in confidence and business performance. By then it is too late. Point B is the inflection point at which the new technology, or model that has previously been looked down on by incumbents, scales to the point where it becomes the dominant way forward. Like a parachutist experiencing ground rush, the new technology ramps more quickly than expected, leaving no time for a lagging, slow moving incumbent to respond in an effective way.

So the answer to this dilemma, of course, is never to get to that inflection point B. And that requires not just episodic innovation initiatives that are instituted in response to rapidly declining performance or an existential threat, but continual experimentation to create the opportunity to ride the next wave before it is too late.

Yet operating in the 'ambiguity zone' (as we have called it) is not easy. It requires not only a heightened level of boldness in being willing to disrupt your already well-optimized model, but the ability to concurrently manage more than one potentially competing business model in the same

Figure 5.1 The ambiguity zone

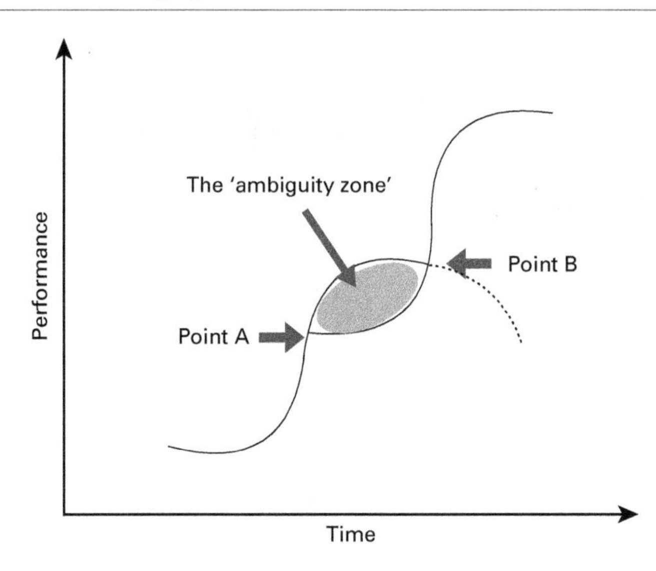

organization, a readiness to allocate precious resources towards continual experimentation and reinvention, and the culture to support all of those elements.

Building velocity through continuous innovation

In the context of the rapidly shifting competitive, company and consumer contexts that we discussed in Part One, the organizational response now required means that the kind of periodic, poorly coordinated innovation efforts seen in many organizations are no longer enough. Digital-native businesses have not only found ways to embed continuous innovation into the fabric of what they do, but also regard it as essential to continuing survival. In this scenario innovation is not compartmentalized into blocks of time any more than it is confined into team silos or individual job titles. This is about orienting the entire business towards continual exploration of potential opportunity and progression, and creating an innovation 'engine' to generate a constant flow of new projects and potential value, and move faster into areas of future opportunity.

Shifting from episodic to continuous, embedded innovation brings challenges that are practical (like day-to-day resourcing), strategic (like the need to resource against a longer-term vision), and cultural (not least that staff need to feel that it is acceptable to spend time on innovative new projects away from business as usual). So what are some of the ways to create the kind of culture that celebrates this way of thinking, doing and being? How do we create the space to originate, nurture and develop a continuous stream of new ideas?

We have all heard of Google's famed 20 per cent time, which encourages employees to spend 20 per cent of their work time experimenting with their own ideas, and which reportedly birthed Gmail and AdSense. But the concept of empowering staff to take the time to work on side-projects is not restricted to Google.

3M, for example, talk about 'Time to Think'[1] and have, since 1948, encouraged employees to spend 15 per cent of their working time on their own projects, utilizing 3M resources:

> *What would you do if you had access to world-class laboratories and scientists, and almost one day a week to investigate a new idea?*

This policy allowed the team that worked on Post-it® notes the space they needed to devote to a development process that had to overcome multiple barriers over the course of 12 years before launch and widespread success. Some of the ideas that come out of Time to Think (six to eight projects, twice a year) are supported by 'Genesis Grants', which can act as research seed money of anywhere between US$30,000 to US$75,000, enabling staff to explore ideas outside of the rigidity of business unit budgets.

The team at the UK Government Digital Service (GDS) have initiated a policy where for a defined period (two weeks or one month) they give the people in the team the freedom to go off the pre-planned roadmap and work on anything they want, as long as it is for the good of GOV.UK – with fewer top-down commitments. The policy, called a 'firebreak', is seen as vital to 'release some pressure from the system', minimize top-down commitments, take a step back, reduce layers of complexity, but also to work on new ideas. As Neil WIlliams, one of the Product Leads at GDS wrote:[2]

> *A whole team working off-roadmap for a whole month might sound reckless or indulgent. But in fact, it would have been reckless not to... Great things can happen when you give creative, passionate people the freedom to explore ideas.*

Ideas, problems and opportunities are collated for a month leading up to the firebreak. Pitch and demo meetings allowed everyone to keep up to date and decide what they wanted to work on. Learnings from the process are captured in wrap-up meetings.

Hackathons and hackdays are focused ways for digital-native organizations to carve out time for new ideas and prototypes. As well as running monthly hackdays when employees can work on anything they want, LinkedIn initiated a quarterly project called (in)cubator[3] where any employee, whether they work in engineering, sales, design or HR, can come up with an idea relating to any part of the business and pitch it to the executive staff. If the project is approved the team can spend up to three months of dedicated time to work on developing the idea. But in addition, the executive staff commit to mentoring the project leads to do everything they can to help it to be successful.

Similarly Apple has an initiative, called Blue Sky,[4] that gives employees two weeks away from their usual job to work on special projects, and Spotify runs regular 'hack weeks' with a similar aim.[5] Facebook has a long (well, since 2007, which is long in Facebook years) tradition of running hackdays[6] (and nights) where engineers and other staff come together to build anything they want, the only rule being that it must not be the same thing that you work on in the day job. Many of Facebook's best-known features (including chat, video sharing, the Like button, and the Timeline) have originated from hackathons. In the run-up to a hackathon, engineers submit potential ideas and groups form organically to work on them. Pedram Kenyani, the engineer who kicked off the practice of all-night hackathons at Facebook has said about them:[7]

> *It's a way to experiment with ideas in a low-cost way. Lots don't make it into products, but every hackathon tends to result in four or five things implemented on the site. A couple have changed the direction of the company.*

Such hackathons go far beyond the traditional company ideas scheme, and are regular and deliberately created opportunities to generate the space to progress ideas from thought into prototype. The practice of carving out dedicated time to focus on innovative projects is not new, but what *is* different is the scale and breadth of how this culture is systematized in the digital-native organization. In this context, these kinds of embedded conventions are seen not as a nice to have, but as essential to the fabric of how the company runs and to its success in the future.

In a digitally empowered world it is simply not enough for innovation to be episodic. Joel Gascoigne, the co-founder of social sharing app Buffer, has written about how the strategy that they have adopted in order to bake innovation into the business and stay agile as they scale.[8] This involves focusing resources on a balance of three key areas:

1. 'Core' areas mean those that are related to the fundamentals of what Buffer already is.
2. 'Expansion' is the term for 'any projects worked on which are logical expansions of what the product already is'.
3. 'Labs' is higher risk stuff that they 'want to just try and see what happens'.

This strategy is an echo of the approach taken at LinkedIn which similarly features 'core', 'expand' and 'venture' projects, and which co-founder Reid Hoffman describes[9] as a framework for keeping the company innovative. Working continuously on all three areas enables both Buffer and LinkedIn to focus not just on incremental improvement and expansion but also breakthrough innovation.

Joel Gascoigne believes that the ratio between these three elements at Buffer is around 50:30:20 but each organization will inevitably need to find their own levels. One alternative split comes from Intuit (the financial software business that thinks of itself as a '30 year-old start-up'). Speaking at SXSWi in 2013, Intuit CEO Scott Cook described a 70:20:10 model for products and budgeting:[10]

- 70 per cent is focused on the core or oldest products, with the objective of incremental growth and maintaining profit. This is the 'rowing team'.
- 20 per cent is focused on young to mid-stage products with an objective of profitable growth. These are the 'white water rafters'.
- 10 per cent is on completely new products, about solving user problems and proving a leap of faith. This is the equivalent of 'diving for sunken treasure'.

Intuit deliberately structure resourcing in this way so that they can successfully bake experimentation into business as usual. Similarly, Google have adopted a 70/20/10 approach to time and focus whereby 70 per cent of management time should be focused on the core business or areas of responsibility, 20 per cent should be on related projects, and 10 per cent on unrelated new businesses or ideas.[11] This is a way of embedding fresh perspectives and different thinking into the company.

Their approach is resonant of three horizons thinking (first espoused in Christian Terwiesch and Karl Ulrich's book *Innovation Tournaments: Creating and selecting exceptional opportunities*):[12]

- **Horizon 1** is about incremental improvements or extensions to existing brands or products. This type of innovation typically focuses on existing markets or utilizes existing technologies that the company is familiar with, and is likely the easiest and most common form of innovation.

- **Horizon 2** innovations are more about adjacencies, next generation products and likely focused on existing markets or technologies but perhaps ones that the company is less familiar with. Because of this, it requires different thinking and techniques from Horizon 1.
- **Horizon 3** innovations are entirely new, breakthrough products or categories that are pushing the boundaries, and pushing the company to explore new markets or technologies.

It is important for companies to focus not just on easier, incremental innovation but to recognize the need for a more comprehensive approach that also recognizes the differences inherent in these different types. While it may not always be necessary to run all three types of innovation concurrently, digital-native organizations are adept at accommodating all three, switching the balance of focus between them as required, and maintaining the kind of thinking, culture and expectations that can enable all three to thrive. An important part of this will be setting realistic expectations for failure (and learning). The failure rate expected in Horizon 1, for example, should be very different from that set for Horizon 3. Unrealistic or poorly planned expectations can kill fragile initiatives before they have even had the chance to properly prove their worth or reveal a larger potential opportunity down the line. Adopting a 70:20:10 approach to resourcing akin to that at Intuit may be challenging in the face of short-term targets and stretched resourcing but is perhaps a more palatable way of supporting potentially breakthrough ideas, and in today's rapidly shifting environment can companies really afford not to do that?

More experimentation = more opportunity

While we have plenty of well-documented examples of businesses that have shown an inability to respond to rapidly changing market and consumer dynamics (RIM/Blackberry, Kodak, Nokia, Blockbuster), there are also examples of companies that are not afraid to reinvent themselves. Apple's revenues have grown dramatically since the return of Steve Jobs to the company in 1997, but so has their composition, not least through a product development programme (iPods, smartphones and tablets) that shows itself to be unafraid of potential cannibalization.

IBM is a business that has reinvented itself multiple times over its 100+ year history from creating punch card systems for payroll data, to originating bar codes and credit card magnetic strips, to developing computer disc drives, chips and a huge mainframe computing business to computing service delivery, a cloud-based offering, technology and digital transformation consultancy, and the development of a design and UX service offering. Their history has not been short of existential crises, but each one of these transformations has involved a reinvention of business models, organizational structure and skills profile.

Yet the pace of innovation and organizational response has dramatically sharpened. Facebook have radically changed their revenue base from a position at IPO in 2012 where they were deriving next to zero monetary benefit from mobile to where, just four years later, 84 per cent of their advertising revenue base is mobile.[13] Their acquisition strategy sees them actively buying up rival services (Instagram, WhatsApp) that pose a potential future threat but instead of then shutting those services down, they enable them to coexist alongside services like Facebook Messenger that have been generated in-house through a continuous programme of innovation.

That innovation is combined with a high-tempo continual improvement of core services – what the Japanese might call 'Kaizen', the culture of continuous improvement.[14] The point here is that investment in continual iteration and innovation creates opportunity at scale, and opportunity that is not always obvious at initiation. Steven Johnson, the author of 'How We Get To Now',[15] tells the story of how Gutenberg's printing press is an example of an invention that had a number of unanticipated effects. One of the impacts of many more people across Europe starting to read was the realization that many people were far-sighted. This resulted in a surge in demand for spectacles, which in turn meant an increase in experimentation with lenses right across Europe, which led to innovations including the telescope and the microscope:

> *Almost immediately there is this extraordinary scientific revolution in terms of understanding and identifying the cell, and identifying the moons of Jupiter and all these different things that Galileo does. So the Gutenberg press ended up having this very strange effect on science that wasn't about the content of the books being published.*[16]

One of the most undervalued consequences of high-volume, high-paced innovation and iteration is the creation of opportunity that you didn't even knew existed.

Marginal and breakthrough innovation

It is easy, perhaps informed by past successes or competitive activity, for companies to think of innovation in relatively one-dimensional ways. We might over-focus, for example, on *marginal* innovation that brings incremental gain and continuous improvement over time. While this can bring huge benefit, it can often be at the expense of *breakthrough* innovation that involves high risk, different thinking, frequent failure but big potential gain. Yet both are, of course, necessary. Both forms of innovation are vital because, in the words of author and economist Tim Harford:

> *marginal improvement is all about climbing the hill you're on... longshots are all about finding new mountains to conquer.*[17]

The biggest problem with an overemphasis on marginal, incremental innovation was neatly summed up by Google founder Larry Page in his 2013 letter to investors:[18]

> *It's... true that over time many companies get comfortable doing what they have always done, with a few incremental changes. This kind of incrementalism leads to irrelevance over time, especially in technology, because change tends to be revolutionary, not evolutionary.*

Later in this section we will focus on ways to break out of incremental thinking and into the realms of the truly disruptive.

The case for a more iterative, emergent approach

> *A complex system that works is invariably found to have evolved from a simple system that worked. The inverse proposition also appears to be true: a complex system designed from scratch never works and cannot be made to work. You have to start over, beginning with a simple system.*
>
> John Gall, systems theorist

'Gall's Law', as expressed above, comes from John Gall's 1975 book *Systemantics: How systems work and especially how they fail.*[19] Gall's work has inspired a number of authors in systems thinking but the book actually focuses more on what we can learn from system engineering failures and how not to design systems. The law (although it was never expressly stated as a law in the book) is essentially an argument in favour of under-specification (so it has a natural affinity to agile thinking which we will discuss later) and argues that owing to the difficulty involved in designing large complex systems accurately, it is far better instead to design smaller, simpler systems that can then develop incrementally based on a continual input and measurement of user interaction and needs.

This was, and is, a simple concept and yet it is quite profound. Think of all the complex systems that we try to design and launch (from large IT projects to government policy implementation) that fail from the outset. As Josh Kaufman has pointed out in his explanation of Gall's Law, complex systems are full of interdependencies and variations that are almost impossible to anticipate but that actually play a significant role in making the system function:

> *Complex systems designed from scratch will never work in the real world, since they haven't been subject to environmental selection forces while being designed... If you want to build a system that works, the best approach is to build a simple system that meets the environment's current selection tests first, then improve it over time.*[20]

Far better surely, to start with something simpler, easier, smaller and evolve from there. This is why, in scenarios characterized by complexity (such as those within which most businesses now operate), prototypical, emergent, iterative approaches work best.

The problem with waterfall

Waterfall development is the classic linear, non-adaptive design-and-build process that has long been applied to software development. Progression in waterfall is linear since once each phase has been completed there is no returning to it. Rather than originating from software design, the process actually originated from other industries (such as manufacturing and construction) where the cost or practicality of making changes to a completed stage was prohibitive.

Waterfall methodologies involve a progression from an (often extensive and lengthy) requirements capturing and analysis process, through (often detailed and protracted) design and build stages, then (frequently arduous) testing and debugging, before finally being installed and becoming operational. While this can work for projects where requirements are rigid and unchanging, there are several key challenges with waterfall processes:

- Requirements-gathering processes are frequently poor at capturing real user need. People do not always know what they want. Many needs are unexpected.
- The detailed, linear, sequential nature of the process (you should only move to the next stage once the previous one has been reviewed) means that it is frequently a very lengthy process.
- This can also mean that functional interaction (for example, between designers and coders) is limited, and concurrent working on the same problem restricted, which can lead to designers designing elements that cannot work, or developers coding without design input.
- Requirements and contexts now change at a faster pace than ever but waterfall is poor at adapting to changing needs (once a stage is complete it is very difficult to go back and make amends), meaning that by the time the end user sees the first version of the product or system updates are required straightaway or it is even no longer fit for purpose.
- Unforeseen problems or needs are less easy to identify along the way since all the requirements capturing has been done upfront.

As we will discuss later, waterfall thinking is emblematic of traditional approaches to strategy, planning and execution that still exist inside most organizations. In a world characterized by accelerating change, the kind of issues that waterfall throws up – inflexibility and linearity, lack of adaptability to changing requirements and contexts, lack of pace and momentum, poor cross-functional collaborative working, are akin to many of the issues that these traditional ways of working now present. Put simply, the problem is not only with the process, but with the mindset, thinking and behaviours that surround it.

The three types of problem in the world

We know that every problem is different but we are often susceptible to misdiagnosing the nature of the obstacle that we are facing, and therefore the correct approach to deriving a solution. American surgeon and author Atul Gawande makes a compelling case in his book *The Checklist Manifesto*[21] for how the quantity and complexity of knowledge required to execute many tasks in the modern world restricts our ability to do it consistently and correctly, and how something as simple as a checklist can be a powerful driver of accuracy, dependability and performance.

Gawande makes a point of acknowledging the importance of recognizing the correct type of challenge that we are facing, referencing the three types of problem in the world delineated in a paper on reform in the healthcare industry by Brenda Zimmerman of York University and Sholom Glouberman of the University of Toronto:[22]

1. *Simple problems are ones like baking a cake from a mix. There is a recipe.*
2. *Complicated problems are ones like sending a rocket to the moon. They can sometimes be broken down into a series of simple problems. But there is no straightforward recipe. Success frequently requires multiple people, often multiple teams, and specialized expertise. Unanticipated difficulties are frequent. Timing and coordination become serious concerns.*
3. *Complex problems are ones like raising a child. Once you learn how to send a rocket to the moon, you can repeat the process with other rockets and perfect it. One rocket is like another rocket. But not so with raising a child, the professors point out. Every child is unique. Although raising one child may provide experience, it does not guarantee success with the next child. Expertise is valuable but most certainly not sufficient. Indeed, the next child may require an entirely different approach from the previous one. And this brings up another feature of complex problems: their outcomes remain highly uncertain. Yet we all know that it is possible to raise a child well. It's complex, that's all.*

Zimmerman and Glouberman go on to contend that we (in the context of the paper they are talking about healthcare experts) often:

> *... implicitly describe complex problems as complicated ones and hence employ solutions that are wedded to rational planning approaches. These often lead to inappropriate solutions because they neglect many aspects of complexity.*

This, say the authors, is like the old joke about the policeman who sees a drunk man searching for something under a streetlight and asks what the drunk has lost. He says that he has lost his keys and so they both look under the streetlight together. After a few minutes the policeman asks if he is sure he lost them here, and the drunk replies, no, and that he lost them in the park. The policeman asks why he is searching here, and the drunk replies, 'this is where the light is'. Our observational bias, and the sophistication of our theories, models and language, say the authors, can be as seductive as the lamplight. They might provide an illusion of clarity but they can also lead to approaches that do not properly take account of complex adaptive systems and situations.

In the context of the modern business environment, which is more than ever characterized by complexity, it becomes essential that we define challenges in the right way, avoid conflating the complex with the complicated, and set about shaping the response to those challenges in the right way.

Complex scenarios require emergent solutions

'Best practice' is one of those terms that, while not inherently bad, has become so overused as to be stretched beyond its rightful application. So it gets applied generically to any scenario where an understanding of the most effective methods to solve a problem is desired. Our wish to create certainty out of ambiguity, and to impose control over the unpredictable leads us to wish to standardize approaches and apply best practice to many distinct types of situation. But as we have shown there is a big difference between simple, complicated and complex challenges.

Figure 5.2 Dave Snowden's Cynefin model

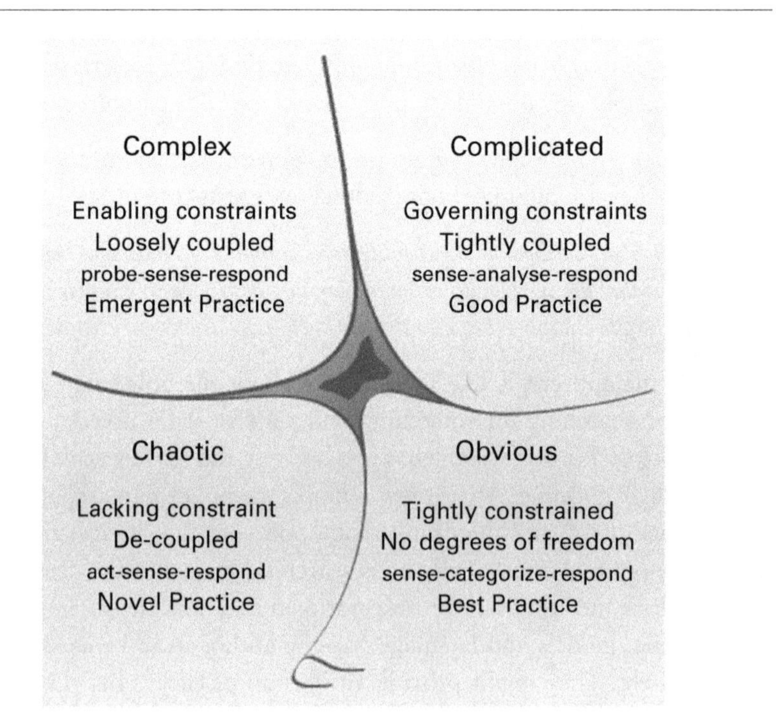

An excellent way of framing the difference in our response to each of these types of challenge comes from Dave Snowden's Cynefin model,[23] a useful framework for decision-making (Figure 5.2).

Simple contexts, characterized by stable, clear cause-and-effect relationships and 'known knowns' are the domain of best practice. Managers, says Dave, might appraise a situation and base a response on established processes. The hazards here come from complacency and entrained thinking, which might blind us to new perspectives.

Complicated contexts may still have a clear relationship between cause and effect but can also contain many applicable answers, some of which are not immediately obvious ('known unknowns'), and so this requires analysis of suitable options and is typically the domain of experts. Good practice is therefore more appropriate than best practice. The danger in this context comes from experts who are biased towards preferred solutions, over-analysis leading to paralysis, or from ignoring potentially innovative ideas from non-experts.

Complex contexts, however, are constantly shifting ('unknown unknowns'). As Dave Snowden notes, the temptation in the face of such unpredictability is to demand certainty in the form of foolproof plans with precise outcomes: to revert to a command-and-control leadership style; to become less patient. But in complex contexts we can only understand why things happen in retrospect and answers are emergent so we need to look for instructive patterns through experimentation. Encouraging the conducting of experiments that are as 'safe to fail' as possible enables informative patterns and a clearer direction to emerge. Imposing a desire for order or a rigidly defined course of action will preempt the opportunity for such instructive patterns to emerge.

In chaotic contexts no manageable patterns exist, the relationship between cause and effect is impossible to define, and so clear, concise and immediate action to establish as much order and stability as possible is what is required. Leaders need to work to transform situations from chaos to complexity where emerging patterns might be identified and suitable responses determined.

If the world of business is increasingly characterized by uncertainty, continuous flux and complex contexts, then the bad side of best practice is that we seek to oversimplify and use it as a way of seeking certainty in situations that require a more emergent pattern of decision-making. As Dave notes, best practice is, by definition, past practice but hindsight no longer leads to foresight after a shift in context. While it may be appropriate in simple contexts, misappropriation of best practice in today's ever-more complex world means that we are in danger of becoming the drunk searching for his keys in the streetlight.

Notes

1 3M, Time to Think, [Online] http://solutions.3m.com/innovation/en_US/stories/time-to-think [accessed 16 October 2016]

2 Neil WIlliams (February 2015) GDS Blog, GOV.UK's Firebreak: How and why we spent a month working differently, [Online] https://insidegovuk.blog.gov.uk/2015/02/06/gov-uks-firebreak-why-and-how-we-spent-a-month-working-differently/ [accessed 16 October 2016]

3 LinkedIn, Incubator, [Online] http://blog.linkedin.com/2012/12/07/linkedin-incubator/ [accessed 16 October 2016]

4 Matthew Panzarino (November 2012) Apple Blue Sky, [Online] http://thenextweb.com/apple/2012/11/12/apple-fires-up-its-version-of-googles-20-time-giving-some-employees-2-weeks-for-special-projects/ [accessed 16 October 2016]

5 Henrik Knowberg (2014) Spotify Hack Weeks, [Online] https://labs.spotify.com/2014/03/27/spotify-engineering-culture-part-1/ [accessed 16 October 2016]

6 Facebook Hackathons, [Online] https://www.facebook.com/hackathon [accessed 16 October 2016]

7 David Sacks, FastCompany (2012) Secrets of Facebook's Legendary Hackathons Revealed, [Online] http://www.fastcompany.com/3002845/secrets-facebooks-legendary-hackathons-revealed [accessed 16 October 2016]

8 Joel Gascoigne, Buffer, (May 2014) How We're Trying to Stay Innovative as a 3.5 Year Old Startup, [Online] http://joel.is/how-were-trying-to-stay-innovative-as-a-3-5-year-old/ [accessed 16 October 2016]

9 Reid Hoffman talks to Matt Mullenweg (February 2014) [Online] https://www.youtube.com/watch?v=LMGb2UoNFYM [accessed 16 October 2016]

10 Martin Bailie, SXSW Themes: Start-up Culture, Code and Data, [Online] http://www.slideshare.net/martinbailie/sxsw-2013-themes-startup-culture-code-and-data [accessed 16 October 2016]

11 John Battelle (1 December 2005) *CNN Money* magazine, [Online] 'The 70 Percent Solution: Google CEO Eric Schmidt gives us his golden rules for managing innovation' [accessed 16 October 2016]

12 Christian Terwiesch and Karl Ulrich (1 June 2009) *Innovation Tournaments: Creating and selecting exceptional opportunities*, Harvard Business School Press, ISBN-10: 1422152227

13 Sarah Frier (2016) Facebook Revenue, Users Top Estimates as Mobile Ads Surge, Bloomberg Technology, [Online] http://www.bloomberg.com/news/articles/2016-07-27/facebook-sales-user-growth-top-estimates-as-mobile-ads-surge [accessed 24 October 2016]

14 What is Kaizen? Kaizen Institute, [Online] https://uk.kaizen.com/about-us/definition-of-kaizen.html [accessed 16 October 2016] https://uk.kaizen.com/about-us/definition-of-kaizen.html" [accessed 24/10/16]

15 Steven Johnson (30 September 2014) *How We Got to Now: Six innovations that made the modern world*, Riverhead Books, ISBN-10 1594632960 ISBN-13 978-1594632969

16 Megan Gambino (30 September 2014) The World Is What It Is Today Because of These Six Innovations, Smithsonian.com, [Online] http://www.smithsonianmag.com/innovation/world-what-it-today-because-these-six-innovations-180952871/?no-ist" [accessed 24 October 2016]

17 Tim Harford (2 January 2013) The Undercover Economist, Wired, [Online] https://www.youtube.com/watch?v=7GHhmgZ0BwQ [accessed 24 October 2016]

18 Sergey Brin (2013) Founders' Letter, Alphabet Investor Relations, [Online] https://abc.xyz/investor/founders-letters/2013/ [accessed 24 October 2016]

19 John Gall (May 1975) *Systemantics: How systems work and especially how they fail*, Times Books, ISBN-10 0812906748 ISBN-13 978-0812906745

20 Josh Kaufmann ©2005–2016 What Is 'Gall's Law'?, PersonalMBA.com, [Online] https://personalmba.com/galls-law/" [accessed 24 October 2016]

21 Atul Gawande (2011) *The Checklist Manifesto: How to get things right*, Profile, ISBN-10 1846683149 ISBN-13 978-1846683145

22 Sholom Glouberman and Brenda Zimmerman (July 2002) Government of Canada, Complicated and Complex Systems: What Would Successful Reform of Medicare Look Like?, [Online] http://publications.gc.ca/collections/Collection/CP32-79-8-2002E.pdf [accessed 24 October 2016]

23 Dave Snowden and Mary Boone (November 2007) A Leader's Framework for Decision Making, *Harvard Business Review*, [Online] https://hbr.org/2007/11/a-leaders-framework-for-decision-making [accessed 24 October 2016]

Digital-native processes 06

If the modern business environment requires more adaptive, emergent and iterative ways of working, there are several foundational concepts which provide us with not only effective, well-proven processes but also ways of thinking that are highly relevant, applicable and instructive. We are talking about agile, lean, design thinking, and the many variant processes that they have spawned. The dynamism, flexibility and non-linearity of these foundational methodologies make them far more apposite for today's complex environments. Small wonder, therefore, that they are expanding beyond startups, innovation labs and technology teams to become embedded in wider business thinking, inspiring new approaches and fundamentally different ways of operating.

Design thinking

The growing importance of design in business has become evident from the heavy investment that companies in a number of sectors are making in design and user experience talent. Not least of these are consulting businesses including Deloitte, Accenture and IBM (IBM have structured frameworks around design thinking to help IBM-ers solve users' problems at speed and scale)[1] who have refocused recruitment and acquisition programmes to serve a far greater requirement for design skills and approaches.

Design thinking was really first adapted for business by David Kelley and Tim Brown, founders of design business IDEO. Tim Brown has defined design thinking as:

> *... a human-centered approach to innovation that draws from the designer's toolkit to integrate the needs of people, the possibilities of technology, and the requirements for business success.*[2]

The process involves a broader application of design methods to business and innovation, using solution-focused thinking, starting with a future goal, and investigating both present and future conditions to iteratively generate multiple ideas and options and simultaneously explore alternative routes to achieving the goal. IDEO, for example, look for the intersection that: 'brings together what is desirable from a human point of view with what is technologically feasible and economically viable'.[3]

Key to design thinking is the successive application of divergent and convergent thinking, the former being about originating multiple possibilities, the latter about narrowing these choices down and selecting the optimal way forwards. One example of a design thinking process incorporates seven stages: define, research, ideate, prototype, choose, implement and learn.[4] This process has similarities to the lean learning loop that we will look at later, but with design thinking these steps are not always linear and may be repeated in order to find better solutions. Like agile and lean, design thinking maintains a strong focus on the user (through empathy) and also teamwork, and some of the tools used including customer journey mapping, empathy mapping, paper prototyping and personas may be applied to add value across all three approaches.

Agile

Published in 2001, the Agile Manifesto[5] arose from a meeting of software developers at the Snowbird resort in Utah who had come together to discuss lightweight development philosophies that had evolved as a counterpoint to more rigid processes such as waterfall. Although iterative, adaptive processes had been around for a number of years, the manifesto helps capture a new way of working that recognized some key shifts in value ('while there is value in the items on the right, we value the items on the left more'):

- Individuals and interactions over processes and tools
- Working software over comprehensive documentation
- Customer collaboration over contract negotiation
- Responding to change over following a plan.

Since then, agile software development practices have grown into widely adopted and extremely robust processes. A number of iterative development methodologies are often categorized under the agile umbrella (including SCRUM, Kanban, XP, Crystal) but agile has revolutionized the way in which technology teams work, and software gets built. The key concepts, characteristics and practices inherent in agile software development methods include (Figure 6.1):

Figure 6.1 Agile software development

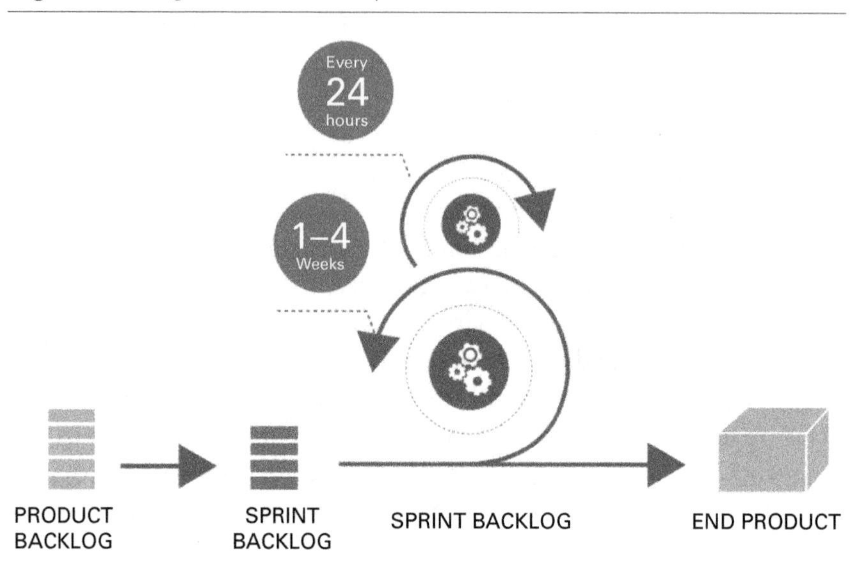

- the use of cross-functional teams drawn from all the key functions (to allow for requirements to change over time, in place of rigorous, rigid, upfront specification
- teams that are are self-organizing, with a high degree of autonomy
- co-location and face-to-face communication prioritized to enable speed
- teams working iteratively in blocks of time or sprints (typically 1–4 weeks) against an agreed set of priorities, which may require multiple sprints to release new features or a product but the objective is usually to be able to release working outputs at the end of each sprint
- working outputs that can be demonstrated to stakeholders whose feedback is incorporated into the next or future work sprints
- the product backlog organizing and prioritizing work based on business and user value – priorities are revisited at the start of every sprint into a sprint backlog
- daily stand-up gatherings (or 'scrums' as they are sometimes called) creating short feedback loops and enabling team members to report daily progress and intentions towards the team and sprint goals, or any barriers to progress that have been encountered
- the product owner as a key part of the team, and the representative of the customer or end user (key stakeholders in the business agree in advance that the product owner can act on their behalf) – they are available to developers to answers questions during the sprint

- transparency is key, with physical displays near the team presenting a summary of progress and current status
- a focus on quality maintained through specific design processes and testing methodologies that are designed to also support agility.

A key advantage of agile methodologies comes from the ability to adapt to changing realities quickly and therefore minimize overall risk. Longer-term goals may be set but there is much greater flexibility built into the path to achieving them. Built-in retrospectives at the end of each sprint ensure that the quality of prioritization and work in the next sprint is as good as it can be. Methods that are more predictive (like waterfall) attempt to plan out the future context or requirements in comprehensive detail that limits the ability to change along the way. In a rapidly shifting environment this carries significant inherent risk, particularly if that early analysis or planning is flawed.

In agile, the principle is to 'release early and often'. Testing is generally conducted on an ongoing basis and incorporated into the same iteration as the coding work rather than being separated out into a distinct phase. This means that end users can have far more visibility of development work and progress, and can better understand the value. This inclusive approach is highly transparent and minimizes the risk of misalignment (which in non-iterative processes can become steadily worse over time), generates better quality feedback through enabling the end users to make better decisions on where the real value/issues are in working outputs (because they can actually use them), and see the progressive build of value over time through frequent releases.

Agile is not without its challenges. Moving to agile working is a significant shift in culture and working practice. It can easily bump up against existing business processes and prioritization. A half-hearted implementation of agile (or what we term later as 'doing waterfall in an agile way') will more often than not fail. There is a healthy dose of delusion in business wrapped up in our belief that we can forecast future needs, situations and outcomes even in highly complex and fluid environments, and yet the apparent lack of long-term predictability inherent in agile can leave many leaders uncomfortable embarking on a roadmap where every step has not already been mapped out. Leaders may also feel uncomfortable having to do without many of the totems of more traditional approaches such as comprehensive documentation in the initial stages of a project. Coaches in agile, and intermediary roles such as the product owner or product manager can often play a key part in mitigating some these risks. But it is important to recognize that the philosophy and principles that surround this methodology and that were expressed in the Agile Manifesto all those years ago do not stop with the technology team running an agile software development process. This speaks to the much bigger opportunity that has inspired this book.

Lean

The foundation for lean thinking was established through lean manufacturing, an approach that considered anything in a production process outside of the creation of value for the end customer as wastage and systematically seeks to remove it. This in turn was inspired by the Toyota Production System (TPS) which had identified 'seven wastes' including defects, inventory (minimizing anything not in process) and overproduction (the idea of 'just in time' production rather than producing ahead of demand) that were then methodically eliminated. Lean manufacturing therefore sought to only bring in necessary inputs to the process at the point they were needed, and identify imperfections in output as early in the process as possible to minimize correction time. TPS and lean manufacturing sit alongside the Japanese practice of 'Kaizen' (meaning 'improvement') which, in the business context, relates to the involvement of employees at all levels in the continuous incremental improvement of the manufacturing process.

In 2008, Eric Ries took some of these ideas and combined them with his own experience in startups to originate the lean startup,[6] the product development methodology that shares some similar overarching principles to agile. Like lean manufacturing, it seeks to eliminate waste. Like agile, the process is iterative with continuous product releases and customer feedback embedded as a key part of the process. Hypotheses about customer need or product features are successively validated through iterative releases or rapid prototyping, thereby minimizing risk and the need for large initial investment, and enabling continuous learning.

Ries believes that the continuous involvement of customers in the development process enables startups (and any business developing new products and services) to inclusively recruit early adopters and solve real customer problems before attempting to acquire scale. The core concepts that sit at the heart of lean are:

- **The build-measure-learn loop:** An iterative cycle that follows a process of identifying a hypothesis (about a specific customer need or product feature), designing a test that will validate that hypothesis (often the simplest possible prototype), testing wherever possible with real customers, and taking the learning into the next learning loop. This methodology is designed to eliminate as much uncertainty as possible from the development process, and to continuously test and learn en route to fulfilling a vision.

- **The minimum viable product (MVP):** In his book, Ries describes the MVP as the 'version of a new product which allows a team to collect the maximum amount of validated learning about customers with the least effort'.[7] MVPs can be developed to test a new hypothesis, but the principle is to create the simplest possible test or prototype to validate that idea and enable progression on to the next learning loop as quickly as possible.
- **Innovation accounting:** Traditional accounting methods work well with established products or propositions but can stifle innovation, a new idea or a startup business by focusing on the wrong metrics (like ratio and cash flow analysis) that set unrealistic expectations about early revenue generation. Innovation accounting focuses on 'actionable metrics' (as opposed to 'vanity metrics' that do not accurately represent the performance and business drivers) that measure early progress and enable better prioritization. These might include customer usage and retention measures.
- **The pivot:** Ries describes the pivot is a 'structured course correction designed to test a new fundamental hypothesis about the product, strategy, and engine of growth'. Pivots might enable a refocusing of the product proposition or key features while still maintaining the guiding vision for the business or product.

While agile software development may be typically used in technology teams, and design thinking and lean mainly applied in the service of product and service development, the principles, practices and philosophy that surround all three have far broader application for the way in which we conduct business and secure competitive advantage.

The principles of agile business

The Agile Manifesto gives us a blueprint for a better way of developing software, but it also speaks to some fundamental principles for doing better business in the complex adaptive environment we know today. The 12 principles of agile business align closely with those that were originated in the manifesto (Table 6.1):

Table 6.1 The 12 principles of agile business

	Agile Manifesto Principle	Agile Business Principle
1	Our highest priority is to satisfy the customer through early and continuous delivery of valuable software	The primary orientation is towards customer need delivered through constant improvement of customer experience
2	Welcome changing requirements, even late in development. Agile processes harness change for the customer's competitive advantage	Strategies and tactics are highly adaptive and responsive, and change is welcomed
3	Deliver working software frequently, from a couple of weeks to a couple of months, with a preference to the shorter timescale	Iterative, sprint working delivers customer value through continuous progress and momentum
4	Business people and developers must work together daily throughout the project	Effective cross-functional collaboration, supported through clear intent, is critical for success
5	Build projects around motivated individuals. Give them the environment and support they need, and trust them to get the job done	Build companies with motivated individuals. Empower teams to deliver through a flexible working environment characterized by trust and comfort with dissent
6	The most efficient and effective method of conveying information to and within a development team is face-to-face conversation	Bureaucracy are politics are minimized, co-location and face-to-face communication maximized wherever possible
7	Working software is the primary measure of progress	Working outputs are the optimum measure of progress and success
8	Agile processes promote sustainable development. The sponsors, developers and users should be able to maintain a constant pace indefinitely	Agile business supports relentless and sustainable innovation and progress. Change and iteration is constant, and the pace of progress never slows
9	Continuous attention to technical excellence and good design enhances agility	Technical excellence and good design are central to maintaining pace and agility
10	Simplicity – the art of maximizing the amount of work not done – is essential	Minimize wasted effort, duplication and resources

(*Continued*)

Table 6.1 *(Continued)*

	Agile Manifesto Principle	Agile Business Principle
11	The best architectures, requirements and designs emerge from self-organizing teams	The best results emerge from small teams with a high degree of autonomy
12	At regular intervals, the team reflects on how to become more effective, then tunes and adjusts its behaviour accordingly	Continuous improvement is achieved through embedded reflection time, and behaviours and culture that support learning

These principles for agile business set out a new orientation for the digitally empowered business. They concern the very fabric of how an organization works.

Developing a learning culture

Agile, lean and design thinking have dramatically changed the way in which technology teams, startups and innovation labs work, but this revolution does not stop with the innovators, entrepreneurs and technologists. The principles and practices that are integral to this more adaptive way of working have much broader application throughout business but just as importantly (as we will go on to discuss in Part Four) in order to deliver real value they all require the organizational culture that can enable them to survive and to flourish.

There is not one right process. Each team or business will find that there are methodologies that they are more comfortable with, and that different scenarios and environments call for different approaches. Rather it is more often about how you can combine different approaches and processes for optimum impact and for the job to be done. Yet all of these ways of thinking and working have commonality in approaches and outlook that are integral to operating in the modern business environment. Not least of these is their need to operate within, and their ability to support and catalyse an organizational culture that is all about learning.

We have all heard the platitudes to 'fail fast', 'embrace failure', or 'fail forwards'. Yet failure in isolation is an unwanted and unnecessary distraction. So let's instead talk about the value of learning cultures. Ed Catmull, President of Pixar, one of the most successful film businesses of all time has said that:

> *Failure isn't a necessary evil. In fact, it isn't evil at all. It is a necessary consequence of doing something new.*

... and

> *If you aren't experiencing failure, then you are making a far worse mistake: You are being driven by the desire to avoid it.*[8]

And he's right. But he also said: 'When faced with a challenge, get smarter'. The point about failure is that we need to use *every* experience, good or bad, as an opportunity to learn so that we get continually better and smarter over time. To paraphrase the venture capitalist Marc Andreesen:

> *The goal is not to fail fast. The goal is to succeed over the long run. They are not the same thing.*[9]

The agile business is one that is continually exploring but also one that is continually learning. Author Jim Collins followed up the bestselling *Good to Great* a decade later, with *Great by Choice*,[10] based on nine years of research into companies that had risen to great things from times of uncertainty. One of the key differences he identified between these companies and others that did much less well was the practice of what he termed 'empirical creativity'. This he defined with a 'bullets' and 'cannonballs' metaphor. Instead of firing cannonballs (putting significant resources behind untested ideas), the more successful businesses began by firing smaller bullets (they prepared the way with lots of low cost, low risk, low distraction tests at a far smaller scale in order to develop learnings about what works and what doesn't). In other words, they made lots of small bets.

This kind of 'empirical creativity', he says, is a blend between creativity and discipline, involving the habit of continually learning from a stream of both successful and unsuccessful experiments and initiatives. On any given day, Facebook are running hundreds of tests concurrently.[11] Each year, Google reportedly changes its search algorithm around 500–600 times.[12] When they launched the first version of their pay-per-click advertising product AdWords in 1999 it initially was not very successful but through constant iteration Google have built a product that is today worth billions of dollars. But iteration doesn't stop. Tens of thousands of quality experiments are still run each year for both search and advertising products.

The agile business is not one that experiments episodically, but instead builds a culture characterized by continuous testing and learning. Whether it is constant testing conducted at high tempo and designed to incrementally improve existing services, or test and learn focused on a perpetual stream of new and potentially breakthrough initiatives, developing a learning culture it seems, is critical not only to performance but also to survival.

Stories from the frontline

Marco Ryan, EVP, Chief Digital Officer, Wartsila Corporation (and digital transformation veteran): Test. Learn. Optimize

Perhaps one of the hardest success factors to implement is cultural change. For many, technology decisions, marketing budgets, investments in websites are easier to measure and easier to understand.

But what will make the transformation stick – what will cause it to deliver the value – is the people. And most organizations struggle with the availability and capability of their talent, to focus on the digital transformation. This is often largely due to approaching it the wrong way. Large-scale process re-engineering projects, tied for example to changes in an ERP system, will absorb both the resources and their appetite for change.

An alternative, and more digital approach, is to continuously 'test, learn and optimize'. This allows shorter timelines, and importantly, enables unsuccessful initiatives to be halted quickly. It is what makes the startups able to outpace the more traditional companies and it can be applied to all parts of the business.

The approach, combined with a hypothesis, good data, the ability to create a pilot, mock-up or prototype, to work in small cross-functional teams often without the need for centralized IT resources, can quickly get a product, idea or service to market, in a high fidelity state that can be tested with a trusted client, improved or perhaps halted. In a digitally transformed company, failure is okay, providing you fail fast, learn from it and improve the next iteration.

Too many companies are afraid to try or lack resources to mentor and coach teams through this new way of working. This can be easily addressed through external input or interims in the short term. But the sin is not to try.

The dangers of systematic survival bias

In 1943, US mathematician and statistician Abraham Wald was part of a group asked to advise the US Air Force on how they might reinforce their planes to prevent so many of them being lost on bombing raids to enemy fire.

The challenge was that there was only a limited amount of armour plating that could be used on the plane if it were to still fly. Research by the military into damage to planes that had returned from missions revealed that bombers were often riddled with bullets in the wings, the centre of the fuselage and around the tail gunner. So they proposed to reinforce these areas where they could see the most damage.

Wald told them that this was a big mistake, and that they should in fact do the opposite. He recognized that what the bullet holes were in fact showing was where a plane could be hit and still survive to make it home. The reinforcement actually needed to be placed in the areas where the surviving planes looked unscathed, since planes hit in these areas never returned. Wald went on to use a complex series of equations to work out the vulnerability of individual parts of a plane. Calculations that are still in use today.

Survival bias leads us to overly focus on the successful, to the detriment or oversight of what we can learn from the unsuccessful, and can lead to false conclusions. In organizations we tend to be exceptionally good at looking at successes as the learning exemplars and exceptionally bad at building in reflection time so that we might encourage the kind of learning culture that can create the kind of advantage that Amazon founder Jeff Bezos talks about when he depicts why Amazon is the best place in the world to fail. If you swing for the fences, he says, you will inevitably strike out frequently but now and then you will hit a home run. What is different between baseball and business though, is that the former has limited outcomes (the most runs you can get is four). In business, however:

> *... every once in awhile, when you step up to the plate, you can score 1,000 runs. This long-tailed distribution of returns is why it's important to be bold. Big winners pay for so many experiments.*
>
> (Bezos, 2016)[13]

Learning to unlearn

It makes intuitive sense that organizations that focus on continuous learning should fair better in complex adaptive environments. But one of the less obvious benefits of learning the new is that it helps you to *unlearn* old habits and practices.

A study from the European Molecular Biology Laboratory and the University Pablo Olavide in Sevilla, Spain, showed that our brains actively erase memories in order to make space for new ones, a process that seemingly only happens in learning situations.[14] In other words we forget through learning.

As we will discuss later, iterative and sprint working methodologies are founded on principles of reflection, learning and application through tight feedback loops from customer interaction or team retrospectives at the end of sprints. In the context of digital transformation the point of adopting new working structures and processes is not only to learn new ways of working but also to help disentangle the company from legacy thinking and practices. We forget the old through learning the new. To quote author, inventor and thinker Buckminster Fuller:

> *You never change things by fighting the existing reality. To change something, build a new model that makes the existing model obsolete.*

In other words (and here to paraphrase the character Socrates from Dan Millman's book *The Way of the Peaceful Warrior*)[15] the secret of change is to focus all your energy not on fighting the old but on building the new.

Fixed and growth mindsets

Stanford Psychologist Carol Dweck (in *Mindset*)[16] has described the fundamental difference in how we view our personality, and between what she calls 'fixed' and 'growth' mindsets. The former, she says, is the view that your intelligence, character and creative ability are static and so cannot change in a meaningful way. If successful, those who have fixed mindsets regard that success as:

> *... the affirmation of that inherent intelligence, an assessment of how those givens measure up against an equally fixed standard; striving for success and avoiding failure at all costs become a way of maintaining the sense of being smart or skilled.*

Those with a growth mindset, on the other hand, relish challenges and rather than seeing failure as evidence of unintelligence, regard it as an opportunity for growth and improving existing capabilities. We can draw clear parallel between individual and organization. The agile business has a growth mindset. It sees *every* initiative as an opportunity to learn.

Embedding reflection time

One of the key ways in which organizations can develop an ingrained learning culture is through embedding the practice of reflective thinking and retrospectives. Unlike critical thinking, which is a way of utilizing different techniques of reasoning and insight in order to increase the probability of a desired outcome or goal, reflective thinking focuses on the analysis of past experiences to draw learning that might be applied in the future.

Two influential thinkers on organizational learning, Donald Schön and Chris Argyris, created a useful way of thinking about the application of what Schön called 'reflective practice', the ability of organizations to not only incorporate as broad a perspective as possible from the experience of individuals and the company itself, but to continually improve through a feedback loop of experience, learning and practice. They considered three key elements:

1. **Governing variables:** the dimensions that people are trying to keep within acceptable or accepted limits.
2. **Action strategies:** the plans and activities used to keep governing values within the acceptable range.
3. **Consequences:** the intended or unintended results of an action.

Learning, they said, involves identifying and correcting errors but when something goes wrong people initially look for an alternative strategy that will work within the existing governing variables in what they called 'single-loop learning'. Single-loop learning is an error and correction process that enables the organization to continue current policies in order to achieve its objectives. So organizations operationalize responses to changing market conditions. 'Double-loop learning' on the other hand, involves questioning the governing variables themselves:

> *Single-loop learning is like a thermostat that learns when it is too hot or too cold and turns the heat on or off... Double-loop learning occurs when error is detected and corrected in ways that involve the modification of an organization's underlying norms, policies and objectives.*[17]

Good reflective practice in the agile business should not only focus on single-loop error and correction, but more fundamental consideration of new and improved ways of working, and challenging and changing established norms.

Reflection is built in to agile methodologies (the last Agile Manifesto principle is: 'At regular intervals, the team reflects on how to become more effective, then tunes and adjusts its behavior accordingly') through the practice of retrospectives. These are used as a simple way to gather the team, typically at the end of a sprint, and hold a (often facilitated) reflection on their work and way of operating and how it might be improved in the next sprint. Actions are captured, made visible and then revisited.

One of the simplest (and therefore best) frameworks for reflection actually originated from the US military. The so-called 'after action review'[18] would be used in de-briefs as a way of improving performance, and features four simple questions that can be answered after an action of some kind:

1 **What did we expect to happen?** Knowing that you have to answer this question afterwards means that you go in with a greater clarity of objective and desired outcome.
2 **What actually happened?** A blameless analysis, that identifies key events, actions and influences, and creates a consensus.
3 **Why was or wasn't there a difference?** What were the differences (if any) between desired and actual outcomes, and why did this difference occur?
4 **What can you do next time to improve or ensure these results?** What (if anything) are you going to do different next time? What should you do more of/the same/less of? What needs fixing? What worked and is repeatable or scalable? The idea is that at least half of the time of the review should be spent answering this question.

Most businesses are pretty bad at taking time out to reflect and learn. There is always pressure to move straight on to the next target, the next priority, the next project. Yet when it is embedded into cultural, behavioural and process norms it is potentially one of the most valuable ways to develop a true learning organization.

Stories from the frontline

John Coleman, agility transformation consultant, coach and trainer: Using agile processes, and bringing people on journey

Even if a client has bought into the significance of more agile working, it's still important to ask 'why agility?'. It's critical that the organization understands what it will gain from being more agile, and yet there will often be different answers to this question, especially from different levels of the business. Senior support for the adoption of new working methods, values and behaviours is key, and it's important to address the 'what's in it for me?' question, so that everyone understands the value.

Benefit will be derived from faster delivery, being more customer focused and innovative, but this needs to be brought to life at a personal, team and organizational level. People need to feel like they co-designed the agility transformation that is to come, since this will help get them through the times when change feels particularly difficult. And there will be difficult times, since most transformation efforts require a number of 'J-curves'[19] to get there. The initial stages of change may well create a period of disruption that can have a short-term adverse impact on performance, before the tangible benefits start to show and long-term gains become apparent. So people need to be aware of where they are on the J-curve, and the fact that there may well be multiple J-curves along the journey.

Once the goal of the first J-curve (no longer than 12 months) is agreed, it's important to then work out the best options to achieve the positive expected outcome at the end of the first curve, and to position yourself as best you can for the second curve. Tools such as the DICE® framework from the Boston Consulting Group[20] are useful in being able to better predict outcomes since it uses four key elements to assess likely results: the duration of the project (longer projects that are reviewed more frequently are often more likely to succeed than shorter ones that are subject to a poor review process); the integrity of the team (quality, skills, capability and configuration); the commitment to change (visible top-down support, engagement at different levels); and the effort of stakeholders (degree of additional demands, which should be as minimal as possible).

The key is then to select a toolbox of methods that best suit the current context, to set the cadence and synchronization pattern that enable regular delivery of value and the mapping of the interventions needed to achieve the medium-term outcomes, to keep your sights on generating early benefit and managing risk, and also 'Black Swan Farming'[21] (the potential to discover features in hindsight that are hundreds or thousands of times more valuable than other features). There are probably several deal breakers, including the acceptance of a half-hearted implementation ('WaterScrumFall' or 'WAgile' for example), a lack of appetite for continuous integration and automated testing, and a lack of appetite for suitable finance support and processes (more regular forecasting/

budgeting, or 'Lean Finance') since this can inhibit long-term gain and the ability to create stable, high performing teams. The main point is to use the right method(s)/frameworks for the right context and to get into a transformation rhythm to get regular wins, pivoting as you discover things that didn't work so well in practice in that context.

And keep on going! Keep it fresh by changing the transformation team by asking more key influencers for help as you go, and as energy dwindles from one focus area and increases in the next one. Be aware of the politics, keep your forecasts on track (re-forecasting monthly at a minimum), use positive peer pressure through informal show and tells, tell stories, spread the word. Above all, leave a legacy so that the transformation continues.

Notes

1 IBM.com (2016) IBM Design Thinking, IBM Design, [Online] http://www.ibm.com/design/thinking/ [accessed 24 October 2016]

2 ideou.com (2016) Design Thinking, IDEO U, [Online] http://www.ideou.com/pages/design-thinking [accessed 24 October 2016]

3 ideou.com (2016) Design Thinking, IDEO U, [Online] http://www.ideou.com/pages/design-thinking [accessed 24 October 2016]

4 Herbert A Simon (26 September 1996) *The Sciences of the Artificial Third*, MIT Press, ASIN B002U60C7S

5 AgileManifesto.com (2001) Manifesto for Agile Software Development, [Online] http://agilemanifesto.org/ [accessed 24 October 2016]

6 Eric Reis (2016) The Lean Startup, The Lean Startup, [Online] http://theleanstartup.com/ [accessed 24 October 2016]

7 Eric Reis (6 October 2011) *The Lean Startup: How constant innovation creates radically successful businesses*, Portfolio Penguin, ISBN-10 670921602, ISBN-13 978-0670921607

8 Ed Catmull (8 April 2014) *Creativity, Inc.: Overcoming the unseen forces that stand in the way of true inspiration*, Transworld Digital, ASIN B00GUOEMA4

9 Marc Andreessen (22 January 2015) Failure – Success is the new failure, Andreesen Horowitz, [Online] http://a16z.com/2015/01/22/failure/ [accessed 24 October 2016]

10 Jim Collins and Morten T Hansen (13 October 2011) *Great by Choice: Uncertainty, chaos and luck – why some thrive despite them all*, Random House Business, ISBN-10 1847940889 ISBN-13 978-1847940889

11 Facebook Engineering (8 August 2012) Building and Testing at Facebook, Facebook Engineering, [Online] https://www.facebook.com/notes/facebook-engineering/building-and-testing-at-facebook/10151004157328920/ [accessed 24 October 2016]

12 Moz (2016) Google Algorithm Change History, Moz, [Online] https://moz.com/google-algorithm-change [accessed 24 October 2016]

13 Eugene Kim (5 April 5 2016) Jeff Bezos: 'We are the best place in the world to fail', Business Insider UK, [Online] http://uk.businessinsider.com/amazon-ceo-jeff-bezos-best-place-in-the-world-to-fail-2016-4 [accessed 24 October 2016]

14 Ray Kurzweil (21 March 2016) We need to forget things to make space to learn new things, scientists discover, [Online] http://www.kurzweilai.net/we-need-to-forget-things-to-make-space-to-learn-new-things-scientists-discover [accessed 24 October 2016]

15 Dan Millman (5 May 2010) *Way of the Peaceful Warrior: A book that changes lives*, Peaceful Warrior, ePublishing B003LBRISM

16 Carol Dweck (2 February 2012) *Mindset: How you can fulfil your potential*, Robinson, ISBN-10 1780332009 ISBN-13 978-1780332000

17 Smith, M K (2001, 2013) Chris Argyris: theories of action, double-loop learning and organizational learning, infed.org The encyclopedia of informal education, [Online] http://infed.org/mobi/chris-argyris-theories-of-action-double-loop-learning-and-organizational-learning/ [accessed 25 October 2016]

18 Douglas Brown (2 October 2012) After Action Review: The most eye-opening business success tool, Post University Insights, [Online] http://blog.post.edu/2012/10/after-action-review-most-eye-opening-business-success-tool.html [accessed 25 October 2016]

19 Clapham, J (2014) David Viney, who did some of the original research on the effect of perceived change, to use his J-Curve in Steve Fullmer's courseware and related delivery, [Online] https://johnclapham.wordpress.com/tag/viney/ [accessed 20 October 2016]

20 Dice: A tool for executional certainty, [Online] http://dice.bcg.com/index.html#intro [accessed 19 October 2016]

21 Arnold, J and Yüce, Ö (no date) Black Swan Farming, [Online] http://blackswanfarming.com/cost-of-delay/ [accessed 19 October 2016]

The agile innovation process 07

In the agile business innovation is not only continuous, its pace is relentless. As we discussed in Part One, today's version of Joseph Schumpeter's 'gale of creative destruction' involves the rapid disintermediation of industries, the unbundling and rewiring of competitive advantage, and burgeoning imbalances in talent. The required response is as broad as it is deep. An agile innovation process requires businesses to be adept at all three stages of Schumpeter's model for technological change: Invention (ideas); Innovation ('the development of new ideas into marketable products and processes' or in other words commercialization); and Diffusion (scaling or adoption). These innovation cycles need to be expedited so that they operate in months, not years, generating a continuous flow of new experiments and initiatives.

Empowering invention

Ideas from anywhere

Creativity and innovation is often considered to be driven by the recombination of previously disparate and unconnected ideas and concepts in new ways. Professor Andrew Hargadon (Professor of Technology Management, UC Davis Graduate School of Management) has described what he calls 'technology brokering',[1] which exploits the social elements within the innovation process and the connections between people, as a way in which people and organizations can apply existing ideas and technologies in new ways by bridging the gaps between existing networks from disparate and potentially distant divisions and even industries. New networks can then be created that can support these creative recombinations.

This concept of empowering new connections combined with a relentless throughput of new ideas is foundational to the innovation process in the truly agile business. Most organizations are pretty bad at harvesting and nurturing great ideas from their employees. Despite its shortcomings, the practice of brainstorming has become so entrenched within organizational behaviour that it is often the unquestioned default protocol for the origination of new ideas and strategy. Such sessions, alongside the convention of the board or team strategy day, often compartmentalize creativity, boxing the formation of ideas and strategy into a small window of time. And yet, as Diehl and Stroebe wrote in 1991:[2]

> *Brainstorming groups produce more ideas than an individual but fewer and poorer quality ideas than from individuals working separately. In other words, brainstorms dilute the sum of individual efforts.*

One of the original rules for brainstorming, first popularized in the 1950s by Alex Faickney Osborn in the book *Applied Imagination*,[3] focuses on quality through quantity. It works on the assumption that the more ideas that are generated, the more likely a radical and effective solution will be found. Yet as Keith Sawyer, a psychologist at Washington University, has pointed out[4] multiple studies conducted over a number of decades have consistently shown that brainstorming groups think of far fewer ideas than the same number of people who work alone and later pool their ideas.

Far better then, to establish a way to continually harvest the best ideas from your people. The creative process at Pixar is empowered by a collaborative culture that combines tight team working with an 'ideas from anywhere' approach. Ed Catmull, President of Pixar, talks about how (since the creative process behind their films involves thousands of ideas) the notion of an idea as a singular thing is a fundamental flaw and instead what is required is a group behaving creatively. So at Pixar, teams of talented people with diverse backgrounds are marshalled around a singular vision.

In outlining his vision for how to build a sustainable creative organization,[5] Catmull gives the example of the head of a major Hollywood studio who told him that his central problem was not finding good people, but instead finding good ideas. This, he says, is a misguided view of creativity that views it as a mysterious solo act and reduces products to a single idea, exaggerating the importance of that initial idea in creating something original. In reality, any kind of complex product development involves continuous creativity from a large number of diverse people and disciplines working effectively together to solve many problems.

In his book on the history of innovation (*Where Good Ideas Come From*),[6] Steven Johnson talks about how ideas, rather than originating from lone creative geniuses that have a sudden spark of inspiration, can mature over time, sometimes laying dormant in the form of 'partial hunches' or half-ideas for years. Since it is the collision of these half-ideas that enables breakthroughs to happen, increasing connectivity is the great driver of innovation. Creating physical and virtual spaces where ideas can mingle is an effective way that companies can capitalize on this.

As an example, Steve Jobs reportedly designed the Pixar building deliberately to enable different people to run into each other, believing that the best meetings are accidental ones (so much so that, as Isaacson wrote about in his biography of Jobs,[7] he positioned the only toilets in the building adjacent to its large atrium to facilitate people running into each other). Informal, random interactions between employees are undervalued.

Another of Osborn's rules for brainstorming focused on the importance of withholding criticism, in the belief that participants will feel more free to express unusual ideas. A study from Charlan Nemeth,[8] a psychologist from UC Berkeley, split 265 students into teams of five and gave them 20 minutes to work on the same problem – how to reduce traffic congestion in the San Francisco bay area. Each team was randomly assigned to work to one of three different conditions: one that specified no further rules at all; one that worked to standard brainstorming rules and emphasized limiting criticism; and a debate condition in which teams were encouraged to criticize and debate each other's ideas. The results for which teams did best were not even close. While the groups that brainstormed slightly outperformed those that were given no instructions, the people in the debate condition generated almost 25 per cent more ideas. When participants were asked later if they had had any more ideas that had been triggered by the earlier conversation, those who had been in this latter group produced an average of seven additional ideas, compared to an average of two from participants in the other two groups.

So it seems that the 'do not criticize' instruction is highly counterproductive. Every morning at Pixar begins the same way, with the animators debating the previous day's work ('ruthlessly shredding each frame' as Ed Catmull describes it) in sessions designed to critique, debate and improve. As well as encouraging the team to fully engage with the work of others, the sessions distribute responsibility for catching mistakes across the entire group, a lesson that Ed Catmull learned from the lean manufacturing process.

Brainstorming is so inherent to traditional business practice that the research illustrating its deficiencies seems counterintuitive. Yet truly agile businesses look far beyond traditional approaches to ideas generation and begin to facilitate more debate, builds and criticism, and embed creative approaches and ideas from anywhere in the fabric of how they work every day.

'Porous enterprise' and the value of fresh perspectives

To encourage the kind of 'technology brokering' that Andrew Hargadon talks about we need to become far more networked as organizations. As companies become larger and face ongoing challenges, they often become very inwardly facing. An increasing proportion of time is spent on internal priorities, managing upwards and company politics. In contrast, being a networked business means generating an outwardly facing perspective, and encouraging the flow of fresh thinking, challenges and ideas into and through the business.

Instead of always focusing on in-sector thinking and examples, fresh perspectives from unrelated and even distant industries can be uniquely valuable here. A great example of fresh thinking from another industry comes from the unlikely combination of a children's hospital and a Formula One team. In the surgical and intensive care units of Great Ormond Street Hospital for Children, doctors knew that improving the 30-minute process to unplug and untangle (in a crowded space) all the wires and tubes from patients in order to transfer them from surgery to the ICU could directly improve patient care. Dr Allan Goldman, the head ICU doctor and Prof Martin Elliot, heart surgeon, were watching a Formula One race in the hospital's staff common room following a 12-hour emergency transplant operation and noticed how a 20-member Formula One pit crew worked seamlessly to change the car's tyres, fill it with petrol, clear the air intakes and send it away in less than seven seconds.

So they invited the McLaren and Ferrari racing teams to work with them to identify how their own handover discipline could be more efficient. The racing technicians' recommendations focused initially on equipment but then broadened out into training and process and resulted in a restructuring of the patient handover procedure, new protocols that detailed who should be the leader in the process (the anaesthetist) and the exact task of everyone involved, diagrams that showed exactly where everyone needed to be positioned around the patient, and rehearsals to make the new processes as seamless as possible. An industrial psychologist monitored 27 operations following the adoption of the protocol and found that the number of technical errors and mistakes in information handover had almost halved.

Encouraging a regular inflow of perspectives however, requires this kind of thinking at scale. In *The Power of Pull*,[9] the authors John Hagel, John Seely Brown and Lang Davison coin the phrase 'porous enterprise' to describe how networked organizations with externally facing, connected employees acting as the conduit for new perspectives, focus on the value that can be derived from the flow of knowledge into and within a business, rather than relying on the stocks of knowledge that already exist within its boundaries and firewalls.

Increasingly, it is the agile, networked business that is best positioned to originate disruptive concepts and ideas from a broader scope of sources, perspectives and re-combinations.

The restless, curious organization

We might describe the porous, networked business as a restless, curious organization – always moving forwards, never being satisfied with the status quo, constantly exploring and reaching out for the next big idea. We are too good, as businesses, at compartmentalizing creativity not just into time segments (like a brainstorming session), but into creative functions, roles and innovation labs. We are too poor, as businesses, at harvesting, assessing, and nurturing concepts from wherever and whomsoever they might arise.

Rather than poorly executed, demotivating suggestion schemes, the creative, curious organization creates an engine of ideation through inclusive, empowering programmes to originate, harvest and grow new ideas. Like people, creativity is not one-dimensional. Research by psychologists Guillaume Fürst, Paolo Ghisletta and Todd Lubart[10] has shown that creativity in individuals requires many different attributes that will often play different roles at various stages of the process. The research identified three 'superfactors' of personality that could predict creativity. These factors speak to the broader components of a truly effective ideation engine:

1. **Plasticity:** traits including extraversion, high energy, being open to experience and inspiration. Whether at an individual or organizational level there is a high drive for exploration, good levels of curiosity, and a willingness to experiment and learn at a fast pace.
2. **Divergence:** non-conformity, and what the researchers termed 'low agreeableness'. As people or businesses this is about independence of thought, a willingness to try new things, to pursue a long-term unique vision even when questioned, to be stubborn.
3. **Convergence:** qualities such as precision, persistence, critical sense and conscientiousness. At an organizational level the discipline to make robust data-driven decisions to validate ideas and concepts, to focus and align direction and decision-making on a strong purpose/mission/vision, to shutter projects and redirect resources towards opportunity when prudent.

The research revealed how creativity is about combining both generative (coming up with lots of original ideas) and selective (being able to critique, evaluate, and elaborate on ideas effectively) skills. Like design thinking, business agility is about imagining lots of different possibilities but also focusing on those that have the most potential value. And it is those that are able to combine these different behaviours and switch between them in flexible ways, that are best suited to world in which we now find ourselves.

The creative organization framework

We have created a practical tool for understanding how the creativity of your own organization maps to the key attributes of agility. Using the canvas below (Table 7.1), workshop the questions that sit at the intersection of creativity (plasticity, divergence, convergence) and agility (velocity, focus, flexibility) to identify areas of strength and weakness.

Table 7.1 Questions to workshop

	Velocity	Focus	Flexibility
Plasticity	We are responsive to new trends and ideas, and move quickly to capitalize on new opportunity	We are outwardly facing, actively exploring and looking for new opportunity	We are open to new ideas, and have a culture and practice that rewards curiosity
Divergence	We are not afraid to adapt quickly in response to shifting contexts	Appetite to consider different ideas, routed in customer needs	We have a culture that embraces different thinking
Convergence	We can swiftly realign resources around opportunity	We use data to test and validate new and different opportunities	Our vision is aligned to and routed in an enabling culture

Innovation is wide, as well as deep

Innovation is often considered in quite one-dimensional ways, and yet it has never been more important to innovate in a multi-dimensional way. In their book *Ten Types of Innovation*[11] the authors Larry Keeley, Helen Walters, Ryan Pikkel and Brian Quinn make the point that while many executives have traditionally overemphasized the association of innovation with the creation of new products and services, the practice of integrating multiple types of innovation enables organizations to develop offerings that are highly differentiated, less easy to copy, and that generate higher returns. Having analysed 2000 successful innovations, they list 10 distinct kinds, grouped into three key areas:

1. Configuration
   a. Profit Model: How you make money. Challenging sector conventions on offering, pricing or revenue generation.
   b. Network: How you connect with others to create value. Network innovations enable companies to capitalize on their own strengths while harnessing the advantage that might be derived from the capabilities and assets of others.
   c. Structure: The organization and alignment of talent, resource and assets. Structure innovations can create unique value or efficiencies. They can improve productivity and collaboration, help attract talent to the company and drive performance.
   d. Process: Developing and implementing unique or superior methods. Process innovations involve a significant level of change from 'business as usual' that can drive greater capability, adaptability or efficiency. The development of unique processes can prove difficult for competitors to access and can yield advantage for extended periods of time.
2. Offering
   a. Product Performance: the development of distinguishing features and functionality. This might speak to completely new products, or significantly improved features, qualities to existing ones.
   b. Product System: the creation of complementary products and services. This is concerned with how separate products or services might be brought together to create new capability or improved scalability. So things like integration, modularity and interoperability are what matter. The development of ecosystems that take value from one place and use it to enhance experience at another is one example.
3. Experience
   a. Service: supporting and amplifying the value of your offerings. Enhancing performance, utility and loyalty through improved design or service provision, fixing customer pain points and helping to ensure seamless customer journeys. This can elevate the average into the exceptional, and create a compelling experience.

- **b** Channel: the way in which your offerings is brought to customers. Channel innovations are focused on finding new or multiple ways to bring products and services to users, creating an extraordinary experience with minimal friction.
- **c** Brand: the representation of your offerings and business. Innovations in the way that consumers might recognize, recall or associate your brand, the distinct identity and 'promise' of your offering. Often incorporating multiple customer touchpoints, these can confer value, meaning and intent to the offering.
- **d** Customer Engagement: fostering compelling interactions. The development of more meaningful customer connections derived from deep understanding of customer aspirations, needs and desires. Helping people to 'find ways to make parts of their lives more memorable, fulfilling, delightful – even magical'.

Taking a broader context around innovation opens the organizational mind toward enabling change that impact not only the outputs (products and services) but also the infrastructure (networks), relationships (partnerships, communications), process, structure and resourcing. Too narrow a consideration of innovation restricts fundamental change and means that transformation will fail.

Defining the problem to solve

Design thinking, agile and lean are all customer-centric methodologies that focus on rigorously defining and responding to customer need. Lean practices, for example, involve removing as many assumptions from a process as possible, and that includes the question of whether you are actually solving the right problem in the first place.

A useful framework here is the '5 Whys', a simple yet very effective way of getting to the root cause of a problem by iteratively asking 'why' five times, each question forming the basis of the next question. It was originally used by Toyota as a technique for problem solving in their manufacturing process, and was one of the fundamental techniques in their scientific approach. Architect of the Toyota Production System, Taiichi Ohno, describes an example of applying it to a robot stopping:

1. Why did the robot stop? The circuit has overloaded, causing a fuse to blow.
2. Why is the circuit overloaded? There was insufficient lubrication on the bearings, so they locked up.

3 Why was there insufficient lubrication on the bearings? The oil pump on the robot is not circulating sufficient oil.
4 Why is the pump not circulating sufficient oil? The pump intake is clogged with metal shavings.
5 Why is the intake clogged with metal shavings? Because there is no filter on the pump.[12]

Similarly, using the 5 Whys in relation to customer problems or organizational challenges helps remove assumptions and focus on the real root cause or issue.

Clay Christensen's 'jobs to be done'[13] concept is another useful way to frame customer needs. 'Jobs to be done' theorizes that what causes us to buy a product or service (or indeed a brand) is that we 'hire' them to do a particular job for us. It is a simple idea, but framing it in this way helps us to understand customer motivations better. Christensen uses an example of the V8 juice drink that was once marketed to compete with (and in a similar way to) other soft drinks like Gatorade, using brand attributes like how refreshing it was. The realization that V8 was being bought instead to fulfil a different job led to a campaign that focused instead on how the drink provided the required daily servings of vegetables. Within a year of this decision, V8 had quadrupled its revenues.

Paul Adams, VP of Product at customer communication platform Intercom (and ex-Facebook and Google) describes how they apply Christensen's framework in the service of product design:

> *We frame every design problem in a Job, focusing on the triggering event or situation, the motivation and goal, and the intended outcome:*
>
> *When _____, I want to _____, so I can _____.*
>
> *For example: When an important new customer signs up, I want to be notified, so I can start a conversation with them.*[14]

These kinds of user stories, simple statements about what a customer wants to do that are framed from their perspective, help ground product development but also connect wider organizational thinking towards the needs of the customer.

First principles and 10x thinking

Another way to really focus on breakthrough ideas is through the application of what Elon Musk (CEO of Tesla Motors and SpaceX and surely one of the most deeply innovative entrepreneurs today) describes[15] as 'first principles' thinking. In Physics or Mathematics, a first principle[16] is 'a basic, foundational proposition or assumption that cannot be deduced from any other proposition or assumption'.

Musk draws a distinction between the common use of analogy in business (ideas that are similar to something that already exists) and first principles thinking (where 'you boil things down to the most fundamental truths... and then reason up from there'):[17]

> *I think it's important to reason from first principles rather than by analogy. The normal way we conduct our lives is we reason by analogy. We are doing this because it's like something else that was done, or it is like what other people are doing. Slight iterations on a theme.*

While reasoning from analogy can help position new ideas, and potentially give some comfort that at least some of the elements of the innovation are founded in existing behaviour or what has worked in the past, it still means that the starting point incorporates existing assumptions. Solving problems in entirely new or disruptive ways requires a lot more mental energy but also starts with the elemental components of a problem and so is far more likely to result in an entirely unique solution to a problem.

Too often in large organizations, the start point incorporates assumptions that have built up over time, become embedded in culture or practice yet have never truly been tested, or that have become outmoded but never challenged. It is difficult to break out of these assumed constraints when the prevailing weight of opinion, relationship capital and organizational habits within a company all act to support them.

In *The Game Changer*,[18] long-time P&G CEO A G Lafley talks about how business schools tend to focus on inductive thinking (based on directly observable facts) and deductive thinking (logic and analysis, typically based on past evidence) whereas design schools emphasize abductive thinking – imagining what could be possible. There is a good chance that as companies grow the balance between these three dynamics becomes skewed and we need to work harder to create more space for abductive thinking.

Google embed what they call '10x' thinking into their innovation process as a way to avoid overly focusing on incremental and marginal innovation. At a key stage in the idea generation process the team focus on answering the question: 'What's the 10x version of this idea?' This forces the team to re-evaluate their thinking on a wholly different scale to identify if there is an opportunity for a truly disruptive solution to be created.

Starting from a problem's most basic elements, and challenging ourselves in order to re-examine what might be possible can yield very different results.

Ingrained commercialization

Structuring for innovation

> *The test of a first rate intelligence is to hold two opposed ideas in mind at the same time and still retain the ability to function.*
>
> F Scott Fitzgerald

Gary Kasporov, the famous chess grandmaster, once talked about how chess, like business, is a balance between the mundane and the unthinkable, and how what separates a winner from a loser at the grand-master level is the willingness to do the unthinkable, to have the courage to explode the game and upend your opponent's thinking:

> *A brilliant strategy is, certainly, a matter of intelligence, but intelligence without audaciousness is not enough... So it is in business: One does not succeed by sticking to convention. When your opponent can easily anticipate every move you make, your strategy deteriorates and becomes commoditized.*
>
> (Kasporov, 2004)[19]

What Kasporov alludes to is a key business challenge: balancing the need to deliver and continually improve on day-to-day execution as well as originate, nurture and grow potentially disruptive and market leading innovations. When the business is oriented to and focused on delivering steady, logical, incremental improvement or development within the market, it can be extremely difficult to have the resource bandwidth, or make room for the challenging thinking necessary to disrupt the market and get that big leap over competition.

Key to this is creating the space for breakthrough innovation. Since the Lockheed Skunk Works came into existence in the 1940s the idea of the corporate innovation lab has become a dominant way for organizations to structure innovation. The risks inherent with compartmentalizing innovation in this way typically lie around a lack of inclusivity and broader organizational learning. But autonomy and separation can catalyse innovation and new ways of working, facilitate genuinely different thinking, and (if resourced properly) prevent early stage ideas from becoming submerged under the weight of slow-moving corporate culture.

The benefits can be multi-dimensional. Research by Cap Gemini among large-scale corporates revealed six key goals for innovation outposts: accelerating the speed of innovation, providing a conduit for fresh ideas, enhancing risk-taking ability, attracting talent, driving employee engagement, and helping to foster a culture of innovation.[20] Silicon Valley entrepreneurs Steve Blank and Evangelos Simoudis describe a typical three-stage development of innovation centres, each needing a clearly defined set of objectives and the right team to match them. The first stage involves networking and partnering, to actively 'sense' innovation and keep pace with technology development. For example, Silicon Valley outposts established by car manufacturers such as BMW and Mercedes to track and engage with self-driving car and other technologies. The second stage moves into inventing, investing, incubating, and acquiring technologies and companies (requiring venture capital or mergers and acquistions capability) in focused, relevant areas. The third stage involves building products, or 'productizing the solution to corporate problems'.

As an example, Walmart Labs ('We're not a retailer competing in Silicon Valley. We're building an internet technology company inside the world's largest retailer'), was created when Walmart acquired Silicon Valley technology business Kosmix. Instead of swallowing the early stage business into the corporate machine they created Walmart Labs,[21] with a mission to redefine e-commerce globally, and in doing so drive the wider organizational capability in digital and mobile commerce. As well as developing a series of new platforms and applications for the mother brand (it is claimed that the internal search engine they developed drove a 20 per cent increase in online sales conversions), Walmart Labs has now acquired over 14 startups.

Other corporates choose to create 'catalyst brands' that are given the freedom to work in different ways to create progressive impetus. In 2013 British Gas launched the Hive Active Heating brand with a mission to make the connected home a reality for everyone. The team use lean startup methodology to keep product development close to customer need, software is built though agile methods so that small bite-sized chunks can be delivered iteratively. In two years their first product, a connected thermostat became the number one such product in the UK with over 200,000 connected home customers.[22]

The Unilever Foundry is a good example of an incubator established by a corporate with a vision for innovators to connect with its brands. Housed in a separate building, the objective is to build and cultivate strategic partners for the future, with Unilever as a partner of choice. As well as office space, Unilever offer mentoring to develop brand and marketing propositions and roadmaps, they run regular hack events focus on Unilever specific briefs, and operate a crowdsourcing platform focused on the company's sustainability challenges. Regular involvement of Unilever staffers in initiatives helps ensure that fresh thinking disseminates more broadly across the company.

The Unilever Foundry, Hive and Walmart Labs are three different examples of how large organizations are creating the space to originate and nurture competing business models in the business at the same time. The real benefit comes when innovation labs are resourced in such a way to make them sufficiently autonomous to have the freedom to develop potentially disruptive concepts and work in new ways, yet integrated enough that it can more inclusively act to champion that new way of working and help disseminate different thinking more widely in the business. They are effective at hothousing new approaches and new ways of working, but it is only when these broaden out more widely than the innovation lab, that real, fundamental change can happen.

The entrepreneurial function

Companies are generally not short on ideas. A greater challenge lies in the harvesting, selection, nurturing and then scaling of these new concepts. A focused innovation lab can be a powerful conduit to introduce new ways of working to an organization and originate step-change ideas. Running working processes in that unit that are based around design thinking, agile and lean can not only improve innovation tempo but also enable the progressive understanding of value.

As ideas are iterated on following an overarching strategic vision but using customer feedback to inform the development priorities, value becomes emergent and organizational risk is mitigated. Companies have the opportunity to explore, test and learn rapidly to validate, and establish early stage products that are already being used by real customers. Instead of untested products emerging from the innovation lab and landing in the wider business, which is then expected to commercialize and scale them, this enables the opportunity for products to become established at an earlier stage with an early adopter audience. Even products that will eventually scale to millions of users should begin with a small market. Facebook, for example, began as a service limited to Harvard students before being opened up to other colleges in the Boston area, Ivy League institutions, and then most universities in Canada and the United States. This requires a change in corporate mindset. As PayPal founder Peter Thiel wrote in his book *Zero to One*:[23]

> *This is why successful network businesses rarely get started by MBA types: the initial markets are so small that they often don't even appear to be business opportunities at all.*

Yet still the move of an early stage product from the innovation lab into the wider business presents a key challenge. A concept might have been rigorously tested and developed in the lab but then it is given to a manager who is not necessarily as invested in it as those who have been on the journey from the beginning and sees it as additive to their already challenging commitments. Worse, the early stage product is shackled with short-term targets and forecasts, and dropped into business as usual where it becomes victim to organizational silos and the drag-brake of bureaucracy. Eric Ries describes this as akin to moving from science to astrology, and suggests that there is a missing function of entrepreneurship in many companies – staff who are responsible for taking ideas out of the lab and have the ability, incentives, time and space to commercialize them, who can manage the process from concept to execution using a disciplined, systematic way of testing new ideas and developments.

The shackling of early stage products with forecasts and targets can contaminate development priorities (you build the feature that you think will make you money rather than the feature that the customer really wants) and eventually strangle the project as it struggles to hit forecasts that often have little foundation in reality. Critical to this stage in a product lifecycle, therefore, is the ability to show progression of value towards the ultimate desired outcome – revenue and profit. Eric Ries's concept of innovation accounting that we discussed earlier is one way of framing this. Another useful framework comes from Silicon Valley entrepreneur and angel investor Dave McClure.

Pirate Metrics

Steve Blank has described how a startup is effectively 'an organization built to search for a repeatable and scalable business model.[24] An early stage product, therefore, might be considered to be a product searching for a market. Tools such as the Value Proposition Canvas,[25] and Lean Canvas[26] are excellent frameworks for establishing product-market fit in early stage products. Yet while revenue is the desired ultimate outcome, the most important objective in the early stages of a product lifecycle is to acquire learning, and so solely using revenue as a measure of success can be distracting and less than helpful.

Dave McClure's Pirate Metrics[27] defines a set of macro metrics that can be used to model the customer lifecycle. While revenue may be one of them, it is not the only one. Pirate Metrics is a sequential 5 metric-model (A-A-R-R-R) designed to represent all of the key behaviours of customers – how many users you are acquiring, how many of them are active users, whether they come back and use it again, whether they tell others about it, and how much money you are able to derive from them. To paraphrase:

- **Acquisition:** What are the ways in which your users become aware of you? What is the rate of customer acquisition?
- **Activation:** How many acquired users actually use/subscribe? What is the activation rate?
- **Retention:** How many activated users come back and use the product/service again? What is the retention rate?
- **Revenue:** How much money do you make from user activity?
- **Referral:** How many users refer other users, or advocate your product/service? What is the referral rate?

These help to define and measure customer value before you actually start capturing some of that value back. In other words they are leading indicators to revenue before actual revenues are realized. And in this sense they can also be used to hold entrepreneurs, and the leaders of innovation projects, accountable. It is a simple model, yet shows the need for flexibility right across an organization if innovation is to succeed.

Scaling, the digital-native way

Large businesses are very comfortable with scale and yet paradoxically some of the best lessons we can learn about scale can come from when we don't have it. For example, the restraint needed to start small, and then get bigger can force us to make difficult prioritization choices and be ruthless about finding the right customer problem to solve. The process of solving a key problem for (and ultimately dominating) a niche market can create indispensable learning that can itself be scaled. The pivot can enable us to make transformational decisions about product features that then catalyse user adoption. Instagram, for example, began life as a multi-featured check-in app called Burbn but when that became too similar to other offerings in the market the founders pivoted to focus purely on mobile photo sharing (founder Kevin Systrom said of the pivot: 'We decided that if we were going to build a company, we wanted to focus on being really good at one thing').[28]

Brian Chesky, founder and CEO of AirBnB tells the story of how Paul Graham (founder of startup incubator Y Combinator) gave them a piece of advice that changed their trajectory – how one of the keys to get to scale is to do things that don't scale, or in other words how it is better to have a hundred people who love what you do, rather than one million who simply like what you do.[29]

Then, as a product or service grows beyond its initial customers and offering, the challenge becomes focused on iterating or pivoting the product offering while still following the ambitious long-term vision. Amazon may have always had a vision to dominate digital retail, but Jeff Bezos very deliberately started with books. So, as Peter Thiel says in *Zero To One*:

> *Sequencing markets correctly is underrated, and it takes discipline to expand gradually. The most successful companies make the core progression – to first dominate a specific niche and then scale to adjacent markets – a part of their founding narrative.*

If one of the key questions is when to scale the answer has to be only when it is right to scale. When your key measures tell you that you are solving real customer problems and your users really care about your product. Then you scale as fast as possible.

Using network effects

Similar to what we now know as network effects, Metcalfe's Law originated in 1980s as a way to express the concept that a network enabled by communications technologies becomes exponentially more valuable as more devices are connected to it. In the 1990s this was expressed as the value of a network being proportional to the square of the number of users connected to that system. A simple example of Metcalfe's Law might be the telephone. If just two telephones existed, that would be of minor use. But as more telephones are added to the network the number of people who can talk to each other using that technology increases, meaning that the value of every telephone increases as the number of connections rise.

Similarly in the internet era, network effects describes the simple but potentially very powerful idea that the more nodes, users or connected points that there are in a network, the more powerful that network becomes. So, like the telephone, the greater the number of users that are using a social network, the more valuable that network becomes to every user. Products that scale using network effects get better and better the more people use it, creating a virtuous circle of growth. Marketing is effectively baked into the product.

The power of open ecosystems, growth hacking and APIs

Restraints are often the drivers of creativity. Being open is often the route to scale. David Weinberger, one of the co-authors of *The Cluetrain Manifesto*, once described the web as 'small pieces, loosely joined'.

APIs are sets of functions, protocols, procedures and tools that enable developers to access the features or data of another service or application. Thousands of APIs exist, connecting thousands of different services and providing an enormously powerful range of easily accessible data sources and building blocks for digital services. There are two ways in which APIs can enable and accelerate growth. Utilizing third-party data via an API can give you access to rich sources of intelligence and data on which can be built services of all kinds. Secondly, if data is a raw material of digital innovation, creating your own API and opening up key parts of your data to third parties can dramatically increase the resource allocated to creating new concepts and services from that raw material. APIs can facilitate not only scale but also new connections between services and companies, creating a networked ecosystem in which value flows as fast as the data.

Open systems and platform business models can create enormous value for both hosts and participants through empowering co-creation or facilitating an exchange of value of some kind. Reducing transaction costs and empowering new forms of collaboration enables businesses to scale in entirely new ways. Apple and Google have created billions of dollars of value for both developers and their own businesses through opening up their respective app stores in the same way as the integration of APIs at launch into countless services has catalysed growth, enhanced value propositions and reinforced innovation.

Yet APIs, open-source, peer-to-peer models, and hacking growth require a different kind of thinking. In the early days of AirBnB, the founders were struggling to create critical mass on both sides of the platform – listings and renters. A traditional approach by a larger business would focus on marketing and advertising, yet the AirBnB founders were severely limited in funding. So they automated a process that when people listed their property on the site it also proposed that they publish it with only one click on Craigslist.com linking back to the original listing. This hack enabled them to leverage the enormous scale that Craigslist had in order to drive their own growth.[30]

Growth hacking describes the process for acquiring and retaining users that combines traditional marketing and analytical skills with those more akin to product development (including test and learn, optimizing successes, discarding dead ends). Its purpose is to drive user growth, particularly in the context of establishing critical user mass and enabling a service to then capitalize on network effects. In their early days Twitter, Facebook, LinkedIn and Quora all employed people to hack their growth.

The concept of growth hacking crosses the divide between marketing and product development teams, utilizing an understanding about how your users discover and adopt your products to build features that will help acquire and retain more users, so making the spending of marketing budget a lot more joined up with the building of product features and vice versa. So it mixes engineering with marketing, combining product management, data science and traditional marketing skills. It is less focused on buying attention in order to drive awareness and interest and more on creating rich and appealing experiences for users. So it is about getting to points of sustainable growth, understanding what the data is telling you about the core patterns from your more active and passionate users, how they became more active, and then building sustainable features and experiences that can help continuously attract new users, and encourage them to be active as quickly as possible.

Well-known growth hacker Josh Elman gives some good examples of how growth hacking can add real value to scaling. Attempting to artificially generate growth, he says, may create spiky numbers but rarely adds long-term value ('It's kind of like eating empty calories').[31] He gives the example of when he worked with Twitter in the early days and how their core challenge was not acquiring users, but getting people who had just signed up to the service to come back and use it regularly. A typical marketing response to this problem would be CRM-based, or re-targeting users with display advertising. Yet when they looked at the analytics around user behaviour they realized that if as a new user you manually selected and followed at least five accounts on the service when you signed up, you were far more likely to return. Rebuilding the on-boarding process and early user experience on Twitter led to a dramatic improvement in retention.

Fluid resourcing

APIs and platform business models are examples of how organizations can move quickly to generate scale and respond to shifting scenarios. In the networked world data and value flow easily between entities in the ecosystem but as we discussed in Part One, businesses that operate in the networked era also require a high degree of fluidity in resourcing.

As Rita Gunther McGrath asserts (in *The End of Competitive Advantage*), if sustainable competitive advantage is shifting to a series of transient advantages then you need to organize your company in a very different way. Towards a strategy of continuous reconfiguration, and orienting the company around being responsive to opportunity rather than simply focusing on efficiency and optimization. McGrath gives the example in her book of Infosys, who reorganize the company every two or three years in order to avoid systemic resistance to changing the way of working.

Rather than extreme downsizing or restructuring, increased fluidity in resourcing brings greater manoeuvrability. While innovation labs can be a great way to hothouse early stage ideas and introduce and catalyse new ways of working, the ultimate goal is to reorient the wider organization around continuous learning, increased velocity, flexibility and structural adaptivity.

In educational theory active learning is a well-known method of schooling in which participants learn through active involvement, experience or doing. In machine learning this is extended to become a type of iterative supervised learning in which a learning algorithm might interact with or query a user or data source in order to obtain improved outputs. But the clue is in the moniker – the key word is 'active'. Organizations may well have digital training programmes that go beyond specialist digital expertise to impact the wider organization. They may even have reverse mentoring or accreditation schemes. But if we are to put any credence in the well-established 70/20/10 model for learning and development[32] which posits that 70 per cent of development is derived from on-the job experiences (actually working on tasks and problems), 20 per cent from interaction and feedback, and 10 per cent from formal training and reading, then by far the greatest individual (and surely therefore organizational) learning comes from active learning: direct hands-on experience and proximity to new ways of working. Key to developing learning and transformation at scale, therefore, is how we extend these new ways of working beyond the innovation lab. How employees from the wider organization might interact with, cycle through, or work alongside the lab and how the new thinking and methodologies might then disseminate wider, and scale beyond the innovation unit.

In Part Four we will consider this broader context of agile resourcing, and some challenging but practical ways in which organizations can structure for manoeuvrability.

Key takeouts

This Part has been focused on bringing to the organization a new level manoeuvrability and responsiveness, a new tempo of innovation, and a new way of working to empower continuous adaptive learning in response to our complex adaptive environment. Some key takeouts include:

1. Have a view on the maturity of your business model. As an exercise, gather the senior team together and get an agreed view on where you believe your organization is on the current 'S-curve'?
2. Create the space for experimentation
   - a Find ways to free up time to dedicate to new thinking, ideation, nurturing early stage ideas, and embed this in cultural norms
   - b Orient resourcing around embedded test and learn. Review and balance the allocation of resourcing towards core business (optimization, efficiency), expansion (extending propositions, related markets), and breakthrough (new territory, high risk)
   - c Assess the cultural and corporeal appetite for risk, experimentation and breakthrough innovation
3. Use digital-native processes such as agile, lean and design thinking to increase the scope, scale and tempo of exploration and experimentation
4. Develop a true learning culture in the organization
   - a Embed reflection time and the practice of retrospectives in working processes
   - b Encourage learning from failures as well as successes – celebrate the learning, not the failure
   - c Encourage an organizational growth mindset that relishes challenge as an opportunity to learn – lead by example from the top, set expectations, ask the right questions
5. Create an agile innovation engine
   - a *Empower invention*: take ideation out of organizational silos and time blocks; maximize the collision of half ideas through physical and virtual spaces; encourage networked employees and the flow of knowledge to empower innovation at the edges; reward exploring behaviours, independence of thought and willingness to try the new; challenge innovation efforts to be broad as well as deep; work hard on finding the real problems to solve then use first principles and 10x

thinking to explode the idea; validate continuously with customers and data

b *Embed rapid commercialization*: use innovation labs, catalyst brands or incubation programmes to hothouse new ways of working as well as early stage ideas; protect early stage concepts as they move from labs to business-as-usual through entrepreneur roles and value driven metrics

c *Scale the digital-native way*: focus on network effects, open ecosystems, platform business models, growth hacking and APIs; encourage active 'learning-by-doing' as a way to disseminate new ways of thinking and working at scale wider through the organization

Notes

1 Andrew Hargadon (1 July 2003) *How Breakthroughs Happen: The surprising truth about how companies innovate*, Harvard Business School Press, ISBN-10 1578519047 ISBN-13 978-1578519040

2 Michael Diehl and Wolfgang Stroebe (September 1991) Productivity Loss in Idea-generating Groups: Tracking down the blocking effect, American Psychological Association [accessed 25 October 2016]

3 Alex F Osborn (1 June 1979) *Applied Imagination*, Scribner, ISBN-10 23895209 ISBN-13 978-0023895203

4 Jonah Lehrer (19 April 2012) Brainstorming: An idea past its prime, *The Washington Post*, [Online] http://www.washingtonpost.com/opinions/brainstorming-an-idea-past-its-prime/2012/04/19/gIQAhKT5TT_story.html [accessed 25 October 2016]

5 Ed Catmull (September 2008) How Pixar Fosters Collective Creativity, *Harvard Business Review*, [Online] http://hbr.org/2008/09/how-pixar-fosters-collective-creativity/ar/1 [accessed 25 October 2016]

6 Steven Johnson (29 September 2011) *Where Good Ideas Come From: The seven patterns of innovation*, Penguin, ISBN-10 141033401 ISBN-13 978-0141033402

7 Walter Isaacson (5 February 2015) *Steve Jobs: The exclusive biography*, Abacus, ISBN-10 034914043X ISBN-13 978-0349140438

8 Charlan Jeanne Nemeth, Marie Personnaz, Bernard Personnaz and Jack A Goncalo (April 2003) The Liberating Role of Conflict in Group Creativity: A cross cultural study, Institute for Research on Labor and Employment, [Online] http://www.irle.berkeley.edu/workingpapers/90-03.pdf [accessed 25 October 2016]

9 John Hagel III, John Brown and Lang Davison (4 December 2012) *The Power of Pull: How small moves, smartly made, can set big things in motion*, Basic Civitas Books, ASIN B00XWQNRWW

10 Guillaume Fürst, Paolo Ghisletta, Todd Lubart (2 August 2014) Toward an Integrative Model of Creativity and Personality: Theoretical suggestions and preliminary empirical testing, Wiley Online Library, [Online] http://onlinelibrary.wiley.com/doi/10.1002/jocb.71/abstract;jsessionid=60ACE13ABA81805AD1D0278AF33DFEA4.f01t02 [accessed 25 October 2016]

11 Larry Keeley, Helen Walters, Ryan Pikkel and Brian Quinn (19 April 2013) *Ten Types of Innovation: The discipline of building breakthroughs*, John Wiley & Sons, ISBN-10 1118504240 ISBN-13 978-1118504246

12 Taiichi Ohno (March 2006) Ask Why Five Times About Every Matter, Toyota Global, [Online] http://www.toyota-global.com/company/toyota_traditions/quality/mar_apr_2006.html [accessed 25 October 2016]

13 Clay Christensen (2016) Jobs to be Done, Clay Christensen Institute, [Online] http://www.christenseninstitute.org/key-concepts/jobs-to-be-done/ [accessed 25 October 2016]

14 Paul Adams (2015) The Dribbblisation of Design, Inside Intercomm, [Online] https://blog.intercom.io/the-dribbblisation-of-design/ [accessed 25 October 2016]

15 Kevin Rose (7 September 2012) Foundation 20 // Elon Musk, [Online] https://www.youtube.com/watch?v=L-s_3b5fRd8 [accessed 25 October 2016]

16 Various (2016) First Principle, Wikipedia.org, [Online] https://en.wikipedia.org/wiki/First_principle [accessed 25 October 2016]

17 Eric Ravenscraft (2013) Use Elon Musk's 'First Principles' Method for Better Brainstorming, LifeHacker.com, [Online] http://lifehacker.com/use-elon-musks-first-principles-method-for-better-br-1476303603 [accessed 25 October 2016]

18 A G Lafley and Ram Charan (3 September 2010) *The Game Changer: How every leader can drive everyday innovation*, Profile Books, ASIN B0041G68R8

19 Gary Kasporov (January 2004) The Unthinkable… and the Mundane, FastCompany, [Online] https://www.fastcompany.com/50914/unthinkableand-mundane [accessed 25 October 2016]

20 Capgemini Consulting (23 July 2015) The Innovation Game: Why and how businesses are investing in innovation centers, Capgemini Consulting, [Online] https://www.capgemini-consulting.com/the-innovation-game [accessed 25 October 2016]

21 Nidhi Subbaraman (30 January 2012) Walmart Labs Brings the 'Two-Pizza Team' Startup Culture to Walmart Empire, FastCompany.com, [Online] https://www.fastcompany.com/1811934/walmartlabs-brings-two-pizza-team-startup-culture-walmart-empire [accessed 25 October 2016]

22 British Gas (15 July 2015) British Gas Makes the Connected Home a Reality With Launch of New Products, [Online] https://www.britishgas.co.uk/media/releases/ReleaseDetailPage.aspx?releaseId=1358 [accessed 25 October 2016]

23 Blake Masters, Peter Thiel, 18 Sept. 2014, *Zero to One: Notes on start ups, or how to build the future*, Virgin Digital ASIN B00KHX0II4

24 Steve Blank (25 January 2010) What's A Startup? First Principles, [Online] http://steveblank.com/2010/01/25/whats-a-startup-first-principles/ [accessed 25 October 2016]

25 Strategyzer A G (2016) The Value Proposition Canvas, strategyzer.com, [Online] https://strategyzer.com/canvas/value-proposition-canvas?url=canvas/vpc [accessed 25 October 2016]

26 LeanStack (2016) Lean Canvas, LeanStack.com, [Online] https://leanstack.com/lean-canvas/ [accessed 25 October 2016]

27 Dave McClure (6 September 2007) Master of 500 Hats: Startup Metrics for Pirates: AARRR!, [Online] http://500hats.typepad.com/500blogs/2007/09/startup-metrics.html [accessed 25 October 2016]

28 Kevin Systrom (12 January 2011) What is the Genesis of Instagram? Quora.com, [Online] https://www.quora.com/Instagram-company/What-is-the-genesis-of-Instagram [accessed 25 October 2016]

29 Chris McCann (8 December 2015) 16 lessons on scaling from Eric Schmidt, Reid Hoffman, Marissa Mayer, Brian Chesky, Diane Greene, Jeff Weiner, and more, Medium.com, [Online] https://medium.com/cs183c-blitzscaling-class-collection/16-lessons-on-scaling-from-eric-schmidt-reid-hoffman-marissa-mayer-brian-chesky-diane-greene-3d6367e63a42#.nxecphpdl [accessed 25 October 2016]

30 Morgan Brown (2014) Airbnb: The Growth Story You Didn't Know, Growth Hackers.com, [Online] https://growthhackers.com/growth-studies/airbnb [accessed 25 October 2016]

31 Josh Elman (28 January 2013) What is 'Growth Hacking' Really? Medium.com, [Online] https://medium.com/@joshelman/what-is-growth-hacking-really-f445b04cbd20#.f0w6cgxf4 [accessed 25 October 2016]

32 Michael M Lombardo and Robert W Eichinger, (January 2000) *Career Architect Development Planner* 3rd Edition, Lominger Limited, ISBN-10 965571246 ISBN-13 978-0965571241

PART THREE
Focus

This Part deals with the importance of vision, direction, strategy, and focus in accelerating pace and creating organizational momentum.

> **Focus** – Progress and momentum towards a distinct direction, clarity of definition, the centre of activity, to pay attention to, to adapt to the surrounding conditions to be able to see clearly.

> *Innovation without Execution is hallucination.*
>
> Thomas Edison

DEFINING FOCUS

Every company wants to move faster. To develop and progress at pace. In Part One we made the case for velocity to be framed in the context of a new kind of agility, responsiveness and manoeuvrability. Yet velocity without focus is foolish. As Peter Drucker said:

> *There is nothing quite so useless, as doing with great efficiency, something that should not be done at all.*

Focus is a ubiquitous concept in business, but rarely applied well. Steve Jobs' biographer Walter Isaacson tells the story of how after Jobs returned to the business in 1997 he was faced with a confused but ample lineup of hardware and peripherals. After numerous product review sessions he had reached the end of his tether and shouted for them to stop. Grabbing a Magic Marker, he went to the whiteboard and drew a two-by-two grid, labelling the columns 'consumer' and 'pro', and the rows 'desktop' and 'portable'. He then told his team that their focus should be on building four great products, one for each quadrant, Everything else should be cancelled.[1]

One can only imagine the bewilderment of the execs in the meeting, but in implementing ruthless focus Jobs saved the business. As he later said to his biographer Walter Isaacson: 'Deciding what not to do is as important as deciding what to do'. Thereafter on Apple senior management retreats he would have the management team list out their top 10 priorities for the coming year, then he would stand up and cross-out the bottom seven on the list and declare that they could only do three.

While we can increase the tempo of innovation and progress through continuous exploration and experimentation, we need a strong, focused vision to create a distinct direction, even if we are then adaptive in our progression towards it.

In this part we reference Amazon a number of times, but for good reason. Few businesses have been quite so adept at maintaining a ruthless focus on a long-term vision ('We seek to be Earth's most customer-centric company for four primary customer sets: consumers, sellers, enterprises, and content creators') while also preserving another important context for focus within the agile business: that of continuous improvement. Author Matthew Syed (in *Bounce*)[2] analysed the factors that determine exceptional success among sporting professionals and concluded that while natural talent and genetic make up do make a difference, the most powerful characteristic exhibited by outstanding performers in sport (and also in other areas) was what he called 'sustained purposeful practice'.

This kind of purposeful practice involves deliberately focusing in a sustained way on the problem areas, things that need correcting, fixing or improving. Science writer Joshua Foer has used the example of musicians to make the same point:

> *When most musicians sit down to practice, they play the parts of pieces that they're good at. Of course they do: It's fun to succeed. But expert musicians tend to focus on the parts that are hard, the parts they haven't yet mastered.'*[3]

Constant application of deliberate practice, focused specifically on improving performance, coupled with the growth mindset that we discussed in Part Two, lead to world-class achievement. Iterative sprint working with in-built reflection time is the organizational form of deliberate practice. Constant, repeated focus reflecting on feedback, defining and solving customer or business problems, or improving ways of working, forms an iterative loop of purposeful practice, and creates its own kind of momentum.

Increased pace may be our desired goal, and a sense of urgency may help to create a reason for change, but it is focus that brings momentum towards a distinct direction. Put simply:

$$\text{Velocity} \times \text{Focus} = \text{Momentum}$$

Momentum is what creates a real impetus for change. It is what creates a highly motivating environment in which to work. And *adaptive momentum* is what creates real competitive advantage and enables you to win.

The wrong side of urgency – Nokia's story

One of the foundational elements of any change process is, of course, to create the reason and urgency for change. Without this, transformation does not even get started. It is the first stage in John Kotter's famous eight-step process for leading change[4] (which we will come back to in Part Five). In this Part we will be discussing the importance of not only organizational pace and manoeuvrability but also generating momentum through a heightened organizational cadence, tempo and rhythm. Creating a sense of urgency helps establish a compelling imperative for change and continued momentum, and can bring focus through prioritization in combining what is important with what requires immediate attention (in much the same way as an importance/urgency prioritization would help create better to do lists in our own time management).

Yet it is essential to draw that urgency from the right place. The story of Nokia's decline is grand testament. Research and analysis (based on an internal perspective from interviews with both senior and mid-level executives and engineers as well as an external one from experts) conducted by Quy Huy, a professor of strategic management at INSEAD, and Timo Vuori, assistant professor at Aalto University in Finland,[5] reveals that rather than the complacency and ignorance to which Nokia's innovation and competitive failures are usually attributed, an organizational culture that at the time was dominated by a climate of fear was instrumental in the company's downturn.

The research indicates that, during the time in question, temperamental leaders created an environment that made it very hard to pass bad news back up the line. The fear that senior management had of the external environment and of not reaching their quarterly targets in a highly performance-driven culture seemingly impacted the treatment of their subordinates, making those middle managers fearful of disappointing the top executives. This 'froze coordination' between senior and middle management to the point where the latter over-promised, remained silent or even directly lied to the former in order to avoid being told that they were not ambitious enough to meet the stretched goals set for them.

The result was a company-wide inertia. Everyone realized that Nokia needed a better operating system for its phones in order to respond to the threat posed by Apple. But middle management, fearful of appearing defeatist and of the reaction of their bosses, avoided publicly admitting the inferiority of Symbian (their own operating system), and the culture led to a 'decoupling of perceptions' between the two groups of top and middle managers about how quickly Nokia could match the iPhone.

This shared fear was exacerbated by a culture of status inside Nokia that equated resources with power. This made everyone want to retain status in order to prevent resources being allocated elsewhere, or to avoid being marginalized by being perceived to be not ambitious enough or willing enough to take on challenging projects or targets. Over-promising became a route to securing more resources, which in turn was perceived as an increase in status. This was not helped by a lack of senior technical competency (at Apple, many of the top brass are engineers), which in turn meant poor assessment of feasibility in relation to goal setting. A disproportionate amount of focus and resources were therefore dedicated towards developing new devices to fulfil short-term market demands at the expense of what was really required – the development of a new operating system.

The conclusion from the authors is that leaders, and particularly those required to lead transformation (and which leader doesn't fall into that category right now?), need to be able to identify 'varied collective emotions' and develop a collective 'emotional capability' in their companies. In other words to be really sensitive to the emotional fallout and resultant impact of the culture within their organization:

> *While modest fear might be healthy for motivation, using it indiscriminately can be like overusing a drug, which risks generating harmful side effects... Fear can only be a useful motivator if management can provide workers with the means to address these fears.*

A positively focused urgency can create real impetus for change but a negatively focused one might overemphasize inputs and action at the expense of outputs. Valuing action over results can lead to shortcuts, micromanagement, declines in proactivity, a reduction in signal vs noise, and a danger that we might value short-term gain over long-term vision.

Notes

1 April 2012, The Real Leadership Lessons of Steve Jobs, *Harvard Business Review*, [Online] https://hbr.org/2012/04/the-real-leadership-lessons-of-steve-jobs [accessed 25 October 2016]

2 Matthew Syed (29 April 2010) *Bounce: The myth of talent and the power of practice*, Fourth Estate, ASIN B003P2WJ18

3 Jocelyn K Glei (ed) (September 2013) *Maximize Your Potential: Grow your expertise, take bold risks and build an incredible career* (The 99U Book Series), Amazon Publishing, ISBN-10: 1477800891

4 Kotter International, The 8-Step Process for Leading Change, Kotter International, [Online] http://www.kotterinternational.com/the-8-step-process-for-leading-change/ [accessed 25 October 2016]

5 Quy Huy and Timo Vuori (28 January 2016) Who Killed Nokia? Nokia Did, INSEAD Alumni Magazine: *Salamander*, [Online] http://alumnimagazine.insead.edu/who-killed-nokia-nokia-did/ [accessed 25 October 2016]

The role of vision and purpose

08

The organizing idea, purpose and vision

At the most basic level digital transformation requires setting a new course. A course that everyone can understand, grasp, get excited about. As we will demonstrate in Part Five, defining an 'organizing idea', an overarching statement or principle which defines the fundamental orientation for the business, or what drives the company at its most elemental level can express this new direction at the simplest and highest level. But beyond this we need to define the vision and purpose that can truly catalyse organizational momentum and bring this idea to life. Mapping purpose, mission, vision and values requires great clarity. Organization design consultancy NOBL has a useful framework that captures the subtle but important differences in definition.[1] To paraphrase:

- **Purpose:** This is defined as *'why you choose to exist together, beyond financial gain'*, and will usually start with the phrase: *'We believe…'*
- **Mission:** The mission represents *'an ambitious yet achievable position in the market or in your customers' lives that recognizes your purpose'*. It is important therefore that this makes it clear what business you are in, and can often start with the phrase *'Be the most…'*
- **Vision:** A company's vision moves beyond its purpose in expressing *'the difference you'll create in your customers' lives or the larger world when you ultimately realize your purpose'*. The vision should be compelling to those both inside and outside the company, and might well begin with the phrase: *'We will…'*
- **Values:** Organizational values are *'the principles and values that will accelerate your progress together'*. These may be succinct and easy to remember, but will often be represented with a verb (eg 'Be committed').

- **Measures:** Often not included in a purpose statement, measures can be the *'things that you can observe that indicate progress, forward or backward'*, and a useful way to bring the purpose, vision, mission and values to life.

Reading the mission statements of the largest companies in the world reveals many that are vague platitudes to shareholder value, customer-centricity, responsibility and competitive advantage. Substituting the name of the company in the statement demonstrates that many of them could apply to any number of large businesses. The most compelling missions are energizing and ambitious, have a clarity, simplicity and uniqueness, but also sit alongside clearly expressed goals, beliefs, character and a reason for being. The most compelling visions provide not only a strong sense of direction but also a motivating clarion call for the best talent, the expectation to shape behaviours, and so enables the basis to move fast. And they need to come from the very top.

Stories from the frontline

Marco Ryan, EVP, Chief Digital Officer, Wartsila Corporation (and digital transformation veteran): If the CEO is not the sponsor, pack up and go home

I've had the privilege to lead two full-scale digital transformations as well as to design or influence nearly eight others over the last 15 years. All too often CEOs do not want to risk the disruption that digital transformation can cause, to be on their watch. They need their time at the helm to be characterized by profitable growth, increased dividends and the achievement of their Long-term incentive Plan trigger price.

But digital transformation is so fundamental to an organization's future success, that if it is not something the CEO sponsors, you should be worried. Worried enough to walk. This is not to say that CEOs have to do the heavy lifting. That's what Chief Digital Officers are for. But they should be confident enough and smart enough to realize they do not have the time or the skills and hire someone that has.

But after that individual is hired, it cannot be 'Box ticked. Job done.' Digital transformation needs the CEO to ensure his direct reports understand the priorities, act with one voice, demonstrate leadership to the organization and prioritize some of the talent and resources to support what is, in effect, a complete remodelling of the business model. It is in effect a leadership issue. It starts at the very top. With the CEO.

The link between purpose and profit

Renowned management consultant and author Peter Drucker once famously said:

The purpose of business is to create and keep a customer.

But he also said:

That business purpose and business mission are so rarely given adequate thought is perhaps the most important cause of business frustration and failure.

The agile business is characterized by a visionary purpose, but one that is strongly connected to strategy and execution. This is not a new idea, of course. Over a decade ago Jim Collins and Jerry Porras demonstrated (in *Built to Last*,[2] which was based on a six-year Stanford University research project looking at 18 exceptional and enduring companies) that companies that were guided by a visionary purpose beyond just making money returned six times more to shareholders between 1926 and 1990 than their explicitly profit-driven competitors.

A more recent survey from a team from at Harvard Business Review Analytics and EY's Beacon Institute (called *The Business Case for Purpose*)[3] found that companies that can harness the power of purpose to drive performance enjoy a significant competitive advantage.

But there was another interesting finding to the research about what happens when that purpose is not clear, or the link between purpose and action not explicit: 90 per cent of respondents in the HBR/EY study said that their company understood the importance of purpose yet less than half thought that it ran in a purpose-driven way. A lack of clarity on organizational purpose, or how it is expressed (or how that translates into action) can mean that it is impossible to measure, properly manage, or even to learn and improve in the journey towards it. And what is the result of having no clear overriding purpose other than profit?

In a subtle alchemical shift, the metrics fill the vacuum, muscling out any wider purpose with the imperative of hitting the numbers. This transposition of ends and means is often disastrous because methods, now geared to meeting the metric, are detached from customer purpose – so banks sell payment protection insurance to people who do not need it, or VW managers manipulate emissions readings to meet targets. Look no further for the reason why companies lose their customer focus.

Clay Christensen characterizes a company's purpose as comprising three parts:

1. Likeness (the vision of the company they want to become)
2. Commitment (the focus to get there)
3. Metrics (the measures of success).

It must be deliberately conceived, chosen and pursued but when that is in place how the company progresses towards that purpose is likely to be emergent.

Hundreds of thousands of words have been written about the importance of purpose in business, yet there are specific reasons why this matters more than ever. A powerful purpose empowers velocity and focus, since everyone knows the direction in which to head, and it supports fast decision-making and autonomy. At the macro level it creates a calling that employees, new talent, customers and investors can get behind (VC Ben Horowitz describes how: 'The story of the company goes beyond quarterly or annual goals and gets to the hard-core question of why... why is the world better off as a result of this company's existence?').[4] At the micro level it removes unnecessary questions and informs group and team strategies and tactics.

Organizational purpose shapes company culture, and seeps into product design and customer experience. A strong purpose enables change to be framed as a choice or presented as a point of view (rather than a response to an existential threat) which in turn empowers the kind of ideas that don't only originate great products but also create new categories. A point of view sets the foundation for change (as the authors of *Play Bigger*[5] describe it, a point of view: 'has to shift people's minds so they reject an old way of thinking and come to believe in something new. It has to reach people on an emotional level'). Above all, a strong purpose enables the whole company to move at speed towards a commonly understood, long-term, ambitious vision.

Taking the long view

In his famous letter to Amazon shareholders in 1997[6] (when the company was only two years old), founder Jeff Bezos outlined his belief that a fundamental measure of success for Amazon would be the shareholder value that they could create over the long term, and how as a result this may mean that they would make decisions differently from other companies:

> *We will continue to make investment decisions in light of long-term market leadership considerations rather than short-term profitability considerations or short-term Wall Street reactions.*

It is a philosophy that in itself proved to have longevity for the company. In a 2011 interview with Steven Levy in *Wired*, Bezos said that when everything you are working on is to a three-year horizon, then you are inevitably competing against a lot of people. But since few companies are willing to invest on a longer time horizon, doing this dramatically reduces the competition:

> *Just by lengthening the time horizon, you can engage in endeavors that you could never otherwise pursue. At Amazon we like things to work in five to seven years. We're willing to plant seeds, let them grow – and we're very stubborn. We say we're stubborn on vision and flexible on details.*
>
> (Bezos, 2011)[7]

And in his 2013 letter to shareholders[8] he said:

> *I think long-term thinking squares the circle. Proactively delighting customers earns trust, which earns more business from those customers, even in new business arenas. Take a long-term view, and the interests of customers and shareholders align.*

Consequently, Amazon's revenues have grown exponentially over the long term, but consistent investment in forward-thinking innovation and infrastructure to continually develop the company's capability and scope has meant that earnings have been minimal. While not every company has the luxury of ignoring short-term shareholder value, the point is that Amazon is buying itself the time and space to invest in not only continual, data-driven, shorter-term marginal improvement, but also large-scale invention. For that, as Bezos has said, you need to be willing to think long term, to start with the customer and work backwards, and even to be misunderstood for lengthy periods of time (as they were when they moved into hardware with the Kindle). For CEOs with quarterly targets and multiple pressing priorities this is not easy. And yet, it is more essential than ever to build the new while optimizing the old. Google CEO Larry Page believes that the main reason behind many company failures is that they 'miss the future':

> *When I talk to most companies, I do think their leaders are pretty short-term focused… It's pretty difficult to solve big problems in four years. I think it's probably pretty easy to do it in 20 years. I think our whole system is setup in a way that makes it difficult for leaders of really big companies.*[9]

Difficult but now critical. The dangers of too much short-termism are akin to that Clay Christensen idea of planting saplings when you need shade – it takes time for the saplings to grow big enough. Prioritizing investment into new sources of revenues only when you need them is too late.

Businesses that work to a long-term horizon have a huge potential advantage, meaning that companies need to have a point of view on the future and their part in it, and that the emphasis of corporate strategy itself is shifting. Author and consultant (and co-founder of the Deloitte Centre for the Edge Innovation) John Hagel has described this shift in emphasis from strategies 'shaped by terrain' to strategies 'shaped by trajectory'. Traditional approaches to strategy are profoundly shaped by the current landscape. While there are still dynamic components to the strategy (such as responses to shifts generated by your own or competitor activities), the starting point is always your current position and the environment that surrounds it.

While strategies of position still matter, in an environment of accelerating change and increasing uncertainty we need, says John, more than ever to have a point of view on the trajectory of change and 'what degrees of freedom we might have in shaping these outcomes through our actions'. In other words to position in the context of the future, not the present. That point of view needs to look from the future towards the present rather than the other way round.

Working back from the future in this way enables us to think far more laterally about our near-term direction and the steps that we need to take now to achieve the future that we envisage. As an example, Netflix is quite open about its long-term view on the future of internet TV and what it sees as its future-facing guideposts, publishing them openly on the web.[10] Businesses are increasingly defined by their futures, not by their pasts. Effective strategies of trajectory take account of fundamental needs and things that are stable over time. Back to Jeff Bezos again who believes that if you want to build a successful, sustainable business, you don't only ask yourself what could change in the next 10 years that could affect your company, but more importantly ask yourself what *won't* change, and then put all your energy and effort into those things.[11]

To be an agile business, you need to have a point of view on the future. To not make oversimplified presumptions about what that future could look like. Strategies of trajectory are not only about what is possible but also about what *could* be possible. In order to take a view on that we need to be paying close attention to underlying shifts in consumer behaviour but also core customer needs that *don't* change, and not simply the latest shiny new technology.

Notes

1. NOBL (2016) How to Define Your Purpose, Vision, Mission, Values, and Key Measures, NOBL, [Online] http://futureofwork.nobl.io/future-of-work/how-to-define-your-purpose-vision-mission-values-and-key-measures [accessed 25 October 2016]
2. Jim Collins and Jerry Porras (1 September 2005) *Built To Last: Successful habits of visionary companies*, Random House Business, ISBN-10 1844135845 ISBN-13 978-1844135844
3. EY (2015) The Business Case for Purpose, EY.com, [Online] http://www.ey.com/Publication/vwLUAssets/ey-the-business-case-for-purpose/$FILE/ey-the-business-case-for-purpose.pdf [accessed 25 October 2016]
4. Ben Horowitz (4 March 2014) *The Hard Thing About Hard Things: Building a business when there are no easy answers*, HarperBusiness, ASIN B00DQ845EA
5. Al Ramadan, Dave Peterson, Christopher Lochhead and Kevin Maney (14 June 2016) *Play Bigger: How rebels and innovators create new categories and dominate markets*, Piatkus, ASIN B010PIF952
6. Jeff Bezos (1999, 1997) Letter to Shareholders, US Securities and Exchange Commission, [Online] https://www.sec.gov/Archives/edgar/data/1018724/000119312513151836/d511111dex991.htm [accessed 25 October 2016]
7. Steven Levy (13 November 2011) Jeff Bezos Owns the Web in More Ways Than You Think, Wired.com, [Online] https://www.wired.com/2011/11/ff_bezos/all/1 [accessed 25 October 2016]
8. Henry Blodget (14 April 2013) Amazon's Letter To Shareholders Should Inspire Every Company In America, Business Insider.com, [Online] http://www.businessinsider.com/amazons-letter-to-shareholders-2013-4?IR=T [accessed 25 October 2016]
9. Vinod Khosla (3 July 2014) Fireside Chat with Google Co-founders, Larry Page and Sergey Brin, Khosla Ventures.com, [Online] http://www.khoslaventures.com/fireside-chat-with-google-co-founders-larry-page-and-sergey-brin [accessed 25 October 2016]
10. Netflix (18 April 2016) Netflix's View: Internet TV is replacing linear TV, Netflix, [Online] https://ir.netflix.com/long-term-view.cfm [accessed 25 October 2016]
11. Jillian D'Onfro (31 January 2015) Jeff Bezos' Brilliant Advice for Anyone Running a Business, Business Insider.com, [Online] http://uk.businessinsider.com/jeff-bezos-brilliant-advice-for-anyone-running-a-business-2015-1 [accessed 25 October 2016]

Agile strategy and planning 09

The key to good strategy

... is to have one. As Richard Rumelt noted in his excellent book on strategy (*Good Strategy/Bad Strategy*):[1]

> *The first natural advantage of good strategy arises because other organizations often don't have one. And because they don't expect you to have one either. A good strategy has coherence, coordinating actions, policies and resources so as to accomplish an important end.*

Many organizations, says Rumelt, substitute strategy for multiple goals and initiatives that may symbolize progress, but in reality lack a coherent approach to actually achieving that progress (apart from, he notes, 'spend more and try harder').

In Part One, we described the key challenge as one characterized by rates of change: Technological change happens exponentially, but organizational change is logarithmic. The way in which we might mitigate this potentially widening gap is through deliberate choices. Yet, as Rotman School of Management Professor Roger Martin has noted,[2] many corporate strategies avoid this:

> *The very essence of strategy is explicit, purposeful choice. Strategy is saying explicitly, proactively: 'We're going to do these things and not those things for these reasons'.*
>
> (Martin, 2015)[3]

The problem with a lot of strategies, he says, is that they are actually full of non-choices. For example, simply saying that your strategy is to be customer-centric is not making an explicit choice about what to do, and what not to do. The way to know when you have made a real strategic choice is if you can easily define what the opposite of that choice is and it doesn't sound ridiculous. Non-choice strategies (and for that matter missions) do lend themselves to confusion, misdirection and apathy, but do not lend themselves to moving quickly.

If effective strategy is about making choices, then effective strategy for the agile business is about signal versus noise, and framing the choices we make through the lens of our three key contexts that we discussed in Part One:

- **Consumer:** We need to be selective about which shifts in consumer behaviour we prioritize, and which customer needs we choose to address first. This means appreciating the difference between a fad (a temporary spike in focus) and a trend (a more fundamental underlying shift). Fads may be focused around technologies, trends around behaviours. Fads may address customer needs in transient ways, trends speak to more fundamental, long-term customer needs and behaviours. Prioritization, and an adept sense of the relative significance of specific changes is key. A company that is closely in touch with the customer, that is outwardly facing and willing to experiment with the new in order to learn, and one that is networked and able to draw on insight from a wide range of sources, is optimized to create the most effective strategy in today's world.
- **Competitor:** We need to make choices about where we play in the market, to lead rather than obsessively follow and benchmark, to make more ambitious choices about who we regard as competition and be more open to who we can learn from.
- **Company:** We need to understand the potential and application of new and existing technologies, and how they might be combined in new ways to create exceptional value. We need to be adept at knowledge flow, and drawing learning from rapid experimentation and iterative working in order to inform the choices we make around strategic direction.

If, as Roger Martin says, developing strategy often becomes 'an exercise in agglomerating initiatives, assigning responsibilities without a coherent set of choices that help bind them'[4] (meaning that most strategic plans are more accurately described as 'budgets with prose'), then we need to be clear that this is not fit for purpose for an uncertain, rapidly moving business environment. Neither is poor communication of strategy, or poor connection with tactics and execution, or conflating a varied set of goals or targets with a coherent strategy. Richard Rumelt said: 'Goals are not strategy. Goals are wishes. Strategies are how one goes about achieving goals', but he also defines what makes a good strategy:

> *A strategy is a coherent set of analyses, arguments and actions that respond to a significant challenge. A good strategy derives from consideration of many plausible courses of action and selects, in a deliberate, reasoned way, one/some of those courses of action to the exclusion of others.*[5]

His 'strategy kernel' combines diagnosis, the creation of a guiding policy, and a coherent set of actions or direction. The agile business combines adept analysis with creative and astute synthesis to be good at all three.

Emergent and deliberate strategy

In order to achieve true agility we need an organizational strategy that retains the right combination of that which is fixed and 'deliberate', and that which is more flexible, or emergent. Harvard Business School professor and author Clay Christensen describes how strategy is 'not a discrete analytical event' or something decided using best-known numbers at the time in a meeting of senior managers. Instead, it is a 'continuous, diverse, and unruly process' that constantly evolves.[6] So the art of managing this is not to dismiss anything that deviates from the original plan but to continually identify better options and then manage resources flexibly to nourish them. Rigid planning processes (particularly in large organizations, where challenging an original fixed plan can often be a political, morale-killing exercise) mitigate the flexibility needed to respond to rapidly changing contexts.

The example Christensen uses to illustrate the advantages of flexibility is the way in which Honda broke into North America. The company's strategy was based entirely around big motorbikes (since that is what US consumers seemed to favour), bringing them into competition with manufacturers like Harley. Some Honda employees started to use a few of the much smaller Supercub models to do a bit of weekend dirt biking in the hills around LA, a Sears buyer sees the interest this generates, decides to stock them in the outdoor equipment department, and a new opportunity for Honda, an innovative distribution strategy, and a whole new genre of biking, is born. Honda refocused their strategy on the Supercub which went on to become the best selling two-wheeler on the planet, in no small part due to their ability to break into the North American market.

Business is increasingly populated with examples of companies that have 'pivoted' in this way, and the high uncertainty and ambiguity that characterizes our modern business environment lends a heightened importance to this kind of fluidity. Image hosting and sharing service Flickr emerged from tools that were created for a web-based multiplayer online game called 'game neverending'. Ludicorp, the game's creators, then shelved the game and pivoted to concentrate on growing Flickr. Pinterest began life as a mobile shopping app called Tote that was arguably ahead of its time but provided the foundations for the service we know today. Twitter grew as a side project out of a podcast company called Odeo. Android, the largest operating system in the world, began with the intention of creating an operating ecosystem for digital cameras.

It is not just technology businesses that need to pivot. Professor Amar Bhidé (in *The Origin and Evolution of New Business*)[7] has shown that 93 per cent of all companies that ultimately become successful had to abandon their original strategy. Companies that survive are able retain a high and consistent level of strategic adaptation and improvisation, even if they occasionally trip up along the way.

The balance between vision and iteration

Jeff Bezos once said:

> *We are stubborn on vision. We are flexible on details... If you're not stubborn, you'll give up on experiments too soon. And if you're not flexible, you'll pound your head against the wall and you won't see a different solution to a problem you're trying to solve.*[8]

Stubborn on vision. Flexible on details. These words capture the essence of agile strategy. The balance between a strong, directional vision that steers, guides and enables, and adaptive, iterative planning that flexes, adjusts and modifies in response to changing contexts and new information.

Iteration without direction is chaotic. The vision should be challenging, clear and compelling, but it needs to give direction to strategic choices and decision-making throughout the business. Change does not come from the CEO standing in front of the company with a PowerPoint presentation. It comes from constant reinforcement through frequent repetition of the vision and continuous communication of goals and progress. It comes from the behaviours and decisions exhibited by senior leaders and those around us. It comes from what we choose to recognize and reward, and how we structure our learning. Every meeting, every update, every communication is a chance to underline, fortify and energize around that vision.

Yet rigidly pursuing a plan with no room for frequent adaptation leads to declining performance, missed opportunities and limited learning. Real change also comes from the continuous iteration that drives progress towards that vision. It comes from the flexibility that allows for enough autonomy and plasticity to adapt planning to continuously learn and improve. Every sprint, every retrospective, every actionable learning is a chance to advance towards bringing that vision to life.

In Part Two, we discussed the analogy of how the high operational tempo of *Blitzkrieg* was enabled through a command methodology that empowered frontline commanders to make quick decisions in the face of rapidly shifting contexts. The underlying goal, intent or focus of effort (the *'Schwerpunkt'*) enabled clarity of objective and direction, and combined with a well-understood level of flexibility for frontline commanders (*'Fingerspitzengefuhl'* or 'finger-tip feel') to enable rapid responsiveness and progression. This is a governance structure built for speed and manoeuvrability.

Using a more modern military analogy, the US Army frame this balance in the terms of a 'Commander's intent' and the 'concept of operations'. The former:

> *... succinctly describes what constitutes success for the operation. It includes the operation's purpose, key tasks, and the conditions that define the end state. It links the mission, concept of operations, and tasks to subordinate units. A clear commander's intent facilitates a shared understanding and focuses on the overall conditions that represent mission accomplishment.*[9]

The Commander's intent is the central objective or idea that pulls everything together, the unifying element of the plan, the Commander's expression of what they want to make happen. The concept of the operation is designed to direct the way in which subordinate units should cooperate to fulfill a mission, and creates the sequence of actions that the force will actually use to get to that objective. The Commander's intent should therefore bridge the gap between the mission and the concept of operations. This system has represented a move away from an over-reliance on a rigid, and therefore increasingly unsuitable methodical planning process which does not work well in situations characterized by uncertainty. Again, it is a governance structure designed for agility.

The agile organization therefore, has a good understanding of what is fixed, and what is flexible, and the critical difference between a strategy and a plan. This latter distinction is best expressed by Sir Lawrence Freedman:

> *Strategy is much more than a plan. A plan supposes a sequence of events that allows one to move with confidence from one state of affairs to another. Strategy is required when others might frustrate one's plans because they have different and possibly opposing interests and concerns... The inherent unpredictability of human affairs, due to the chance events as well as the efforts of opponents*

and the missteps of friends, provides strategy with its challenge and drama. Strategy is often expected to start with a description of a desired end state, but in practice there is rarely an orderly movement to goals set in advance. Instead, the process evolves through a series of states, each one not quite what was anticipated or hoped for, requiring a reappraisal and modification of the original strategy, including ultimate objectives. The picture of strategy... is one that is fluid and flexible, governed by the starting point and not the end point.[10]

So a strategy should be fluid, and open to creating many potential routes to success ('You don't make strategy so that there's one path to victory; you make it so that as many paths as possible lead to something which isn't loss,' said Nick Harkaway in his novel *The Gone-Away World*).[11] So the *pace* of change at which each element evolves and adapts is key:

- **Mission and purpose:** are fixed and do not change.
- **Vision:** is compelling, and largely fixed.
- **Strategy:** characterized by choices, changes and evolves to take account of shifting contexts and new information, but does so more infrequently or slowly.
- **Plans or tactics:** are highly fluid, iterative and adaptive to feedback, learning and new information.

Agility and adaptiveness increases the closer we get to execution, but the strategy and governance that frames planning, tactics and delivery is flexible enough to allow responsiveness throughout the organization. Leaders need to set the expectation, establish the governance that acknowledges necessary boundaries but removes barriers to progress, and empower teams with required tools and resources. And then GET OUT OF THE WAY.

The customer-centric organization

Above all else, align with customers. Win when they win. Win only when they win.

Jeff Bezos

In the agile business, the customer is the guiding beacon for the organizational mission, vision and strategy, but also the operational priorities, tactics and execution. Every company believes that they place the customer at the heart of their business, yet so often the orientation and prioritization is derived from what is easier and more efficient for the company, rather than better and more effective for the customer. Businesses are frequently organized in ways that make little sense for the customer (ever had a customer service representative need to transfer you to another department because they cannot action your query?). In resourcing prioritization, too much emphasis is placed on business efficiency over customer satisfaction. Too much customer-facing resource is focused on dealing with a failure of the organization to do something or do it well (failure demand), rather than helping to create more value (value demand). Poor application of automation, use of scripts or inflexible rules and systems make for bad customer service (many businesses still bury contact details on their website or even worse, charge their customers to talk to them).[12] Too many customer experiences are not joined up, resulting in duplication of effort for the customer and missed opportunity for the company.

We have already discussed how digital-native processes such as agile and lean are naturally customer-centric, involving the customer along the development process. Yet real customer-centricity stretches into every aspect of the business, from process and strategy to culture, measures and even structure (we will discuss more about customer-centric structures in Part Four).

Earlier we showed how Amazon takes the long view on innovation. But they are also an exceptional exemplar for what true customer-centricity really means (remember that the Amazon mission is: 'We seek to be Earth's most customer-centric company for four primary customer sets: consumers, sellers, enterprises, and content creators'). This is brought to life throughout the operating model, measures and culture. As Jeff Bezos puts it:

> *We're not competitor obsessed, we're customer obsessed. We start with what the customer needs and we work backwards.*

Early in Amazon's life, Jeff Bezos would famously bring an empty chair, which represented the customer (or the most important person in the room) into meetings. Each year thousands of Amazon managers (including the founder) spend time in the call-centres to help ensure a culture of not just listening to, but understanding, customers. Team objectives and metrics are aligned to customer experience, and data-driven decision-making used to continuously improve against those measures. Performance at Amazon is tracked via 500 measurable goals, with almost 80 per cent of them relating to customer objectives.[13] Its highly tuned algorithms create an unparalleled degree of content personalization across a customer base of hundreds of millions of users. Customer experience is taken so seriously that even the tiniest delays in web page loading time become a significant focus to improve (they believe that a 0.1 second delay in page rendering can result in a 1 per cent drop in customer activity). The Amazon obsession with efficiency is driven by the desire to deliver better prices for customers, Bezos waging war on 'muda' (the Japanese word for waste). Everything Amazon do as a business is oriented towards the customer. The point is that saying you are something doesn't make it so. And customers can see that.

Customer-centricity can be a central driving force for digital transformation. The UK Government Digital Service (GDS) are a small team of people sitting at the centre of multiple government departments but who have brought an unprecedented level of agility to what would typically be a distinctly un-agile environment. From the beginning their approach has been characterized by transparency, user-centricity, and solid service design practice, as exhibited by their 10 design principles[14] which read like a manifesto for not just exceptional digital design, but a truly digital-native way of working. To summarize:

1. **Start with needs** – user needs, of course, not government needs.
2. **Do less** – only do what you can do and concentrate on the 'irreducible core'. Make what works shareable and reusable to minimize duplication of effort. Build platforms that others can build on, develop APIs, link to the work of others.
3. **Design with data** – use data to demonstrate real behaviour, to learn, to reduce assumption, to drive decision-making. Continuous iteration using data to prototype, test and improve services. Analytics should be embedded, always on and easy to understand.
4. **Do the hard work to make it simple** – work hard to make complex systems easy for people to use, challenge toxic assumptions.
5. **Iterate. Then iterate again** – 'start small and iterate wildly'. Test minimum viable products and prototypes with real users. Make constant improvements using customer feedback. Don't be afraid to remove or move on from what doesn't work: 'Iteration reduces risk. It makes big failures unlikely and turns small failures into lessons'.
6. **This is for everyone** – services should be accessible, inclusive, legible.
7. **Understand context** – design for people, not screens. Consider the context in which services might be used.
8. **Build digital services, not websites** – connect the digital world to the real world, consider all aspects of a service, make no assumptions about platform.

9 **Be consistent, not uniform** – consistency in language and design patterns, but respect shifting circumstances.

10 **Make things open: it makes things better** – the sharing of knowledge, code, ideas, failures brings unforeseen benefit.

The traditional approach to service design was government-centric: start with the government policy, then consider the process needed to fulfil the policy, and then the systems needed to support that. User need came far down the list, but this method led to overly detailed input, 'digital versions' of existing practices, poor customer journeys, lengthy and complex procurement procedures and inflexible solutions based on traditional thinking.

The new approach turned that on its head: user needs provided the foundation, services are designed around those needs, the systems needed to support those services then considered, and then a check that the service is delivering to government policy. GDS do the research, they analyse the data, they talk to and observe users to make sure that they make no assumptions, and are focusing on real needs (combining *claimed* behaviour, or traditional forms of research such as surveys, polls and focus groups, with *real* behaviour, assessed through observation or analytics, leads to a more three-dimensional understanding of customer need). This fundamental shift in approach not only ensures that service design is grounded in a solid empathy with, and understanding of, user need (thereby leading to better services), but catalyses a much broader philosophical and organizational shift towards orienting processes, culture and resourcing towards the customer. Executive Director at GDS Stephen Foreshew-Cain describes this transformation thus:

> *The upshot will be services that shape government, not the other way round. Because we're putting users first, and because we're working in an agile way, and because we're making data easier to use, government itself will have to change.*
>
> (Foreshew-Cain, 2016)[15]

This 'organizing idea', he says, is not about incrementally making existing things a little better; it is about completely rethinking the way that they work. Combining service design methodologies with small, multidisciplinary teams working in short, iterative sprints can bring a new breadth and depth of customer-centricity to an organization, which can in turn lead to *real* transformation.

'P' is for Prioritization

One of the key challenges with any digital transformation programme is the prioritization of limited resources. Good prioritization can make the difference between a successful transformation and complete failure and yet there are some immediate pitfalls that many fall into. Poor technology literacy among the senior leadership of an organization, for example, can easily lead to poor decision-making about technology or project development prioritization. In the age of horizontal innovation and accelerated, non-incremental change, in-sector competitive activity can be disproportionately significant in determining organizational priorities and a time-suck on company resources. While competitive positioning and strategies are important, so much management time in organizations is wasted analysing what the competition are doing. Google founder Larry Page has talked about how he thinks of his job as getting people *not* to think about what Google's competition are doing because rather than think about the things that already exist he would rather his staff focused on the things that have not been thought of yet. It is, he says, hard to find examples of amazing things that have only happened because of competition, and if the focus is simply on crushing another company that does almost the same thing, that does not make for the most compelling place to work:

> *That's why most companies decay slowly over time. They tend to do approximately what they did before, with a few minor changes. It's natural for people to want to work on things that they know aren't going to fail. But incremental improvement is guaranteed to be obsolete over time.*
>
> (Page, 2013)[16]

One of the key inputs to prioritization, of course, is customer need. When the Government Digital Service began the huge task of redesigning the UK government portal they faced a massive prioritization challenge that covered 660 services involving 1.3 billion transactions over 16 departments. The team looked not only at what users wanted from those services, but also prioritized projects based on usage patterns. The data told them that there was a real long-tail to service usage with 26 per cent of services (or 4 per cent of the total services) accounting for 90 per cent of transactions,[17] so they took the top 25 and made those the initial ones to focus on. This ensured that they could have the biggest impact in the shortest possible time. Russell Davies, who was Director of Strategy at the Government Digital Service during the key period of early transformation, describes how you need to start with a firework (an impactful win that can get people excited), followed by some quick fixes ('you need to make some stuff work surprisingly well, surprisingly quickly and cheaply'), then move rapidly out of innovation and fireworks into fixing the basics ('transforming the basic reality of the organization'), and focus on fundamentals such as digital infrastructure (hiring, procurement, contracts, management), analytics and measurement (including tracking key indicators), organizational blockers, governance and reporting ('an essential element of transformation is likely to be dissolving the existing corporate silos – that can't be done from within one of them'), and of course, culture.

Stories from the frontline

Russell Davies: Prioritization in digital transformation

If you're really doing digital transformation, you have to do everything first. Everything's connected. So you have to do everything.

Some things will happen first, but you have to start as much as you can as soon as you can.

So, for instance, the plan to transform government publishing with GOV.UK was part of a larger plan to transform government services as a whole. That was prioritized since it was thought to be relatively quick, cheap and easy to do. It would be very visible and would reach a lot of people.

Within the GOV.UK project itself there were then many other prioritization decisions that were informed by a mixture of easiness and impact. And those changed over time.

What you prioritize for the alpha – when you're learning what to do and trying to persuade people to let you do it – is different to when you have full control and you're grinding through the programme. For the alpha, things that Ministers would immediately care about were prioritized. Once their backing was secured, then came the stuff that would really matter. On the whole we optimized for momentum – it was known that eventually the machine would wake up and try to slow things down, so we tried to change as much as we could as quickly as possible, so it would be harder to unpick.

And then, inside the project itself there were a ton of decisions: What services do we start with? Which departments should go first? It's fractal – priorities within priorities. Eventually you solve that by trusting the team doing it. You describe some outcomes, emphasize some things over others (MOMENTUM!) and let them work out their own delivery priorities. Setting specific priorities at every level is counter-productive, it becomes a version of waterfall or (dread phrase) a Target Operating Model.

And, of course, zooming out again, if you're doing proper transformation you can't set these priorities in isolation. In order to transform publishing you need digital specialists, which means you need to hire different people, which means you need to change the HR practices, which means you need to change hiring guidelines and recruit different HR people and rewrite all the ads and find a way round the salary restrictions. And you have to give people the right tools which means you have to persuade IT to allow people internet access and to change accounting practices so people can use a government purchasing card to sign up to Heroku ($99, 30 seconds) rather than use the single source hosting contract ($ millions, months). That's all at the apparently trivial level, but it actually makes a huge difference. And at a more apparently 'transformational' level you probably have to fire, disempower, or sidestep the existing IT organization and their suppliers. Which may well mean changing the composition of the board. You'll probably have to change the way procurement works and re-educate them about what a good IT contract looks like. You might need to extract all kinds of digital stuff from the marketing and sales organization. It goes on and on.

Prioritization via impact and effort is not new, but becomes particularly important when the requirement is to demonstrate early value in a digital transformation programme. Put simply, showing big impact in a short space of time buys you more time, particularly if you can show the tangible benefit not just to the business but also from the perspective of the customer (nobody can argue with customer data). As well as impact and effort, a third dimension to prioritization is, of course, time. As Dwight D Eisenhower famously said:

> *What is important is seldom urgent, and what is urgent is seldom important.*

The Eisenhower matrix (Figure 9.1) is a simple but powerful way of balancing these two criteria to define what we should pay attention to first.

It is, of course, important that we ensure we are not constantly ignoring or scheduling for later development priorities that might not be urgent now, but are fundamentally important for long-term capability or advancement.

Figure 9.1 The Eisenhower matrix

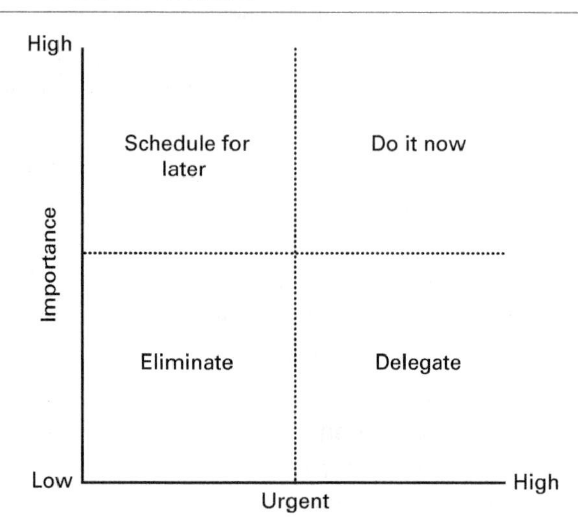

Ring fencing resource and allocating to short- and long-term needs helps mitigate this, and simple scorecard approaches (including, for example, an assessment of customer impact, risk, cost, time and profit contribution) can be highly effective in prioritizing development. Any broader innovation or transformation programme can be significantly undermined by poor, nonsensical service design and delivery and so fixing basic but poorly designed customer or product experiences and unnecessary barriers to seamless customer journeys can often be a powerful driver for change. Remember, innovation is no substitute for basic competence.

Clarity of roadmap ownership and governance, robust prioritization methodologies and capacity planning against set criteria are essential to prevent capacity overload and development precedence being given to inappropriate internal priorities (like from those who shout loudest) rather than those that make sense for the customer.

But when is it not right to listen to our customers? It is, of course, a myth that Apple do not do research, but Steve Jobs famously described the limitations of customer feedback when designing the new:

> *It's really hard to design products by focus groups. A lot of times, people don't know what they want until you show it to them.*

Henri Seydoux, Founder and CEO of technology and drone business Parrot describes how there are times when they have no consideration of the user, and other times when they are extremely sensitive to user need:

When your idea is totally new, you cannot ask the user... if you ask people to dream with you, they not will understand with you, or the dream will not be serious.[18]

Seydoux relates the story of how an idea for a connected picture frame rapidly became overcomplicated by focus groups who relayed all kinds of additional features that they wanted to the point where it became untenable. Yet for a developing or existing market, continuous customer feedback is key. As Clay Christensen said:

Working harder, being smarter, investing more aggressively, and listening more astutely to customers are all solutions to the problems posed by new sustaining technologies. But these paradigms of sound management are useless – even counterproductive, in many instances – when dealing with disruptive technology.[19]

The secret is to design with vision and optimize with feedback.

Strategy as an ever-changing algorithm

Everybody has a plan until they get punched in the face.

Mike Tyson

We have discussed how the agile business is stubborn on vision but flexible on details, and how strategy is about making choices, continually defining better options, evolving in response to shifting contexts but changing more slowly than the highly fluid and adaptive planning process. Noah Brier, the founder of marketing software business Percolate, describes strategy as an ever-changing algorithm and it is a useful analogy. If algorithms create a set of rules that enable problems to be solved, then strategy 'is really about building algorithms that help drive optimal outcomes in decisions'.[20]

If we think about strategy as an ever-evolving algorithm, then the rules or guidelines that we set should help us to navigate the terrain that we need to cross. Just as algorithms constantly change to take account of new inputs, so a strategy should be emergent, constantly taking account of new contexts and what data and insight is telling us in order to find the path to the optimal solution. Google updates the search algorithm hundreds of times a year but periodically undergoes a major overhaul that impacts how it works in more fundamental ways, in the same way that strategies continuously morph but periodically need a significant correction to keep us on track when we are in danger of getting thrown off-course.

While rigid, top-down strategy is the more traditional domain, the requirement in the agile business is both to set the strategy in such a way that it can evolve utilizing a continuous stream of insight, data and feedback from customer facing teams, and in an environment of increasingly transient competitive advantage to be ready to disengage and refocus, even when the business is still viable. As Rita Gunther McGrath describes it:

> *One of the most significant differences between the assumption of sustainable competitive advantage and more dynamic strategy is that disengagement – the process of moving out of an exhausted opportunity – is as core to the business as innovation, growth, and exploitation are.*[21]

So just as we should work to increase the pace of change and responsiveness in the way in which we work, we need to take more account of the tempo of change in our strategy and planning process and find ways to embed this practice and thinking. A useful framework for this has been created by ex-Global Head of Brand Design at Facebook and now VP of Product at Intercom Paul Adams, who describes an effective way of thinking about your product roadmap by delineating over three timelines: the next six years, next six months, and next six weeks. Paul applies the framework in the context of a product roadmap but it is just as applicable to a more adaptive approach to strategy:

- **The next six years:** this is your view on the shape of the world six years out, taking account of how key trends and your own actions will have changed it. This is your strategy of trajectory.
- **The next six months:** your focus here is on your plans for building, creating or executing things that will materially impact on progress towards your long-term strategy. This is a rolling timeline that can evolve so that at the end of the six months, says Paul, you may have built 50–75 per cent of what you set out to do, but the remaining 25 per cent is made up of new things that you had not thought of before.
- **The next six weeks:** the immediate plan which is known well, and is being worked on in detail right now, and changes iteratively as a rolling timeline every week or two.

The timescales used in the '666 roadmap' are less important than the three-timeline concept (although aligning it with the 'number of the beast' no doubt creates plenty of opportunity for amusement among product teams) which allows for a directional view on the future, a mid-term adaptive strategy, and a highly iterative short-term plan.

Discovery-driven planning

Processes such as agile and lean are designed to remove as many assumptions from development as possible. With an exponential increase in the quantity of available data, applying that data in the service of challenging assumptions (particularly the hidden, or 'toxic', assumptions that go unquestioned) is an essential requirement in helping the agile business get to the outcomes it desires. If, alongside this, we are tracking back from our vision of the future in order to reimagine our present priorities (rather than extrapolating from a past which may be defined by out-of-date assumptions) then we have a more solid basis for crafting our agile strategy. But there are times, such as when we are entering new or poorly defined areas, when the ratio of assumptions we are forced to incorporate relative to the knowledge we already possess is likely to be unusually high. Emergent, iterative strategy and planning helps to mitigate risk, but it is still critical to identify as many avoidable, or hidden, assumptions as possible.

Rita Gunther McGrath's discovery-driven planning[22] is a useful concept that forces you to identify a desired outcome, and then ask what needs to be true in order for that outcome to happen. Conventional planning is based on a premise that future results can be accurately extrapolated from the predictable platform of past results and so may be useful in a stable, incremental or known scenario. Discovery-driven planning focuses on establishing the key truths that are needed for an outcome to be achieved and so is much more useful for those ventures that are new, more unknown, or characterized by a greater degree of uncertainty.

McGrath uses a great case study to illustrate the folly of using conventional planning techniques for a new venture – the launch of Euro Disney Resort (what is now Disneyland Paris). The launch in 1992 was something of a disaster, with numbers of visitor-days falling far short of expectations. Two years after launch it had accumulated losses of more than US$1 billion and only achieved its target of 11 million admissions after a drastic drop in ticket prices.

In the planning process Disney had used assumptions based on their extensive knowledge derived from their experience running parks in other parts of the world (United States and Japan). There were some pretty big assumptions around the admissions price that punters would be prepared to pay, how European customers would want to eat, and the type of merchandise they would buy. But the really punishing assumption was that (based on their experience in other markets) they had assumed that people would stay an average of four days in the park's hotels. And yet the average stay in the early days was only two days. Euro Disney opened with only 15 rides, compared with 45 at Walt Disney World. People could do all the rides in a single day and so had little reason to stay longer.

In order to avoid such outcomes, McGrath defines a number of disciplines including: specifying a clear frame for the project (including quantifiable goals); the importance of basing plans in market and competitive reality; to translate strategy into specific, implementable actions (working backwards from what you have to deliver); to document, test and revisit assumptions; and finally planning to learn at key milestones.

> *In discovery driven plans, the whole plan is organized around converting the maximum number of assumptions to knowledge at minimum cost.*

As the novelist E L Doctorow once said:

> *Writing a novel is like driving a car at night. You can see only as far as your headlights, but you can make the whole trip that way.*

With discovery-driven planning we have enough knowledge to plan in detail to the next major milestone but not beyond it, so the key is to test assumptions as you go at key milestones. Much like agile and lean, this approach is motivating, giving people freedom to test and learn rather than shouldering them with an obligation to justify divergence from a flawed original plan. The key question to always ask: What needs to be true in order for this outcome to be achieved? This form of emergent strategy has never been more appropriate than it is today.

Notes

1 Richard Rumelt (9 June 2011) *Good Strategy/Bad Strategy: The difference and why it matters*, Profile Books, ISBN-10 184765746X ISBN-13 978-1847657466

2 Roger Martin (21 January 2015) Roger Martin's Unconventional Wisdom, Bridgespan Group, [Online] http://www.bridgespan.org/publications-and-tools/strategy-development/roger-martins-unconventional-wisdom.aspx#.VRvHoBB4r7R [accessed 25 October 2016]

3 Roger Martin (21 January 2015) Roger Martin's Unconventional Wisdom, Bridgespan Group, [Online] http://www.bridgespan.org/publications-and-tools/strategy-development/roger-martins-unconventional-wisdom.aspx#.VRvHoBB4r7R [accessed 25 October 2016]

4 Roger Martin (21 January 2015) Roger Martin's Unconventional Wisdom, Bridgespan Group, [Online] http://www.bridgespan.org/publications-and-tools/strategy-development/roger-martins-unconventional-wisdom.aspx#.V9ZVyJOU3-b [accessed 25 October 2016]

5 Richard Rumelt (9 June 2011) *Good Strategy/Bad Strategy: The difference and why it matters*, Profile Books, ISBN-10 184765746X ISBN-13 978-1847657466

6 James Allworth, Karen Dillon and Clayton Christensen (10 May 2012) *How Will You Measure Your Life?*, HarperCollins, ASIN B006I1AE92

7 Amar V Bhidé (16 October 2003) *The Origin and Evolution of New Businesses*, Oxford University Press, USA, ISBN-10 195170318 ISBN-13 978-0195170313

8 John Greathouse (30 April 2013) 5 Time-Tested Success Tips From Amazon Founder Jeff Bezos, Forbes.com [Online] http://www.forbes.com/sites/johngreathouse/2013/04/30/5-time-tested-success-tips-from-amazon-founder-jeff-bezos/#3ad6bc73351a [accessed 25 October 2016]

9 Major Richard Dempsey and Major Jonathan M Chavous (December 2013) Commander's Intent and Concept of Operations, United States Army Combined Arms Center, [Online] http://usacac.army.mil/CAC2/MilitaryReview/Archives/English/MilitaryReview_20131231_art011.pdf [accessed 25 October 2016]

10 Sir Lawrence Freedman (31 October 2013) *Strategy: A history*, OUP USA, ISBN-10 199325154 ISBN-13 978-0199325153

11 Nick Harkaway (4 September 2008) *The Gone-Away World*, Cornerstone Digital, ASIN B0031RS8JE

12 BBC (6 August 2013) Complaints Call Costs to be Capped, BBC News, [Online] http://www.bbc.co.uk/news/uk-politics-23590778 [accessed 25 October 2016]

13 George Anders (4 April 2012) Inside Amazon's Idea Machine: How Bezos decodes customers, Forbes.com, [Online] http://www.forbes.com/sites/georgeanders/2012/04/04/inside-amazon/3/#3ec60390650f [accessed 25 October 2016]

14 Gov.UK (2016) Design Principles, Gov.uk, [Online] https://www.gov.uk/design-principles [accessed 25 October 2016]

15 Gov.UK (2016) What GDS Is For, Gov.uk, [Online] https://gds.blog.gov.uk/2016/06/29/what-gds-is-for/ [accessed 25 October 2016]

16 Steven Levy (17 January 2013) Google's Larry Page on Why Moon Shots Matter, Wired.com, [Online] https://www.wired.com/2013/01/ff-qa-larry-page/all/ [accessed 25 October 2016]

17 Tom Loosemore (5 June 2014) Government Digital Services, Slideshare.net, [Online] http://www.slideshare.net/intscotland/tom-loosemoregovernment-digital-service [accessed 25 October 2016]

18 Mike Murphy (11 September 2016) This French Drone Company Innovates By Knowing When To Ignore What Consumers Want, Quartz.com, [Online] http://qz.com/753538/how-parrot-the-french-drone-company-comes-up-with-new-products/ [accessed 25 October 2016]

19 Clayton M Christensen (22 October 2013) *The Innovator's Dilemma: When new technologies cause great firms to fail* (Management of Innovation and Change), Harvard Business Review Press, ASIN B00E257S86

20 Noah Brier (26 November 2014) Leadership: Strategy as Algorithm, Percolate.com, [Online] https://blog.percolate.com/2014/11/strategy-as-algorithm/ [accessed 25 October 2016]

21 Rita Gunther McGrath and Alex Gourlay (14 May 2013) *The End of Competitive Advantage: How to keep your strategy moving as fast as your business*, Harvard Business Review Press, ASIN B00AXS5EBY

22 Rita Gunther McGrath (August 1999) Discovery Driven Planning, ritamcgrath.com, [Online] http://ritamcgrath.com/ee/images/uploads/Discovery_Driven_Planning.pdf [accessed 25 October 2016]

Linking strategy to execution 10

The five questions

To understand a company's strategy, look at what they actually do rather than what they say they will do.

Andy Grove

In the agile business, the link between strategy and execution is critical to enabling the organization to move fast, yet misalignment, or worse, confusion about what the corporate strategy is and how it relates to team strategy and execution often prevails in many companies. Roger Martin has described how strategy is the answer to five key questions that cascade logically:

1. What are our broad aspirations and the concrete goals against which we can track progress?
2. Across the potential field available to us, where will we choose to play and not play?
3. How will we choose to win against the competitors in this chosen place?
4. What capabilities do we require to win?
5. What management systems are needed to build, operate and maintain these key capabilities?[1]

The key to applying these five questions successfully, he says, is to understand that since the questions are interlinked and cascading, so the answers should be consistent, linked and reinforcing. The challenge comes in appreciating that this interlinking means that an iterative approach is often required. It may be difficult to start at the top with a compelling vision, for example, without some idea of the answers to the next two questions. So this requires iterating back and forth between the five questions, using the answers we are getting in one area to inform the answers in the others. This kind of iteration actually makes strategy easier:

> *It will save you from endless visioning exercises, misdirected SWOT analyses, and lots of heroically uninformed big thinking. Crafting your strategy in relatively small and concrete chunks and honing the answers to the five questions through iteration will get you a better strategy, with much less pain and wasted time.*[2]

Rather than leadership being like the brain (making key choices, controlling everything) and the rest of the organization being like the body (delivering what the brain tells it to), a more useful conception of the corporation sees cascades of the five questions (and answers) operating at the corporate, strategic group and individual level, all linked together to ensure strategy is tied closely to execution (Figure 10.1).

Figure 10.1 The five questions as cascades

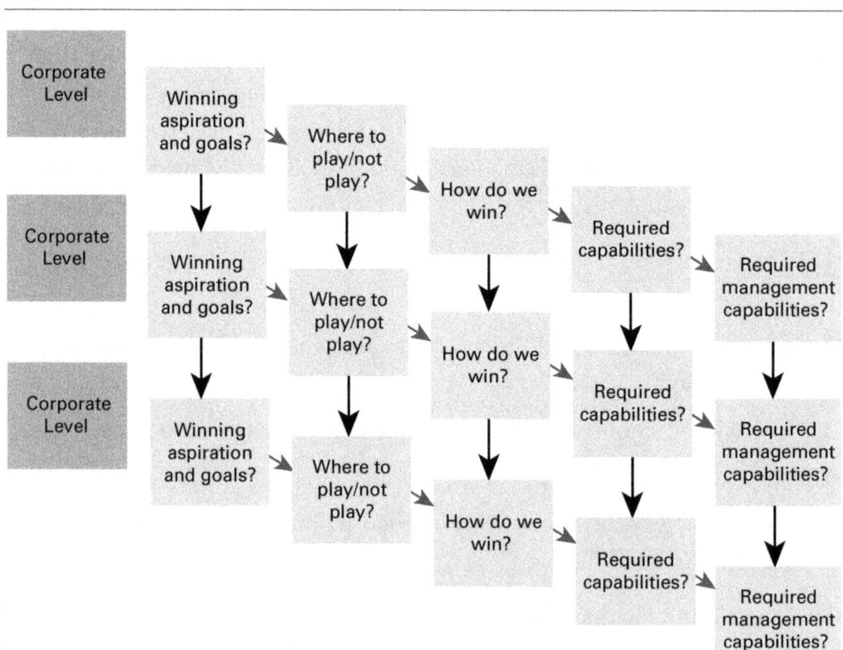

Strategy and tactic trees

Another way of framing this concept is the idea of strategy and tactic trees. Many businesses set a company-wide strategy and then regard everything else as a tactic that contributes toward that strategy. Not so. Dr Eli Goldratt (in 2002)[3] observed that strategy itself has a hierarchical structure, and that

Figure 10.2 Strategy and tactic tree

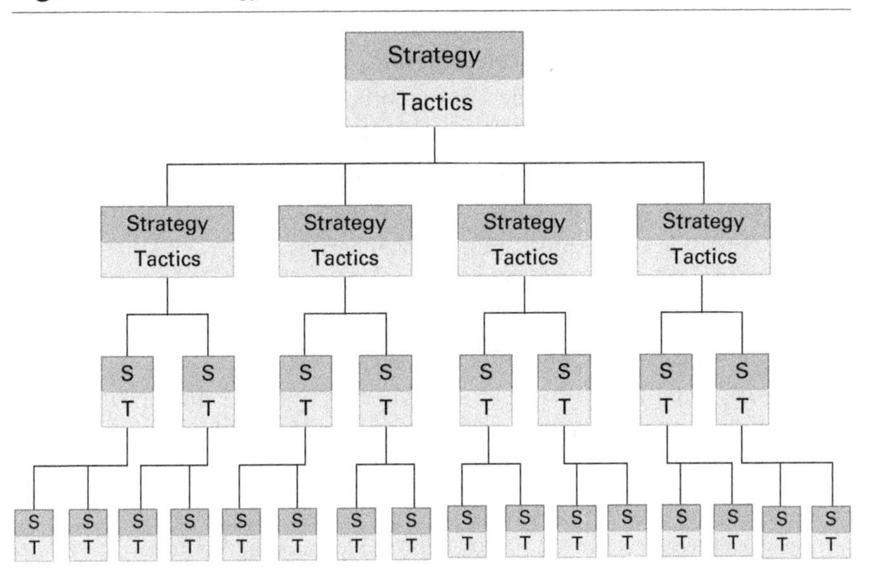

there might be several layers of strategy that are each connected by necessary conditions. In this way, objectives at a lower level are prerequisites for objectives at a higher level – the former more specific or detailed than the latter (Figure 10.2).

Goldratt defined strategy as the answer to the question 'What for?' (in other words the overarching direction needed to get to an objective), and tactics as the answer to the question 'How to?' (the steps in the process needed to pursue the strategy). In defining his strategy and tactics trees, he argued that if strategy was hierarchical, every strategy should have an associated tactic and the two should always exist in pairs at every level of the organization. Thus, a strategy can be brought to life and related to specific actions at every level. As an addendum to this concept, we should also consider the role of measures, aligned to tactics and strategies at every level of the organization, in order to ensure that our metrics too are linked, coordinated, and that strategy truly aligns with execution.

OKRs: bringing the team with you

OKRs, or Objectives and Key Results, is a methodology for connecting company, team and individual goals and measurable results that was originally introduced at Intel in the 1970s. John Doerr, an Intel executive and

Google board member introduced the framework to Google early in the company's journey as a way of helping them align objectives and direction across the business as they scaled rapidly. They are still in use at Google today, and have since expanded out to other technology sector businesses (including LinkedIn, Oracle, Twitter) and beyond.

The system involves setting quarterly measurable, definitive objectives at a company, team and individual level, and then supporting those objectives with quantifiable key results, against which performance is measured. OKRs are generally transparent (at Google for example, everyone's OKRs from Larry Page the CEO down are available to see on the internal directory) but provide a clear directional focus and expectations, ensure alignment at every level, and a high level of awareness of what others priorities are. This brings greater empathy and understanding for individual or team priorities, and giving focus to how an individual might make their own priorities align with someone else's in order to get stuff done.

Between three and five ambitious, achievable and time-bound objectives are set at each level. Each objective is supported by three or four measurable results that are clearly quantifiable, stretching while attainable, and can provide the basis for grading performance. The grading against each result can be scored 0 to 100, or 0 to 1.0 according to the level of achievement. These result indicators can be updated regularly throughout the quarter, perhaps weekly, but are designed to be stretching. When objectives are scored, we might consider them as not ambitious enough if 100 per cent of results have been achieved, but instead if we have achieved a score around 70 per cent, we can consider this to be successful. OKRs may be operational or more aspirational (fixed against bigger, longer-term goals) but can be regularly reviewed to ensure that they remain ambitious, and that they are always aligned to evolving strategic needs.

If your mission and vision provide the long view, this might then be expressed in a limited number of objectives and key results at an organizational level, which in turn can then be delineated in team and individual OKRs (Figure 10.3).

Figure 10.3 An organization's OKRs

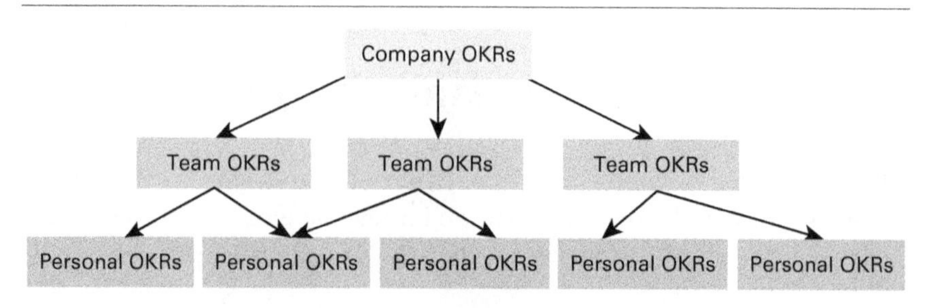

The key benefit to the OKR system is that it clearly aligns strategy with execution and measurement at every level of the organization, ensures disciplined thinking around major goals, demonstrates to everyone very clearly what is important to the organization, enables transparency around individual and team priorities, and ensures regular review of objectives and motivates and tracks progress towards them. In this way, OKRs can play a key role in transformation, and towards becoming a more agile business.

Stories from the frontline

Duncan Hammond, Delivery Director at Guardian News & Media: Using OKRs to drive change

In 2015 the Guardian appointed a new Editor in Chief, Katharine Viner, and a new CEO, David Pemsel. This was the biggest leadership change in many years and it gave the Guardian a great opportunity to take stock and review its strategic priorities.

The Guardian will be 200 years old in 2021. So Katharine and David posed a simple question; what will the Guardian be at the age of 200? This led to a six-month strategic review, named Project 2021, which culminated in a new three-year strategic plan designed to change the organization and set us on a sustainable path to the future. We called our three-year plan The Relationship Strategy.

The Project 2021 process revealed some difficult realities about the challenges facing the Guardian, we called them The Unvarnished Truths. These truths were major blockers to achieving sustainability.

One of the unvarnished truths stated our organization was too complex and insufficiently agile. With complexity came a lack of clarity on what our strategic priorities were; how we allocate our resources for the greatest impact; how we express our intent and measure success, or failure; and how we ensure the right people are collaborating at the right time, focused on the right things.

In the year prior to unveiling The Relationship Strategy we had been experimenting in small pockets of the organization with the Objectives and Key Results framework, also known as OKRs. OKRs were invented by Intel in the late 1970s and famously adopted by Google in 2001. It's a simple framework which introduces a consistent approach to setting aspirational goals and measurable results to judge success (or failure). We had some successes with OKRs in these small experiments and had aspirations to adopt them more widely as part of our new strategy.

The first step we took was to set five organization-wide objectives (OKRs), to focus us for the first year of the new strategy. These directly cascaded from the vision the Editor and CEO had crafted for the Guardian. If we could deliver these five objectives, we would be on a trajectory to deliver the Relationship Strategy successfully over the following years.

Next, we introduced the concept of huddles. Huddles are small, cross-functional teams, focused on delivering an OKR of their own. They're normally expected to deliver over three months. They have the freedom to approach the challenge as they see fit, and take a test-and-learn approach to delivering the best possible solution.

A huddle's OKR directly cascades from one of the organization-wide objectives. This ensures we're focusing on the ideas that have the biggest impact on the strategy. It's clear how the huddle's work fits into the bigger picture. And the huddle members should be able to see how their day-to-day tests are impacting on the overall vision of the Guardian.

Having a common approach to setting objectives for huddles, and a shared language, has helped democratize the quarterly process. It has forced new behaviours and encourages teams to be more strategic in their thinking, ensuring the work they prioritize has the most impact on our strategy. And it has enabled the organization, and our leaders, to be clearer in their approach to prioritization and resource allocation.

The OKR framework has improved our focus and working in huddles has increased the diversity of ideas and approaches to delivering an objective. These two things alone won't solve all the challenges we face, but they have gone a long way to improving the way we deliver our strategic priorities at the Guardian.

Sprint working as a driver of change

Working in iterative time-blocks, or sprints is, of course, central to agile and lean processes, each sprint forming a repeatable cycle of work that is confined to that unit of time and characterized by one iteration of the process. Working in sprints has a number of not insignificant benefits including:

- **Clear focus on a set of expected outcomes to be delivered by the end of the sprint** – each sprint commits to a set of deliverables, with review and reprioritization at regular intervals.

- **Embedded feedback loops and learning** – testing with real customers (wherever possible) and regular retrospectives empower learning and data-driven decision-making.
- **Multi-disciplinary working** – most teams working on sprints will be small and multi-disciplinary, comprised of the key functions needed to enable the outputs, which maintains continuous progress, ensures better communication and contributes to team spirit.
- **Greater velocity** – clarity of direction towards tangible, achievable outcomes, blocks of time for 'doing' and a focus on removing barriers to progress all ensure a heightened level of velocity. Constant iteration and focus on continuous improvement enhances pace and performance.
- **Improved transparency** – the defined tasks, level of difficulty, and progress against specific tasks are typically made visible to the whole team (and others), the practice of daily stand-up meetings enables blockers to be addressed at the earliest opportunity.
- **Greater accuracy** – working in cycles helps challenge and remove assumptions and improves forecasting accuracy.
- **Energizing and motivated working** – participants can see both working outputs, and clear progress against longer-term objectives which is both galvanizing and empowering.

Sprints can operate to different timescales and it is important to define for your own context the blocks of time that will be short enough to enable rapid progress and long enough to ensure useful working outputs at the end of each one. In agile methodologies such as Scrum for example, sprints may be two weeks long, but some development sprints may be as short as one week. The Google Ventures Design Sprint,[4] for example, is a five-day iterative sprint process:

1. **Day one – Understand:** agree the goal and target, map the challenge, draw in insight, analytics and research to inform.
2. **Day two – Diverge:** draw in inspiration, ideate, remix ideas, envisage solutions.
3. **Day three – Decide:** critique solutions, converge on the best idea, storyboard that idea.
4. **Day four – Prototype:** turn the storyboard into something you can test, create the simplest possible prototype.
5. **Day five – Validate:** with real users wherever possible, learn what does and doesn't work.

Sprint working is central to the agile business and has far wider application than simply technology and innovation teams. It is a naturally empowering, energizing, motivating way of working that can drive organizational momentum, invigorate innovation, and act as a catalyst for new mindsets and behaviours that can support greater agility and 'transformation through doing'. Don't keep that confined to the technology team.

Data-driven decision-making

> *Typically information is defined in terms of data, knowledge in terms of information, and wisdom in terms of knowledge.*
>
> (Jennifer Rowley)[5]

Data-driven decision-making is essential in the agile business. Data is central to the flow of knowledge into and within a business, to governance processes, performance optimization and customer experience delivery. The fallacy of 'big data' (extremely large data sets that require specific techniques to analyse computationally in order to reveal associations, relationships and patterns) is that most organizations do not have the volume or variety of data or the velocity of data processing (the so-called '3Vs')[6] required to qualify to join the 'big data' club. Nonetheless, companies are awash with data, typically with small proportions of it being analysed and applied in the service of business optimization. An oft-quoted study by IDC from 2012 found that less than 1 per cent of the world's data was being analysed.[7]

In order to structure an approach to deriving value from data, we need to understand the hierarchy of value at the simplest level. The Data, Information, Knowledge, Wisdom (DIKW) model is a straightforward way to position this. Raw data, observations, measurements at the bottom of the pyramid have little value until you are able to put some structure around the data, and turn it into information. Information is capable of answering simple who, what, where, when questions. Applying meaning, understanding relationships and connections turns it into knowledge. Knowledge answers the 'how' question but still has limited value. Wisdom, at the top of the pyramid is attained through the application or use of knowledge and answers the 'why'.

The opportunity apparent in the smart application of knowledge through data is manifold and yet few companies invest time and resource in creating an integrated data strategy. Key areas within a data strategy that require focus include:

- **Collection of data** – What data do we need to drive business outcomes? What questions do we ask? What sources? What level of detail?

- **Storage, management and access** – What technologies, processes, governance, privacy rules, location, security?
- **Architecture, integration and flow of data** – structure, network, breaking down data silos.
- **Insight, analysis and application** – What information and knowledge is required by whom? What needs to be real-time? How do we align with organizational objectives? What skills, resources, roles, responsibilities? How can we ensure insight is actionable? What is the role for algorithms, automation and dashboards?

As business moves from simple analytics to data science, so it is shaping entirely new requirements not just for technology, but also for capabilities, roles and business processes. Agile businesses are establishing robust infrastructure and resourcing alongside intuitive interfaces and dashboards that enable analytics (often real-time) to become central to the governance, performance and operations of the business. But in the words of the UK Government Digital Service, do the hard work to keep it simple. Success through data depends on widespread process and practice adoption, comprehensive strategy and application, but also on supportive behaviours. It needs to be embedded in the culture.

Technology as a barrier to change

New technology is usually viewed as both a driver and an enabler of change. But sometimes the reverse is true. Large businesses often feel comfortable making big decisions about big spends on big solutions (this is akin to the 'Bigger-Higher-Faster-Farther' philosophy prevalent among the US Air Force hierarchy that John Boyd fought so hard against). To draw a metaphor from *Star Wars*, we might call this the 'Death Star' IT approach. When technology is seen in companies as the solution to a business need, the answer can often look like a large, expensive, proprietary software system.

Since it is expensive, the system is complex enough to require a lengthy training course to understand how to use it and is accompanied by a thick user manual that few people ever read. Since it is complex, when people (being people) make errors it requires valuable management time to unpick them. Since it is inflexible to changing requirements, it attempts to mould people to its needs, rather than moulding itself to the needs of the people that use it. Since it is not open-source (because it comes from a world where value has traditionally been generated through protected proprietary assets), it struggles to update at the pace required to keep up with shifting requirements and contexts. Since it is designed to fulfil a specific function in a specific way, the cost of adaptation is high, and when adaptation is required (as it inevitably will be) new functions get added in layers so that it becomes more unwieldy over time, not less.

Adding more users to the system simply makes it more expensive, not more powerful. Because of its high cost, it is retained by the business for an extended period of time, and eventually required to fulfil functions that it was never designed to do. So it does them badly. Perhaps it is one of several such systems within the organization. Systems that likely don't talk to each other. At least not intuitively. So data and outputs are difficult to join up. And more management time is spent dealing with anomalies. Sometimes a big expensive system is the right way to go. But the consequences and opportunity costs of the choices we make are often hidden. If you make it expensive to change, you will likely not. And nothing endures but change.

Technology as an enabler of change

In 2013, the UK Government Cabinet Office engaged the Government Digital Service in a process to develop a different way to deliver technology to government departments and the civil service. At the start of the process, GDS defined an aim to 'deliver modern, flexible technology services that are at least as good as those people use at home',[8] and ones that were less expensive than those currently in place. They set out some guiding principles that provide a blueprint for technology acquisition and transformation, and speak of the fundamental need not for rigid, detailed, upfront planning processes, but of flexibility. Rather than the 'Death Star' IT, we might think of this as the 'X-Wing fighter' approach to technology. To paraphrase:

- **Start with user need** – don't start buying things until you understand what users want.
- **Design with choice and flexibility in mind** – offer solutions that benefit individuals as well as teams.
- **Make the process transparent** – ensure users and stakeholders understand key approaches by being open about decisions and actions.
- **Architect loosely coupled services** – allow for greater flexibility, less dependency and duplication ('a key success measure for the programme is that we should never have to do it again'), services that can independently be replaced or swapped in and out.

- **Favour short contracts** – to enable flexibility in response to the rapid change in technology capability.
- **Bring the best of consumer technology to the enterprise** – devices and cloud applications that intuitive and contemporary.
- **Make security as invisible as possible** – security is important, but it shouldn't get in the way of user experience.
- **Build a long-term capability** – don't rely on a single outsource vendor, establish necessary skills in-house to support ('technology delivery doesn't end with the programme').

Technology can be a powerful enabler of change, with significant opportunity deriving from three complementary but overlapping elementals:

1 **Analytics, tracking and measurement:** It was sociologist William Bruce Cameron who said 'Not everything that can be counted counts. Not everything that counts can be counted'[9] (a quote often attributed incorrectly to Einstein) which is why we should spend at least as much time focusing on what to measure, as we do measuring it. Data should inform but not dictate strategy, insights need to be actionable, we should focus on measuring what really matters rather than vanity metrics (those that may have large numbers but which are ultimately superficial or easily manipulated). In physics, momentum is the product of the mass and velocity of an object, and so when tracking momentum of change we should focus on measuring not only the pace of progress but also the elements that add weight to create momentum change (behaviour and attitude change).

2 **Automation, communication and infrastructure:** From dynamic pricing systems to self-driving trucks to new communication tools, technology can facilitate, network, notify, optimize, distribute, aggregate, filter. From business process automation, to communication and notification systems, customer service interaction, marketing automation and lead management, workflow automation can bring powerful efficiency benefits, augment human decision-making, and automatize uniform, repetitive tasks. Yet we need to remember that not every business process can be automated, and that human oversight, intervention and strategic or creative input is never very far away from the most adept application of machines.

3 **Artificial intelligence and machine learning:** Taking simple automation to new levels, agile businesses will increasingly apply machine learning to enable pattern recognition and continuous improvement in areas as diverse as customer insight, forecasting, production, service optimization,

information flow and distribution, and demand anticipation. While machine learning is already being applied to help solve simple problems, or as a valuable part of more complex decision-making flows, the adept use of ever-more sophisticated artificial intelligence capabilities will create the competitive advantage of the future.

If a business is to be truly agile, no employee should be coming into the workplace bemoaning the fact that the technology is worse there than it is at home. Technology stacks should be malleable enough to bend easily to the inevitable shifts in requirements. Interfaces should be intuitive and simple to learn. Communication technologies should facilitate agile, fast conversation, connection and distribution (think IM and chat services like Slack, rather than entirely relying on e-mail). The guiding principles for technology as a driver for change are flexibility, adaptability and scalability.

Agile budgeting

A last word (for this Part) on budgeting. We can establish highly flexible, adaptive and iterative working practices but they will fail if not supported by suitably flexible, adaptive and iterative budgeting.

As we discussed in Part Two, traditional accounting methods may work well for established propositions but new ventures characterized by increased uncertainty, iterative value, and test and learn should not be shackled to short-term targets, over-burdensome reporting and inappropriate measures. Like Eric Ries's 'innovation accounting', we need instead to focus on actionable, early stage metrics that can show value before revenue, and demonstrate sufficient progress towards the ultimate goals of customer satisfaction and profit. But more broadly financial resourcing needs to support an orientation towards experimentation, and the fulfilment of not only short-term objectives, but longer-term, breakthrough goals.

The politics of budgeting can act as a drag-brake on agility. Overly hierarchical decision-making on financial controls slows progress. Overly bureaucratic budget setting processes act as a time-suck for management. Siloed control of financial resources reduces flexibility and manoeuvrability. As Rita Gunther McGrath expounds, it is about investing in flexibility:

Firms built to thrive under transient-advantage conditions handle resources differently from firms designed for exploitation. In an exploitation-oriented firm, reliable performance, scale, and replication of processes from one place to another make a lot of sense because you can operate more efficiently and gain the benefits of scale. Resources, therefore, are directed to support these goals, and changing these resource flows is painful and difficult. A transient-advantage-oriented firm, on the other hand, allocates resources to promote what I call deftness – the ability to reconfigure and change processes with a certain amount of ease, quickly.[10]

Financial resourcing that is oriented not only towards efficiency and optimization, but towards finding the next star product, the next breakthrough, the next curve. Financial resourcing that supports the mitigation of risk through investment in multiple test-and-learn scenarios to explore new opportunities, rather than the 'Bigger-Higher-Faster-Farther' school of financing. Financial resourcing that is fast and flexible enough to support the truly agile organization.

Key takeouts

In this Part we have focused on building a heightened momentum within the organization through enhanced velocity allied to a reinvigorated focus, brought to life in new ways of working. Key takeouts include:

1. Map out the organizational purpose, mission, vision and values. Make them unique, compelling and easy-to-grasp. An ambitious, motivating call-to-arms.
2. Create a *positive* sense of urgency to drive continuous change towards that compelling vision. Communicate the vision repeatedly, bring it to life at every opportunity, live it, breathe it, exhibit it in leadership actions and behaviours.
3. Create the space to pursue that long-term vision, to solve the big problems, to enable breakthrough innovation. Fight the suck of resources to short-term targets and priorities.
4. Have a point of view on the future. Pay attention to what *doesn't* change, as well as what is changing. Work back from that vision of the future to empower different thinking and shape near-term priorities towards long-term goals.
5. Create clarity in strategy through making definitive choices shaped by consumer, competitor and company contexts.
6. Be stubborn on vision, but flexible on detail. Combine emergent strategy with highly fluid, iterative planning.
7. Orient strategies, processes, resourcing, operational priorities and execution towards the customer. Don't sacrifice customer experience

for efficiency gain. Use short, fast customer feedback loops inherent in processes such as agile and lean to embed customer focus in development and operational working. Put user need at the centre, start with the customer and work backwards, but design with vision and optimize with feedback. Use data in the design process to validate and drive decision-making.

8 Be ruthless about prioritization. Know your competitors but don't follow them. Balance importance to the organization with impact to the customer. Fix flawed customer experiences before investing in shiny innovation.

9 Use a three-timeline strategy framework to align short-, medium- and long-term strategy and planning. Work to remove as many assumptions as possible. Ask what needs to be true in order to achieve a desired outcome.

10 Link strategy to execution at every level of the organization using strategy and tactic trees and OKRs.

11 Build organizational momentum by using sprint working as a driver for change, to shift behaviours and mindsets as well as processes, and to catalyse innovation, new ways of working and transformation.

12 Develop a robust data strategy to support transformation and performance.

13 Take a user-centric approach to technology, guided by principles of flexibility, adaptability and scalability.

14 Support change with fast, flexible budgeting that enables the space to experiment and the adaptability to manoeuvre fast.

Notes

1 Roger L Martin (May 2005) Five Questions to Build a Strategy, *Harvard Business Review*, [Online] https://hbr.org/2010/05/the-five-questions-of-strategy [accessed 25 October 2016]

2 Roger L Martin (May 2005) Five Questions to Build a Strategy, *Harvard Business Review*, [Online] https://hbr.org/2010/05/the-five-questions-of-strategy [accessed 25 October 2016]

3 Eli Goldratt, Rami Goldratt and Eli Abramov (2002) Strategy and Tactics, Washington State University, [Online] https://public.wsu.edu/~engrmgmt/holt/em534/Goldratt/Strategic-Tactic.html [accessed 25 October 2016]

4 Google Ventures (2016) The Design Sprint, Google Ventures, [Online] http://www.gv.com/sprint/ [accessed 25 October 2016]

5 Jennifer Rowley (April 2007) *The Wisdom Hierarchy: Representations of the DIKW hierarchy*, Sage Publishing.com, [Online] http://jis.sagepub.com/content/33/2/163.abstract [accessed 25 October 2016]

6 Diya Soubra (5 July 2012) The 3Vs That Define Big Data, Data Science Central, [Online] http://www.datasciencecentral.com/forum/topics/the-3vs-that-define-big-data [accessed 25 October 2016]

7 John Burn-Murdoch (December 2012) Study: Less than 1% of the world's data is analysed, over 80% is unprotected, theguardian.com, [Online] https://www.theguardian.com/news/datablog/2012/dec/19/big-data-study-digital-universe-global-volume [accessed 25 October 2016]

8 Tom Read (13 November 2013) Technology at Least as Good as People Have at Home, Gov.UK, [Online] https://cabinetofficetechnology.blog.gov.uk/2013/11/13/technology-at-least-as-good-as-people-have-at-home/ [accessed 25 October 2016]

9 William Bruce Cameron (1963) *Informal Sociology: A casual introduction to sociological thinking*, Random House, ASIN: B001A9FCWQ

10 Rita Gunther McGrath (4 June 2013) *The End of Competitive Advantage: How to keep your strategy moving as fast as your business*, Harvard Business Review Press, ISBN-10: 1422172813, ISBN-13: 978-1422172810

PART FOUR
Flexibility

In this Part we consider the role of people, culture, structures, resourcing in enabling and facilitating change.

> **Flexibility** – adaptable, able to be easily modified to respond to altered circumstances, to bend without breaking, workable, malleable, supple, ready and able to change.

DEFINING FLEXIBILITY

In 2014, author and social innovator Charles Leadbeater wrote a paper (The London Recipe: How systems and empathy make the city)[1] that attempted to define the key facets or ingredients that combined to create a successful city. Some of the best recipes, said Leadbeater, comprise two key ingredients (like eggs and bacon or fish and chips) and so it is with cities that a combination of two factors that determine success or failure – systems and empathy:

> *Systems oil cities. Without effective power, transport, health and education systems, cities fall apart. But it's empathy that makes cities human.*[2]

We need systems to 'bring together disparate interacting components to achieve a common purpose', to have processes and methods, to make everything work easily and reliably at scale, and to gain efficiencies. Life is chaotic without shared systems. And yet we also depend on the 'dark matter' of empathy, our capacity for insight, affinity, rapport, to understand and find common ground, to collaborate, cooperate and engage in sharing and exchange.

The city, Leadbeater said, is at its absolute best when it combines both of these things, where 'lots of people use efficient systems to have a highly convivial, charged, shared experience' (Figure P4.1).

Figure P4.1 Systems and empathy

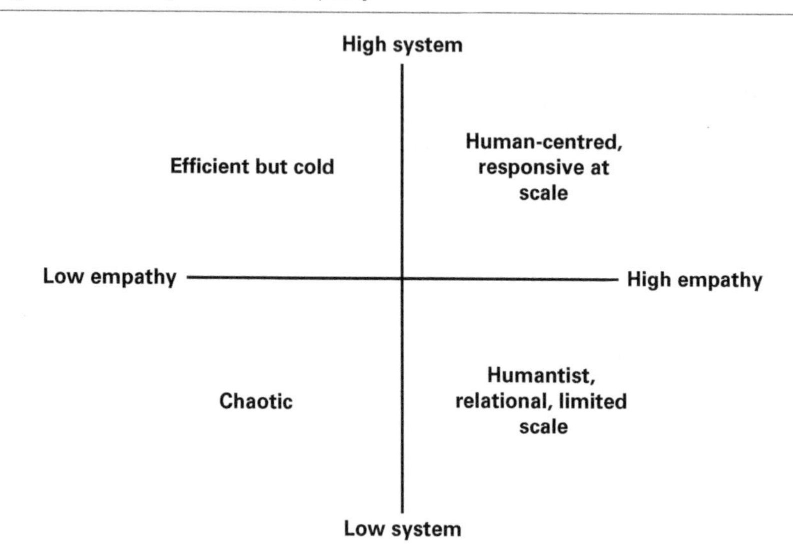

Success comes from this combination of both systems and empathy (Leadbeater used the London Olympics in 2012 as an example of when efficiency of large-scale systems combined with very human connections and approaches to great effect). System-heavy entities may look impressive but they can often feel dead. Empathy brings in the countless small and large acts that make large systems human.

In his paper, Leadbeater talks about how a key challenge when building systems is how to scale empathy. A city, like a large organization, is a social system in that it comprises lots of people interacting in different ways. Interactions between elements over time become systems when they naturally evolve to develop a set of understood and recognized boundaries that help define them. These emergent conditions help to guide and shape the way in which the system operates and may then become more rigidly defined rules. But as this scales the factors that once created the value in relations and interactions can be challenged, undermined or corrupted so that we lose connection, intimacy and empathy.

Organizations are systems but in the digital age, now more than ever, they need empathy at scale to survive and thrive. To become a truly agile organization, therefore, we need structured systems and efficiency but we need to combine that with human-centred approaches, processes and experiences. Trying to introduce agile into a non-agile culture will not work unless we face the human-centred challenges that will inevitably arise. Trying to create change without bringing people on the journey with you will lead to failure. Attempting to become more responsive as an organization without accepting the need to think differently about the fluidity of resourcing will not work.

To become more agile we need the human-centred flexibility in culture, resourcing and behaviours to create the environment in which change can really happen. Put simply:

$$(\text{velocity} \times \text{focus}) - \text{flexibility} = \text{failure}$$

Notes

1 Charles Leadbeater (1 April 2014) The London Recipe: How systems and empathy make the city, Centre for London.org, [Online] http://www.centreforlondon.org/publication/london-recipe/ [accessed 25 October 2016]

2 Charles Leadbeater (29 April 2014) Charles Leadbeater: It's small things that make our big city what it is, *Evening Standard*, [Online] http://www.standard.co.uk/comment/comment/charles-leadbeater-it-s-small-things-that-make-our-big-city-what-it-is-9301446.html [accessed 25 October 2016]

Agile structures and resourcing 11

The decisions we make around how we choose to build, structure and apportion our capability have a fundamental impact on our ability to deliver our strategy but also our capacity to be more agile. So what do we mean by agility in resourcing? Traditional approaches are often characterized by rigid functional or divisional silos, inflexible roles and job descriptions, a focus on owned assets and exploiting existing positions, large downsizing programmes, restrictive approaches to career mobility, demotivating performance review systems, control over resources being seen as commensurate with power and influence, and change disliked and avoided.

Our historical approaches emphasize the optimization and aggregation of vertical craft and experience expertise into functional groupings which, while valuable, comes at the expense of flexibility and effortless cross-department or division working. So in a rapidly shifting environment we need to work harder to find new and more agile ways to combine that vertical expertise, blend it with more generalist skills, and establish a far greater degree of fluidity in our resourcing. We need easier collaboration between disciplines. Easier flow between centralized and decentralized resources. Greater internal employee mobility. A move on from rigid functional roles to a more skills-based approaches that can attract, retain and combine required skills in more adept ways. Smarter outsourcing and use of external capability to reduce reliance on owned assets. Continual modification to free up resources and refocus on new projects and initiatives. Change welcomed as an opportunity. And as Rita Gunther McGrath described, we need key resources that are managed under central control and not held hostage by local business units, and faster, more responsive organization around opportunity rather than opportunities being squeezed into existing structures.[1]

Greater advantage now comes from information efficiency, or establishing tight customer feedback loops, easy access to key analytics, and reducing the number of information exchanges that are needed to respond to opportunity or demand or other key processes. It is more essential than ever that our organizational structures reflect and enable progress towards our vision. Strategies that are customer-centric, for example, will struggle unless structures are adapted to also be customer focused (most, as we have already discussed, are not). Rather than supporting limited, episodic innovation and singular initiatives, resourcing needs to enable continuous experimentation and multiple projects that combine to create momentum and change. Table 11.1 summarizes the key differences between legacy and agile.

Table 11.1 Key differences between legacy and agile

Legacy	Agile
Organized around exploitation, execution and optimization	Organized around continual experimentation, exploring and learning
Rigid functional silos, difficult cross-division cooperation	Easy cross-team collaboration
Large, single-discipline departments	Vertical expertise combined with small, multi-disciplinary teams
Fixed job descriptions, rigid functional roles, restrictive career mobility, directed learning	Self-learning, ownership mindset, flexible role boundaries, skills-based approaches, high career mobility
Emphasis on vertical aggregation of expertise	Easy cross-discipline aggregation, vertical combined with generalist skills
Periodic overhaul of balance between centralized and decentralized resourcing	Continual flow between the centre and local capability
Focus on owned assets, in-house headcount and capability	Asset-light businesses, networked ecosystem of talent and resource
Change seen in negative terms, new initiatives fitted to established structures	Change welcomed, continuous regeneration, oriented around opportunity
Functionally oriented structures, poor information efficiency	Customer-facing structures, tight feedback loops, high information efficiency

Companies achieve great efficiencies and craft expertise through organizing in vertical functions (marketing, sales, finance, engineering, and so on). As organizations scale and become multi-product companies these vertical expertise areas exist as functions within divisions that group products together into logical areas. These multiplying silos enable functional focus and efficiency to work at scale, but faced with rapidly shifting contexts we need to be far more adept at combining functional expertise in different ways to gain advantages in velocity and focus. We need more of our expert resource to be working concurrently with other functions, far greater emphasis on small, multi-disciplinary teams to be used to address key challenges, energize experimentation and develop new capability, and we need to greatly improved fluidity between central and localized, in-house and outsourced resourcing in order to be truly responsive and to open up new opportunity.

Concurrent running, co-located working

Traditional methods of working can often involve waterfall-driven processes with one department completing their part of the project before handing off to the next function to work through theirs. A product development process, for example, may involve designers passing an initial look and feature set to the engineers (who find ways to make it actually work), and then on to manufacturing (who work out how to produce it), and then sales and marketing (who decide how to sell it).

Yet as the innovation writer Steven Johnson has pointed out, the ubiquity of this model comes from the fact that it works very well in situations where efficiency is the most important consideration but it kills creativity since original ideas get chipped away at every stage. In contrast, Apple's development model involves all the groups (design, engineering, manufacturing, sales) meeting continuously throughout the process in an approach that is messier and more chaotic in the early stages, but which avoids great ideas being slowly hollowed out and becoming ghosts of themselves:

> *The process is noisy and involves far more open-ended and contentious meetings than traditional production cycles – and far more dialogue between people versed in different disciplines, with all the translation difficulties that creates.*[2]

In the same way that single-team waterfall processes (like an IT development project) can move too slowly and fail to take account of shifting contexts and adapt accordingly, so multi-team waterfall working can make for sluggish, arduous, and overly rigid process and progress. Sometimes it is necessary. But often there is a better way.

Concurrent, co-located working, with all the key skills and disciplines working on solving problems at the same time and in the same room carries a number of key advantages. It acts to break down departmental silos and align priorities cross-functionally since the group is working towards a common goal. It enables different disciplines to spark off one another and catalyse the creative process. It circumvents issues around key input not being available when required. It allows simultaneous input from multiple perspectives, and an 'ideas from anywhere' approach (the best ideas don't always come from where we most expect them to). It simplifies communication and can enable greater transparency and accountability on progress.

Co-located working with external partners (such as innovation or marketing agencies) can enable a combined team to move at pace through greater efficiency of communication, improved understanding of each other's priorities, demonstrable commitment, shared goals, smoother workflow. In other words, a real partnership. AstraZeneca, for example, partnered with the digital agency DigitasLBi to form a co-located Digital Innovation Group to tackle the 'wicked problems' in healthcare:

> *A wicked problem has innumerable causes, is tough to describe, and doesn't have a right answer... Not only do conventional processes fail to tackle wicked problems, but they may exacerbate situations by generating undesirable consequences.*[3]

Owing to the complex nature of these problems, conventional working in a linear, sequential way gave way to iterative, highly interactive, agile working involving a continuous process of insight gathering, building and learning in rapid sprints throughout a 12-week innovation cycle. A highly social, collaborative process between AstraZeneca stakeholders, the DIG teams and the end beneficiaries, the 12-week cycles kick off with an immersion phase, followed by rapid concepting and prototyping (Figure 11.1). This enables multiple ideas to be worked on in parallel, using a series of gate meetings to filter out ideas that do not deliver on the agreed conceptual promise.

DIG has launched a succession of new (and award-winning) projects and services including ones to help drug trial participants and heart-attack

Figure 11.1 AstraZeneca's 12-week cycle

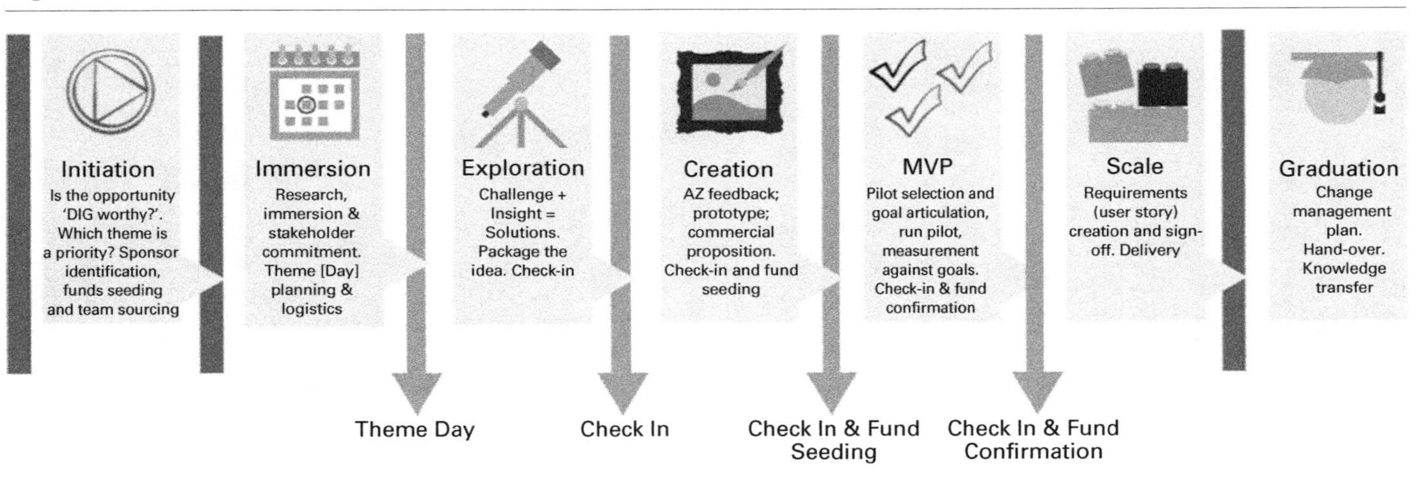

patients, new social networks for lung cancer survivors and ethnographic health studies in Africa, and has begun to have a positive impact on the wider AstraZeneca organization.

As we will go on to discuss, if the teams working on challenges are small, kept to a core group, not allowed to become corpulent with members whose contribution is peripheral or required only periodically, and then empowered to work iteratively towards a solution, then they can really move fast. The opportunity provided by small, multi-disciplinary teams to accelerate organizational tempo is vastly undervalued. We need a new way of working that places far greater emphasis on their role as catalysts for a new type of organization.

The insourcing and outsourcing dynamic

The dynamic of what companies choose to do in-house and what they outsource to partners and third parties is a continually shifting one, yet there is a distinct trend for organizations to facilitate greater agility by establishing more sophisticated, nuanced and outwardly facing approaches to partnering and outsourcing. The obvious advantages behind insourcing include more immediate control, responsiveness and consistency, and the opportunity to build owned capability and value over time. In many areas (notably when dealing with areas of critical importance to the business like the effective integration of people, data and technology that relates to key areas of competency or customer experience, reputation or compliance) keeping capability close at hand leads to improved responsiveness and agility.

It often seems that with the empowerment of digital technology, companies are doing more and more in-house. Yet the picture is more nuanced than this suggests. A more sophisticated approach to outsourcing can open up the opportunity to leverage a broader range of expertise, assets and resources (wherever they sit) in ways that are more flexible, scalable, and even cost efficient. The growth of cloud-based services has been the great exemplar of this for a number of years, but it is just one example of how agile organizations are cultivating increasingly networked ecosystems of partners and resources from which they can draw. Whether it is utilizing third-party data or stitching together remote services through APIs, or accessing specialist expertise, assets and resourcing remotely to fulfil specific functions, such networks can dramatically enhance organizational capability, help build in-house learning and capability (as a key output of an agency or consultancy engagement, for example), and bring new levels of flexibility and agility.

External resource can add value both at the centre (incremental improvement of existing products, processes and services through efficiency gain, automation, optimization) and at the edges (new ideas, consultancy around developing new propositions, early stage capability). But you should never outsource the future. The critical thinking, decisioning, hiring of talent, and essential elements of customer experience – in fact, any capability that is crucial to the long-term success of the business – should not go outside. As example of what can happen, Clay Christensen describes how Dell in the early 1990s were a disruptive force in part because they were able to outsource key capabilities to Asus in Taiwan. As time went on, however, and spurred on by Wall Street who smelled greater efficiencies, Dell expanded their outsourcing programme to more critical parts of their business including the management of their supply chain and the design of the computer. By 2005 Asus had got so good at so many parts of Dell's business that they were able to create their own brand of computer. Over the years, says Christensen, Dell had 'slowly outsourced its way to mediocrity in the consumer business'.[4]

One example of this is the growing approach for organizations to create talent networks to augment internal capabilities. A combination of new technologies, remote working capability, improved support networks and infrastructure such as the growing global proliferation of co-working spaces, and new business models including algorithmically managed workforces like Uber, and crowdsourced micro-task services like Amazon's Mechanical Turk and Task Rabbit, have led to a notable rise in freelancing and contracting. One study from Intuit predicts that by 2020, over 40 per cent of the American workforce (equivalent to 60 million people) will be independent workers.[5] Huge value exists in being able to tap into specialist expertise on a more flexible basis, whether that is through the growing number of freelance consultants, or the global range of technical outsourcing solutions. An advanced talent network may draw from three key sources: full-time, permanent employees; a wide-ranging pool of specialist freelance expertise; and a pool of contracted or associate partners and consultants (Figure 11.2).

Each organization will structure its own talent network according to its own unique needs, but the aim is always the same: flexibility, scalability, cost efficiency, agility.

Figure 11.2 Advanced talent network

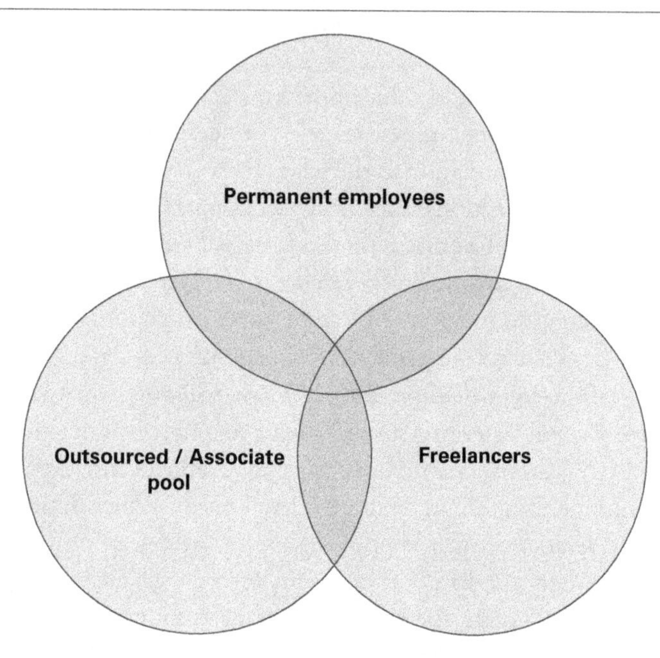

Centralization vs decentralization, specialists and generalists

In a digital transformation process there are key dynamics that will inevitably see a continually evolving balance. Our ever-more complex, digitally enabled business environment, for example, requires increasing levels of technical and functional specialization. We need deep, vertical expertise in key areas to optimize specific capability. But there is also greater value in more horizontal, generalist roles that can bring diverse specialist expertise together and marshal that capability towards achieving a shared goal.

Similarly, the dynamic between what resource is held at the centre, and that which serves more localized needs or discrete divisions and audiences is continually changing. The centralization of digital resource, for example, can bring significant advantages in a transformation process including improved governance, standards and control, greater consistency, scalability and efficiency, and more emphasis, clarity and focus. But the risks inherent with centralization can include a lack of integration with wider activity, and a lack of learning in the broader business. Often, a centralized digital team will begin to devolve executional resourcing and responsibility out to localized areas (in a 'hub-and-spoke' model), and this may even eventually involve more strategic-level decision-making. It may often be the case, for example, that strategic direction and broad capability development sit at the centre, while discrete strategy, plans and tactics sit locally. Overarching governance and standards may reside centrally, but compliance and specific rules are local. And process design is likely to be centralized, but implementation local. But above all, there remains a requirement for a heightened level of fluidity in resourcing between these two areas to effectively orient resourcing to capitalize on not just exploitation but also opportunity.

The power of small teams to drive big change

> *From the Founding Fathers in politics to the Royal Society in science to Fairchild Semiconductor's 'traitorous eight' in business, small groups of people bound together by a sense of mission have changed the world for the better.*
>
> Peter Thiel

When attempting to increase tempo and momentum within organizations, teams that work in small multi-disciplinary units (or 'pods', as we might call them) can be disproportionately powerful in demonstrating new, agile, iterative ways of working and helping to drive transformation across the business.

Work by author, Harvard professor, and specialist in team dynamics Richard Hackman has shown the challenges inherent in attempting to accelerate pace using large teams, the issues not only relating to the size of the team itself, but the number of links between people and the growing burden of communication.[6] As group size increases, the number of unique links between people also increases, but exponentially. So while a small team of 6 creates 15 links between everyone, a larger team of 12 will generate 66 links, and a team of 50 has no fewer than 1225 links to manage. This exponential increase means that coordination and communication costs are soon growing at the expense of productivity.

Leaders, says Hackman, may often create oversized teams in the faulty assumption that 'more is better' for team effectiveness, or due to emotional considerations such as sharing responsibility and spreading accountability across larger numbers of people, or for political reasons such as ensuring that all relevant stakeholders are represented. You may then have a politically correct team, but likely one that is incapable of moving at pace towards its objective.

Hackman defined four key features that are critical to create an effective team in an organization:

1. Common team tasks that work towards fulfilling a compelling vision.
2. Clear boundaries in terms of who is in the team, information flow, and alignment with other resources, priorities, policies and teams.
3. Autonomy to work within these boundaries.
4. Stability.

These qualities take on a heightened level of significance when trying to move fast within the agile organization. The difference, for example, that Hackman delineates between a 'co-acting group' and a real team. A great deal of organizational work is performed by groups that are commonly called teams, but in reality are more like co-acting groups that have members who sit in close proximity, may have the same leader, but where each member has an individual job to do and the completion of that job does not depend on what the others in the group do. The hope is that managers can gain the benefits of teamwork while still directly managing the behaviours of individual members but this is, he says, misplaced: 'If you want the benefits of teamwork, you have to give **the team** the work'.[7]

In the agile organization, far greater emphasis is placed on small multi-disciplinary teams where the interdependencies, work and individual responsibilities between team members intertwine in the course of concurrent working towards a common, shared objective. Work by Wharton Management School professor Jennifer Mueller[8] has shown that individual performance in larger teams can suffer in comparison to those in smaller teams due to 'relational loss', or the perception that individual team members are less able to get as much support, ease of access to information or recognition in a larger team. Momentum comes from teams becoming a real unit, improving iteratively over time, focused on clear outcomes. As the UK Government Digital Service was always fond of saying: 'the unit of delivery is the team'.[9]

Similarly, it is essential for the team to have clear boundaries in order to move fast. While the work doesn't always need all team members to be in the same location at the same time for progress to be made, lack of clarity over who is on the team will act as a brake on momentum if key members are juggling multiple priorities or missing from key meetings. Attempting to establish new ways of working through a half-hearted adoption of cell-based working that sees key members allocating only part of their time to the new team is likely to be problematic. It requires commitment. The team needs to be sufficiently bounded to profit from clear direction and comprehensive participation, while sufficiently porous to enable beneficial cross-boundary exchanges. More than ever, agile teams need focused objectives, clear ways of monitoring advancement towards achieving those objectives, and then the freedom to define how they will work to create that progress.

Stories from the frontline

Gareth Kay, Co-Founder, Chapter SF: The new unit of work

It's been widely accepted for some time that the atomic unit that unlocks the potential of any organization is the team. What we've failed to realize is that the very nature of the team has changed dramatically as technology has allowed people to work together in new and better ways.

We are not unlocking the full potential of our teams because we are using the wrong map to understand organizational structures today. Despite all our talk of agile working processes and the democratization of the 'bottoms up' workspace, we still envision teams operating in a rigid, post-industrial hierarchy of command and control. Org charts are the still dominant way we shape and present those who work with us. We see teams being bounded, at best, by the organization and at worst by their department or discipline.

The organizations that unlock their potential see their teams quite differently. They see the team as a group of people who come together around a common goal. Yes, this could be a department but more likely it will be a group of people from different disciplines, potentially working in different countries and even different companies, who are working together to achieve something together they wouldn't otherwise be able to.

Research by Amy Edmonson at Harvard Business School shows that the nature of teams is changing dramatically in response to a more fluid world. As much as we talk about them, stable, bounded, clearly defined teams are less and less in evidence. What she sees more of is 'teaming', a dynamic activity, not a static, bounded entity. A verb rather than a noun. If we use this map of the world, then some very different needs emerge about how to build a world class team (of teams).

First, we need to be far more radical in our approach to bringing different people together in different ways. We should be looking at how we can truly diversify the talent, skills and experience we bring around a problem. This means looking outside the 'usual suspects' inside an industry and looking for inspiration outside. We should look at how we can break the approaches and working processes we repeat every week and replace them with new ways of collaborating at different tempos (not everything should perhaps be a sprint). If we are to find new solutions we need to approach different problems with different processes, approaches, mindsets and people.

Second, organizations have to accept that their greatest ability to create value is to act in a way that may feel initially antithetical to everything they've done before. Great organizations today understand that they are no more than a network of teams. This changes their approach to management. They become more open and permeable and accept that talent lies outside the organization not just within; that a coalition of talent can get further, faster. They are less obsessed about process and more obsessed by creating the environment and organizational underpinnings that allow people to recombine and shapeshift without losing the knowledge that used to be guarded within the team or department.

The team may be an old concept but teaming is the new unit of work. If we're to thrive we need to design and build our organizations for it.

Two pizza teams

Amazon is a technology company. We just happen to do retail.

Werner Vogels

Amazon are fixated on staying agile as a business as they scale. Werner Vogels, Amazon CTO has outlined one of the key ways in which they do this.[10] Scaling quickly had always been the key priority for the company. More of a priority, he says, than maintaining a coherent architecture, which led them to developing services based around APIs rather than direct database access. This in turn lent itself to an organizational structure focused around small teams typically comprised of no more than seven to eight people. These small, nimble groups were called 'Two-pizza teams' since they were typically the number of people who can be fed easily with two large pizzas. There are hundreds of such teams in the business, each behind specific services that go to comprise the wider Amazon offering. The Amazon home page, for example, requires about 200 to 300 such services to construct the page.

This strategy comes right from the top of the organization, from founder Jeff Bezos, who believes that small, nimble, networked, task-based teams are the best way of maintaining a high degree of focus and agility. People in small teams are more easily able to stay in touch with what other members of the team are doing whereas in most large teams, regular meetings are required to achieve the same goal. Meetings, believes Bezos, slow teams down. This decentralized structure also brings focus. From the earliest beginnings of the company, Bezos wanted:

> *... a decentralized, even disorganized company where independent ideas would prevail over groupthink.*[11]

Amazon structure two-pizza teams in such a way to allow for focus through objective and direction, autonomy in prioritization and execution, and accountability through performance measures. Each one of those small teams was established with a 'fitness function', a key business metric agreed between the senior leadership and the team lead that gives the team focus. This autonomy enables greater entrepreneurialism, the opportunity for greater ownership and growth.

It is a structure that is built for speed. Amazon are able to bring a new service or product to market in 10 to 15 days. Vogels has depicted how Amazon deliberately design for flexibility, for on-demand and, where appropriate, for automation. Processes are distilled into their simplest form because they have to be and it means that they can enable a culture of continuous innovation (for example, Vogels describes Amazon Web Services, their cloud computing division, as resembling 'a collection of 15 or 20 or 40 startups') and a relentless customer focus. Any benefits accrued from additional scale are passed on to customers, and innovation is focused on the things that will always be important to those customers.

Amazon launches a continuous stream of new products, often with minimal initial feature sets, and then develops additional features through close cooperation with customers and data from customer interaction. Despite building a huge business, Amazon have been able to retain the flexibility and adaptability of a startup. In a world increasingly characterized by the need to respond to and design for on-demand, there is a lesson in that for all of us.

Self-organizing, multi-disciplinary teams

> *The best architectures, requirements, and designs emerge from self-organizing teams.*
>
> The Agile Manifesto

The principle of self-organizing teams is one of the foundational tenets of agile and, like many of the practices inherent to this way of working, has broadened out beyond the distinct agile practice area. The not insignificant advantages inherent to self-organization include increased staff motivation, productivity and ownership (you have, after all, chosen to work on this project so are naturally invested and feel greater responsibility for the outputs).

But it is when self-organization is incorporated as part of a wider adoption of new ways of working (such as agile or Scrum) that it can catalyse greater change and continuous learning. As teams work iteratively, for example, there is regular opportunity to optimize working patterns, processes and behaviours. The process of embedded reflection through retrospectives helps the self-organized team to learn and become more efficient over time through constant inspection and adaptation without delay. Combining the multiple disciplines needed to progress outputs in the same team, working can be concurrent and fast. Key roles in the team can help it to function well. Product owners or managers might act as the voice of the customer, interface with the rest of the business, and work to prioritize and re-prioritize the work backlog. In agile methodologies like Scrum, the 'Scrum master' helps to oversee, not micro-manage but instead ensure that rules and boundaries are respected and that barriers to progress are removed.

Richard Hackman described four key functions that must be accomplished by an organizational unit that has work to achieve: executing work; monitoring and managing progress; to design the performing unit (structuring tasks, organizing application of resource and required support, establishing norms of behaviour); and setting the direction for the team out of which fall the necessary tasks. How we separate up these tasks and responsibilities across management and team, he said, gives us an authority matrix that we can use to describe different levels of authority that we might give the team:

- **Self-governing teams:** the team-members have responsibility for all four aspects (like a startup or a worker's cooperative).
- **Self-designing teams:** managers set the direction but the members have authority over all other aspects so can modify the design of their team and/or aspects of the organizational context in which they operate on an ongoing basis.
- **Self-managing teams:** team members are responsible for execution but also monitoring and managing progress.
- **Manager-led teams:** Managers do everything except task execution, which is left to team members.

A key benefit of higher levels of autonomy and self-organization in teams is the ability to more easily and continuously adapt to a changing environment as resources are focused on achieving the job at hand rather than being at the mercy of organizational and managerial politics. Greater adaptation and more emergent, fluid structures lead to greater resilience.

The process of self-organization tends to naturally align and bring together the necessary talent needed to achieve a goal that the team is setting out to pursue, but we need to balance this with the need to ensure specific expertise is dedicated towards solving key challenges. Heightened levels of self-organization can empower teams to move quickly, but as we have seen there are different gradients of self-organization and manager/team responsibility.

Concepts such as Holacracy apply the idea of self-organization and flat hierarchies but at scale. Holacracy is presented as the 'complete, packaged system for self-management in organizations', replacing traditional management hierarchy with 'a new peer-to-peer "operating system" that increases transparency, accountability, and organizational agility'.[12]

The system may seem like it lacks leadership or management, but as Frederic Laloux has said: '... the absence of dominator hierarchy is not the same thing as the absence of any hierarchy'.[13] In Holacracy, collective intelligence informs decision-making reducing the ability of one person to unnecessarily put the brake on a process or hold an idea or budget hostage. Transparency comes through visibility of responsibility rather than power. Team members are responsible for what needs to be done, but also monitoring and managing the progress of each other and the team as a whole. Difficult decisions are worked through at a team level rather than pushed up the line. It attempts to replace traditional 'dominator hierarchies' with 'actualization hierarchies' focused on recognition, influence and skill.

While Holacracy has to date been adopted by mainly smaller-scale organizations, we can all learn from exploring different ways of devolving responsibility and ownership throughout the organization rather than decisions always emanating from the top. Finding the right balance is about creating as much freedom as possible at all levels through greater autonomy and flexibility around resourcing, while still establishing clear direction, boundaries, governance and accountability. Above all, the over-arching principle (again) should be to keep the unit small.

The composition of multi-disciplinary teams

Careful consideration needs to be given to the composition of these small cell units. The key rule is to take a skills-based, rather than purely functional, approach. Don't feel pressured to include staff who are there to represent a function but whose input may be incidental or infrequent. The only people who should be included in the team are those whose skills are central to making outputs happen, those who have direct, tangible and ongoing input. Above all the unit should be kept to 'two-pizza' size.

Eric Schmidt of Google describes the people who he believes can have the biggest potential impact within organizations (he calls them 'smart creatives')[14] as those who can combine a triumvirate of key skills' areas: technical knowledge, business acumen and creativity. We will talk more about 'smart creatives' later, but this troika of skills areas has the potential to be transformational at not just at an individual level, but at a team level as well. While the specific roles or job titles may differ, the pattern of combining these key capabilities in a small multifunctional team is repeated again and again. And for good reason. We need business acumen (strategists, product managers, product owners and so on) to align to business needs and inputs, provide direction and prioritization, and a commercial perspective. We need technical skills to code, build, make, engineer. And we need creative skills to ideate, imagine and design for user need. While the balance in composition may differ according to need, this triumvirate of skills can work on a problem through every stage but with no single practice area leading. Each area amplifies and extends the capabilities of the other. As Tim Malbon, founder of product innovation agency Made By Many, has described it:

> *It's a force multiplier... we've created a machine that renders insights and ideas into code in almost-real-time on a continuous and self-correcting basis.*[15]

This is the modern blueprint for a multi-disciplinary team.

Notes

1. Rita Gunther McGrath (4 June 2013) *The End of Competitive Advantage: How to keep your strategy moving as fast as your business*, Harvard Business Review Press, ISBN-10: 1422172813, ISBN-13: 978-1422172810
2. Steven Johnson (29 September 2011) *Where Good Ideas Come From: The seven patterns of innovation*, Penguin, ISBN-10 141033401 ISBN-13 978-0141033402
3. John C Camillus (May 2008) Strategy as a Wicked Problem, Harvard Business Review, [Online] https://hbr.org/2008/05/strategy-as-a-wicked-problem [accessed 25 October 2016]
4. James Allworth, Karen Dillon and Clayton Christensen (10 May 2012) *How Will You Measure Your Life?*, HarperCollins, ASIN B006I1AE92

5 Future of Small Business, Intuit, [Online] https://http-download.intuit.com/http.intuit/CMO/intuit/futureofsmallbusiness/intuit_2020_report.pdf [accessed 25 October 2016]

6 David M Messick and Roderick M Kramer (22 September 2004) *The Psychology of Leadership: New perspectives and research*, Psychology Press, B000SMD1IS

7 J Richard Hackman (10 July 2002) *Leading Teams: Setting the stage for great performances*, Harvard Business Review Press, ASIN B0106P71WI

8 Jennifer S Mueller (January 2012) Why Individuals in Larger Teams Perform Worse, Science Direct, [Online] http://www.sciencedirect.com/science/article/pii/S0749597811001105 [accessed 25 October 2016]

9 Russell Davies (17 April 2013) A Unit of Delivery, Russell Davies, [Online] http://russelldavies.typepad.com/planning/2013/04/the-unit-of-delivery.html [accessed 25 October 2016]

10 Werner Vogels (5 October 2011) Werner Vogels: Amazon and the Lean Cloud, Hack Fwd, [Online] http://blog.hackfwd.com/post/11060764003/werner-vogels-amazon-and-the-lean-cloud [accessed 25 October 2016]

11 Richard L Brandt (15 October 2011) Birth of a Salesman, Wall Street Journal, [Online] http://www.wsj.com/news/articles/SB10001424052970203914304576627102996831200 [accessed 25 October 2016]

12 HolacracyOne, How It Works, Holacracy.Org, [Online] http://www.holacracy.org/how-it-works/ [accessed 25 October 2016]

13 Frederic Laloux and Ken Wilber (9 February 2014) *Reinventing Organizations: A guide to creating organizations inspired by the next stage of human consciousness*, Nelson Parker, ASIN B00ICS9VI4

14 Eric Schmidt and Jonathan Rosenberg (12 March 2015) *How Google Works*, John Murray, ISBN-10 1444792490 ISBN-13 978-1444792492

15 Tim Malbon (March 2016) The Solution to Design Thinking [Online] https://medium.com/the-many/the-solution-to-design-thinking-42e8f1b59022#.i117lomra [accessed 6 March 2017]

Scaling agility 12

Big is a collection of smalls.

Nigel Bogle

New ways of working such as Agile, Lean, and Scrum and operating in small, multi-disciplinary teams are not only the domain of startups. With rapidly shifting contexts *every* company needs to become more adaptive, iterative and emergent, and work to combine functional expertise horizontally across the organization in smarter, more fluid ways. As Silicon Valley entrepreneur and academician Steve Blank has pointed out a startup is not a smaller version of a large company.

As an organization scales, functional groups are an excellent way to optimize efficiency and craft. As it scales and diversifies further to become multi-product, divisions (which each house their own functional groups) allow these efficiency and expertise gains to be extended. But this comes at the expense of structuring for the benefit of the organization, not for the customer. Customers are horizontal. They don't care about the differences between sales, customer service, or marketing. They don't care about how company divisions are structured. They just want products that work, and to be able to find solutions to problems easily and quickly. So the need for more seamless customer experience and greater agility creates a heightened horizontal tension and obligation to counteract the constraining impact of organizational silos. Adept collection and application of data can mitigate this (utilizing a 'single customer view' in order to join up customer touchpoints and help interaction to be more personalized and intuitive, for example). But the organizational response needs to stretch deeper into processes, culture and, of course, structures.

This means finding better ways to combine the benefits we can derive from unifying expertise in functional groups (HR, finance, sales, marketing, operations), with the ability to capitalize on the agility and momentum that can come from small, multi-disciplinary pods. Organizational systems and ideology are weighted heavily towards optimizing efficiency through functional groups. We need to find a new balance, one that reflects a greater emphasis on learning, velocity, focus and flexibility through agile, iterative, multi-functional pod working.

More commonly iterative methodologies and pod working seeds first in technology teams, centralized digital units, innovation or product development labs and incubators, or standalone catalyst brands that are established to enable a large organization to experiment with new approaches. But confining these ways of working to small units or single teams misses the huge opportunity that companies have to scale agility far more broadly across the organization. We can represent this progression of agility through several distinct stages:

1 **Dispersed mavericks:** Restless change agents in dispersed areas of the business recognize the need for different approaches and start to question the status quo and agitate for change. This may initiate pilot projects or minor revisions in local areas efforts are not joined-up and substantive change is difficult in the face of a lack of senior support, and wider organizational complacency.
2 **Focused agility:** As the strategic imperative for change takes root at senior levels, investment and resources are allocated towards digital capability development and innovation. New agile ways of working become established in specific areas such as innovation units, catalyst brands, technology teams and digital centres of excellence. Centralization brings focus, a visible statement of intent, easier prioritization, efficiency, better governance and commonality of approach. Iterative, sprint working in small, multi-disciplinary teams enables faster learning and greater experimentation, agile culture and behaviours are nurtured and protected through senior backing and 'translator' roles.
3 **Scaling agility:** As the need to scale agility becomes more pressing, small multi-functional pod working, and iterative experimentation is expanded beyond tightly focused innovation, technology or digital areas more broadly into the wider organization. This is accompanied by senior vision, communication and support, along with a clear link between corporate and team strategy, objectives, execution and measures. Over time the proportion of the workforce that is working in this way increases.
4 **Dispersed agility:** As agility naturally scales ever wider, it becomes essential for the business to manage the ever-fluid proportion of staff that are working in multi-functional pods, and continually balance that with the efficiency and craft benefits gained from functional groups. Ongoing sensitivity to the type, scale and scope of customer needs, and the ability of the business to respond to these and other contextual challenges is key.

The stage when we are looking to scale agility can be particularly challenging. It is at this point that we are expanding new approaches, behaviour and culture beyond an isolated area, so a senior mandate, permission to fail-safe but to orient to learning becomes critical to success. Initial focus may be on setting up small multi-functional teams to address key business challenges through iteration and experimentation. Or establishing areas at a divisional level that can enable the introduction of these new ways of working focused on divisional priorities – more of a hub-and-spoke model to scaling agile working.

Exposure to agile working and culture can support wider adoption over time. This might come via staff, functions and teams that interface regularly with already agile areas (osmosis). Or wider assimilation through deliberately including an ever-wider coterie of staff to experience agile working and be included in pod team working (diffusion). Or encouraging the larger organization to learn from catalyst brand initiatives (mother-learns-from-baby).

Businesses cannot go from a rigid, functionally oriented state to a highly fluid, agile, learning-oriented organization overnight. The staged approach allows for proper establishment of supporting structures and cultures, and the proportion of workforce that is ultimately working in pod-like structures is likely to be fluid.

To see an exemplar of scaling agile structures, we can look at Spotify. Agile and organizational coaches at Spotify, Henrik Kniberg and Anders Ivarsson, have detailed an approach that the company has adopted successfully, focused on what they call Squads, Tribes, Chapters and Guilds.[1] Spotify has scaled more rapidly than most companies but the structure that they have adopted in their engineering teams is specifically designed to maintain an uniquely advantageous level of agility across 30 teams and three cities.

The basic unit of development at Spotify is the 'Squad', a small, nimble, multi-disciplinary, autonomous self-organizing team that is designed to feel like a mini-startup. Squads are co-located and focus on specific areas of the product or service, incorporating all the tools and skills they need to take an idea from design to test to release and production. Much like Amazon's two-pizza teams, Squads are clearly focused on a specific task and KPI.

Squads are grouped together into related product areas called 'Tribes'. Tribes are like the incubator for the squad mini-startups and designed to be no larger than 100 people. Specific processes help minimize the potential of dependencies to slow things down.

'Chapters' and 'Guilds' link Squads horizontally together, enabling some economies of scale without sacrificing autonomy, and acting like the glue that binds the company together. Chapters group together people with similar functional expertise and meet regularly to share learnings. The Chapter lead is the line manager for chapter members and has more traditional staff-management responsibilities, but is also a member of a Squad themself so stays in touch with the work. Guilds are looser, more organic and wide-reaching communities of interest that can stretch across the whole company (rather than just how a Tribe like a Chapter does). They enable knowledge and tool-sharing across a wider group.

As Kniberg and Ivarsson describe it, it is like a matrix organization but one that is weighted towards delivery. The structure is a departure from typical organizational approaches in that rather than people being grouped into vertical silos defined by function, the vertical dimension is customer and product focused, and defined by those multi-disciplinary, self-organizing, co-located Squads, while the horizontal dimension is all about sharing knowledge, best practice, learning and tools.

The risk in having a looser organizational structure focused around small, nimble teams is that an increased level of complexity is created through a greater number of dependencies, coordination issues, a possible lack of focus on developing vertical functional expertise, and the difficulty in effectively sharing learning horizontally across the organization. What's interesting about Spotify's approach is that it specifically finds ways to avoid those potential pitfalls, while making for a customer focused structure that is far more flexible and empowering, and one that can be far more adaptive at scale.

Managing core teams and dependencies

When scaling agile working and small multi-functional teams through the organization we need to remove barriers to ensure that they can move fast. An important part of this, as we have discussed, is being ruthless about keeping the team small. But we also need to ensure that teams have the necessary support and input they require, what they need when they need it, in order to generate and maintain momentum.

The model of Agile team onions (Figure 12.1), originated by Agile practitioner Emily Webber, is a way of structuring dependencies which, in a large organization may be required functional inputs (perhaps ops, legal, finance and so on) that are involved in some way in delivery but which are still situated in vertical silos, around the core team.[2] The onion is a way of creating understanding about who is in the wider team, and inviting them in without disrupting the small (and effective) size of the core team:

> *This isn't just a stakeholder map, it is about bringing the organization in and having shared responsibility for what you are creating together.*

The onion is classified thus.

Figure 12.1 The Agile Team Onion

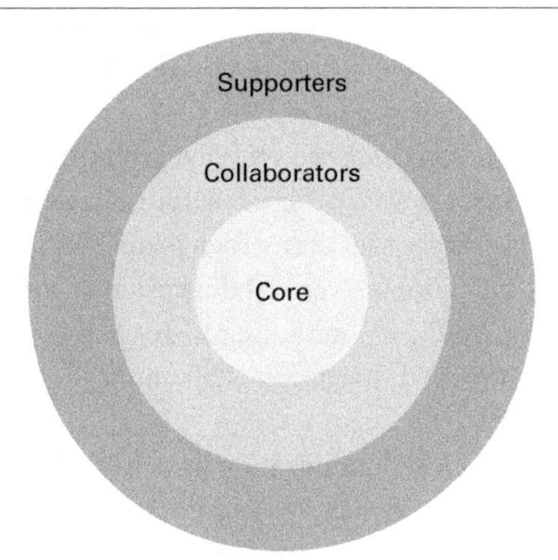

SOURCE The Agile Team Onion © Copyright 2016 Emily Webber @ewebber. Published as The Agile Team Onion: A model for Agile teams in large organizations, July 2016 http://tacit.pub/agileteamonion

Core team

- Purpose: delivery of digital services
- Communication: daily (all stand-ups, retrospectives, planning, show and tells)
- Co-located: daily, all day
- Types of people: product owner, scrum master, developers, designers, etc.

Collaborators (who might be working on multiple teams)

- Purpose: bring in specialist information to assist the team, assurance as needed, reduce dependencies and blockers (open doors)
- Communication: regularly, they come to some agile meetings
- Co-located: on a regular basis (as a guide ~2 days a week) – this also depends on what is needed and the phase of project – but enough to be able to not block anything
- Types of people: other delivery teams working within the same portfolio, security liaison, policy liaison, portfolio manager, operations, suppliers, etc.

Supporters

- Purpose: keep informed, feed into broad organizational priorities
- Communication: every sprint/iteration (show and tells, ad-hoc when needed)
- Co-located: monthly or as needed
- Types of people: steering groups, wider organization.

Mapping out your team onion, inviting people in, agreeing expectations and protocols establishes the right footing for it all to work. So, ultimately, an organization may consist of many overlapping onions (Figure 12.2).

In this way, the core team is kept at a suitable size to maintain velocity, collaborators provide necessary inputs to maintain momentum, and supporters remove barriers and provide direction to empower agility.

Figure 12.2 Overlapping onions

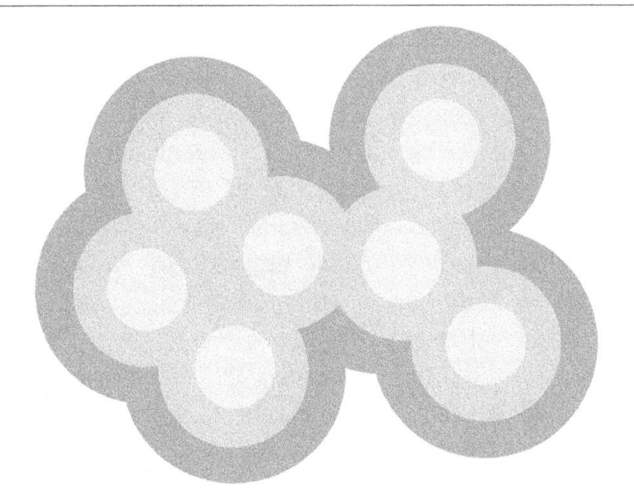

SOURCE The Agile Team Onion © Copyright 2016 Emily Webber @ewebber. Published as The Agile Team Onion: A model for Agile teams in large organizations, July 2016 http://tacit.pub/agileteamonion

Getting the right mix: pioneers, settlers, town planners

David Smith, of Global Futures and Foresight, has written about[3] achieving effective change through a model which positions the right person in the right place at the right time. It's interesting, says David, that the business world has more recently prized leadership over managers and entrepreneurs when, of course, all three are critical to the effective running of a business. Yet they are very different beasts:

- The Entrepreneur: dreams about the future, is strong on ideas, and brilliant at vision.
- The Leader: plans for tomorrow, is strong on people and brilliant at behaviour.
- The Manager: delivers today, is strong on process, and brilliant at capability.

Entrepreneurs in companies are the ideas people who often end up being put in charge of building new capability or business units. But once those units are established they require managers to extract the full value or generate sustainable sales or greater ongoing efficiencies.

Conflict can occur between entrepreneurs and managers as the former struggle to get the latter onside with new ideas, and the latter despair of getting the former to appreciate the nuances of running the ongoing business. As entrepreneurs are focused more on the ideas of tomorrow, and managers more on the business of today, the former may see the latter as 'change blockers'. Once a new venture has been created, entrepreneurs may be less equipped or enthused to optimize the venture on an ongoing basis and so may be moved out of the business rather than be assigned the next entrepreneurial challenge, resulting in innovation loss for the company. For this reason, says David, more entrepreneurs feel that they don't belong on corporate world and so end up in SMEs.

But all three are, of course, essential. Leaders need entrepreneurs (to identify and capitalize on ideas), and entrepreneurs need leaders (so that they are not working in isolation). Both need managers who can take innovations and make them work, and managers in turn need leaders and entrepreneurs. Everyone has a profile that mixes these three attributes to a greater or lesser degree, and it goes without saying that where things go wrong is where someone's profile is mismatched to the role that they find themselves in. In the context of achieving change, awareness of the profiles enables you to identify where support for the change will come from, and where there might be blockers. In the context of a senior team in the corporate environment, leadership may be overvalued (everyone wants to be a leader) at the expense of entrepreneurs and managers, resulting in an imbalance.

We need to ensure that our best talent is oriented towards opportunity, not just to efficiency. Putting the right people to work on the wrong thing can have a disastrous impact. Take Microsoft, a business that many believe badly trailed its competitors in its development of key technologies including mobile. In a 2014 *Vanity Fair* article on Microsoft, Steve Ballmer talked about the cost of the misalignment of the talent that the company had:

> *The worst work I did was from 2001 to 2004. And the company paid a price for bad work. I put the A-team resources on Longhorn, not on phones or browsers. All our resources were tied up on the wrong thing.*[4]

Researcher Simon Wardley has described an approach that brings together the unique combination of resourcing characteristics needed to bring products and services to life (in a concept itself adapted from Robert X Cringely's description of companies in terms of Commandos, Infantry and Police).[5] Pioneers, settlers and town planners are each brilliant in their own way, but demonstrate different attributes:

- **Pioneers:** have the ability to explore uncharted territory and generate entirely new concepts: '*They show you wonder but they fail a lot.*'
- **Settlers:** can turn incomplete ideas into something useful for a larger audience, make prototypes into products, commercialize, build understanding and trust: '*They make the possible future actually happen.*'
- **Town planners:** are able to industrialize young products to capitalize on economies of scale: '*You trust what they build. They find ways to make things faster, better, smaller, more efficient, more economic and good enough.*'[6]

While pioneers will be experimenting iteratively, prototyping in-house, using agile working and techniques, settlers may be utilizing more off-the-shelf technologies, tapping into ecosystems, using lean methodologies, and town planners will likely be using existing tools to drive efficiency, perhaps outsourcing, and maybe even using more traditional waterfall development. Each of these stages are critical in the agile organization, and great people are needed in each of these roles to create the right combination that can not only generate new ideas, but also commercialize and scale them at pace. There is even the potential to deploy small, multi-functional pods to fulfil each stage of this process.

While the pioneers may logically sit within the innovation area or digital team, and the town planners within vertical functions, the settler stage is a key one. During this phase the concept or project may start as an early stage prototype that has established an early value proposition and product-market fit, but then needs to be properly commercialized, and the business

Figure 12.3 Attributes of pioneers, settlers and town planners

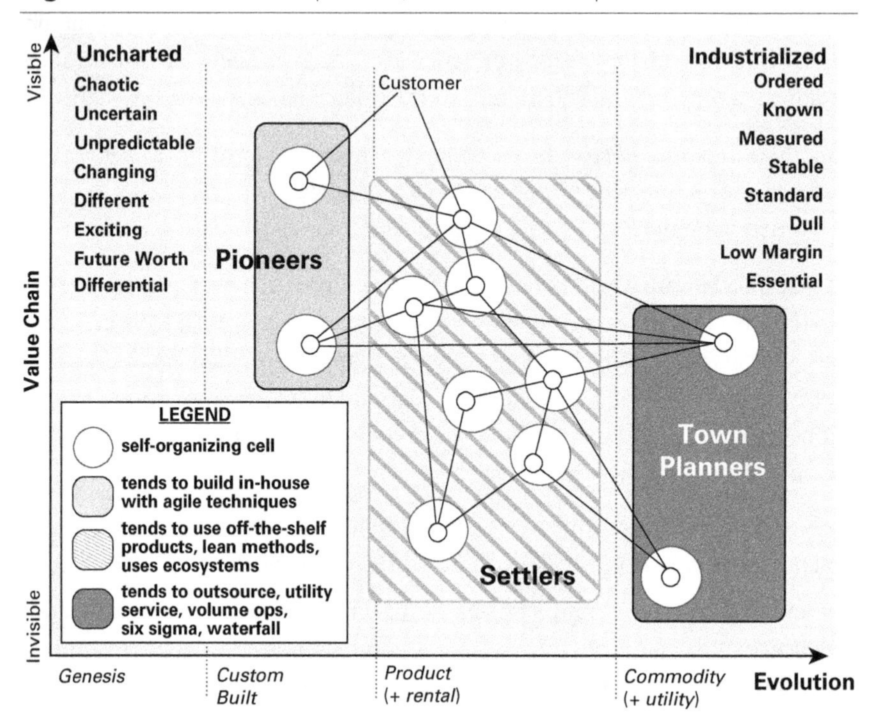

model and proposition developed to make it repeatable and ready for scale. The inherent dangers at this point are that the concept moves out of the innovation area, straight into business-as-usual functions where it is saddled with a short-term profit target and given to a functional leader and staff who have not been invested in the idea from the start. Under these burdensome conditions, the idea (even if it is a great one) will often wither and die. There are several factors that can instead contribute to success:

1. A clearer metrics journey that can show early stage value before revenue (see 'Pirate Metrics' in Part Two).
2. Senior patronage, and a clear understanding of the role of the new initiative in progressing towards a long-term vision.
3. A continuum of resourcing on the project – key people who have been there from the start continuing to work on it. The balance here is ensuring that pioneers, adept at ideation, rapid experimentation and prototyping, are not being forced unnecessarily to play the role of the settler.
4. Resourcing dedicated to the commercialization of early stage ideas. Sometimes, with the right support, the same team can take an idea

through from initial concept to commercialization. But even a startup adapts its skill base in tune with these critical stages. So more commonly in a large organization we need committed staff with the right expertise, or a multi-functional team specifically focused on establishing scale and economic viability. We need not only systematic ways of testing new ideas, but also disciplined ways of commercializing the ones that show early stage promise.

We need to create the conditions in which each phase can feed off the others. This is about building a systemic way to orient the organization towards not only continuous experimentation but also continual commercialization and scaling of early stage ideas.

Agile decision-making: flatter structures, quicker decisions

The primary purpose of the organizational hierarchy in a company is decision-making efficiency.

Ben Horowitz[7]

Here's a scenario. The CEO needs to do a big review presentation. So they ask five of their direct reports to help put it together. Those five leaders brief five of their subordinates to compile the material. Those five subordinates brief out another five of their juniors asking for specific information. Each of those stages requires just two meetings between each of the individuals involved (briefing and review), and perhaps five e-mails. A not unreasonable scenario and yet that is already 156 people, 310 meetings, 775 e-mails for one presentation. Over-burdensome hierarchy creates its own over-burdensome process. And it can be paralysing.

Consider a second scenario. A team wants to implement a change that will support one of their objectives but which impacts another team's activity. In an overly hierarchical business the proposal gets passed up the line to the department head, who engages the head of the other team in trying to win support for their initiative. The other department head consults their own team to understand the implications of the change. In the absence of appropriate data, the decision becomes drawn out and protracted as the department heads go back and forth to negotiate a solution they are both happy with. Instead of being dealt with quickly at an appropriate level, multiple decisions are passed up the line, across, down the line, and back again. Time passes. Projects are stalled.

In order to move quickly it is essential in a large organization (particularly in the context of leading transformation) to invest time in understanding where decision-making and influence resides. In other words, to know 'who's who in the zoo'. Attempting to implement change that carries dependencies without the support of key stakeholders or influencers within the organization will at best slow things down and at worst result in failure. Simple frameworks such as RACI (Responsible, Accountable, Consulted, Informed) are useful not only in assigning and managing responsibilities, but also in determining the required actions necessary to smooth the process of change and ensure continued support.

Over time, the number of managerial layers in large organizations seems only to increase; yet flatter structures reduce unnecessary communication and expedite speed of decision-making. The secret is to have *just enough* hierarchy. Yet reaping the benefits of a flatter business is not just about formal structures. Decision-making needs to be empowered with ease of access to relevant data, and the kind of culture that is not suffocated by internal politics. Effortless access to the right data at the right time (through dashboarding, for example) can bring agility by supporting and removing contention around a proposed course of action. Teams that have access to relevant data make better decisions. Companies that make that data easy to access enable their staff to make those better decisions faster.

Similarly, senior perks and other visible symbols of status might make a few staff feel self-important but are largely counter-productive to open communication and can be a barrier to just getting the job done. Are executive floors, large exuberant offices, and other visible perks of seniority really necessary?

When he was CEO of successful work productivity company Evernote, Phil Lipin said that such signals: 'create artificial barriers to communication. They create artificial things that people focus on rather than just getting their job accomplished'.[8] Eliminating all distractions so you can just focus on achieving means that you attract people who are primarily motivated by how much they achieve.

We should all be passionate in the pursuit of maintaining decision-making structures that enable clarity of responsibility and authority while preventing redundant or avoidable hierarchy and process.

Agile governance and the digital board

If the rate of change on the outside exceeds the rate of change on the inside, the end is near.

Jack Welch

Slow decision-making can be anathema to effective digital management and transformation. As the pace of digital development accelerates and pressure on resources intensifies, one of the key challenges that arise in organizations undergoing digital transformation is the effective prioritization of digital projects and developments. There is just so much to do, so many different (and potentially competing) priorities that it can be hugely difficult for those at the top tier to know the right thing to do (especially if their level of knowledge of all things digital is not what it could be).

The issue is often not about the level of comparative significance attributed to digital developments by the company board, nor their visibility among the most senior staff of the company. A more likely scenario is that while an organization may already have digital development as a strategic pillar of the corporate strategy, the difficulty comes in taking account of multiple dependencies or risk factors and in elucidating and defining a priority list that will ensure that the most meaningful and impactful changes are prioritized above those which may have less significance. Sometimes impact is difficult to demonstrate or even to determine. Sometimes changes that have short-term impact might be unfairly or misguidedly prioritized over those with potentially much larger long-term impact. Sometimes involvement of multiple senior-level stakeholders slows the decision-making down to the point where the impact of development is negated.

Companies might try to mitigate this risk by appointing digitally savvy people to the board, or having a board member take responsibility for becoming a digital 'champion'. Both of these options can help. Yet there can be little substitute for a board that is conversant and experienced as well as informed. The broader this capability across the board the better. Every company is operating in a digitally empowered world, which means there is now little excuse for lack of board level competency and proficiency.

Outside of board meetings, decision-making structures need to be agile in support of an empowered board. Clear delineation of responsibility helps. Peter Thiel has said:

> *The best thing I did as a manager at PayPal, was to make every person in the company responsible for doing just one thing. Every employee's one thing was unique, and everyone knew I would evaluate him only on that one thing.*[9]

While the clarity, focus and simplicity that this brings may reap dividends for startups and small businesses, as a company scales applying this approach to small teams rather than individuals is likely to be easier. Clear and sensible escalation procedures also help.

More formalized decision-making and feedback structures such as the creation of a 'digital board' can, however, prove to be extremely valuable in facilitating agile governance while providing a crucial link to most crucial decision-making body in the company: the main board.

A 'digital board' might typically comprise key main board members (the board 'digital champion', or Finance Director or perhaps even the Managing Director or CEO) and other principal digital stakeholders, and becomes the main decision-making body for the digital development roadmap, meeting regularly to make key investment and strategy decisions.

This ensures the ongoing commitment, involvement and engagement of key senior staff including the CEO, CFO, and/or the IT and Operations Director, provides a crucial link between digital operations and the main board, while still keeping the decision-making process as agile possible.

Notes

1. Henrik Kniberg and Anders Ivarsson (October 2012) Scaling Agile @ Spotify, with Tribes, Squads, Chapters and Guilds, [Online] https://dl.dropboxusercontent.com/u/1018963/Articles/SpotifyScaling.pdf [accessed 25 October 2016]
2. Emily Webber, 14 May 2016, The Agile Team Onion. How many pizzas does it really take to feed your team?, Emily Webber http://emilywebber.co.uk/agile-team-onion-many-pizzas-really-take-feed-team/ [accessed 25 October 2016]
3. David Smith (26 October 2016) Effective Business Change: Right person, right place, right time, Global Futures and Foresight, [Online] http://thegff.com/Articles/205178/Global_Futures_and/Methods_and_tools/Effective_Business_Change.aspx [accessed 25 October 2016]
4. Bethany McLean (November 2014) The Empire Reboots, *Vanity Fair*, [Online] http://www.vanityfair.com/news/business/2014/11/satya-nadella-bill-gates-steve-ballmer-microsoft [accessed 25 October 2016]
5. Robert X Cringely (4 April 1996) *Accidental Empires: How the boys of Silicon Valley make their millions, battle foreign competition and still can't get a date*, 2nd revised edition, Penguin Books Ltd, ISBN-10 140258264 ISBN-13 978-0140258264
6. Simon Wardley (13 March 2015) On Pioneers, Settlers, Town Planners and Theft, Gardeviance.org, [Online] http://blog.gardeviance.org/2015/03/on-pioneers-settlers-town-planners-and.html [accessed 25 October 2016]
7. Ben Horowitz (24 April 2014) *The Hard Thing About Hard Things: Building a business when there are no easy answers*, Harper Business, ISBN-10 62273205 ISBN-13 978-0062273208

8 Adam Bryant (7 April 2012) The Phones Are Out, but the Robot Is In, New York Times, [Online] http://www.nytimes.com/2012/04/08/business/phil-libin-of-evernote-on-its-unusual-corporate-culture.html?pagewanted=all&_r=1 [accessed 25 October 2016]

9 Peter Thiel and Blake Masters (16 September 2014) *Zero to One: Notes on startups, or how to build the future*, Crown Business, ISBN-10 804139296 ISBN-13 978-0804139298

Building the culture to move fast

13

Agile is not just a process, it defines a culture

Agile is a working process that has revolutionized the way in which technology teams (and increasingly a wider set of functions) work but it is far more than that. Agile defines a broader opportunity to change mindsets, behaviours, and yes, organizational culture.

Agile practitioner Michael Sahota has written about a key distinction in this respect: the difference between *doing* agile, and *being* agile – in other words between adoption and transformation.[1] Change agents, he says, talk of adopting agile but rarely about transforming the culture of a company to support the agile mindset. And without that, it fails. Sahota builds on a model from William Schneider[2] that maps four distinct organizational culture types against a two-by-two matrix which positions people versus company-oriented businesses on the horizontal axis against reality versus possibility oriented companies on the vertical (Figure 13.1).

So, for example, the 'cultivation culture' is about succeeding by growing people who fulfil a compelling vision, collaboration culture is about succeeding by working together, control by getting and keeping control, competence by being the best and so on. No one culture is better than another but while companies may have characteristics that originate from multiple culture-types, they are likely to be routed in one. Other cultural elements may be encouraged as long as they serve the dominant culture. This also enables us to see a relationship between different culture types. Controlling organizational cultures, for example, are more compatible with competence and collaboration cultures than they are with cultivation.

Figure 13.1 Schneider's two-by-two matrix of organizational culture types

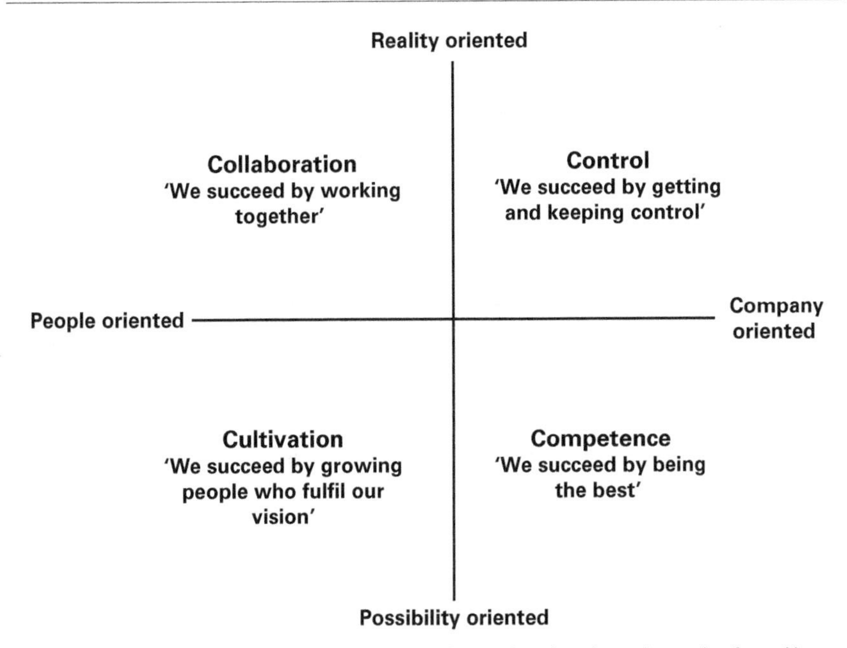

SOURCE Adapted from William Schneider (May 1994) *Reengineering Alternative: A plan for making your current culture work*, Irwin Professional Publishing, ISBN-10: 0786301201

The model is useful in thinking about where your company culture is routed, but also in identifying potential areas of conflict. Agile culture is focused more on collaboration and cultivation, and so arguably plays less well with controlling cultures in particular. Conflict can arise when individual teams or departments may have a subculture that is different to the dominant organizational culture. These cultural mismatches can kill off new ways of working before they have even had chance to prove their value, or cause a long-term drift back to the old ways of doing things. It is like when a virus is introduced into the bloodstream in our bodies, the white blood cells cluster around it and try to kill the foreign body off. Similarly, an organization can reject the introduction of a foreign culture system and work hard in order to maintain the status quo.

The role of 'translators', or 'interpreters' here is key. These are roles that can help make the new way of working make sense to the rest of the business (and avoid triggering the antibodies). Job roles such as product managers and project managers can help fulfil this need in these early stages.

What is digital-native culture?

> *You don't create a culture. Culture happens. It's the by-product of consistent behaviour... real cultures are built over time. They're the result of action, reaction, and truth. They are nuanced, beautiful, and authentic. Real culture is patina.*
>
> Jason Fried[3]

Organizational culture can be the one of the biggest enablers, but also blockers, to change. We cannot deliberately create culture overnight, nor can we change a company's culture at whim. But we *can* recognize that there are certain essential characteristics and behaviours that are fundamental to organizational agility, and frame the context in which they can thrive. We can set expectation, recognize, amplify and reward, and demonstrate through the choices that we make, the questions we ask, and our own behaviour. In this sense, it is not about creating a digital-native culture, but enabling a culture that is fit for a digital world.

To describe the essence of this culture, we can draw together a number of essential ingredients. We can talk about being entrepreneurial, innovative and experimental. About continuous learning. About being non-hierarchical and collaborative. The importance of commercial focus, data-driven decision-making and accountability. About openness and transparency. Staff who benefit from a high degree of empowerment and autonomy. An organization that is passionate, hungry, outwardly facing and curious.

All of these things are important. But so is how we choose to bring this to life. Nolan Caudill, Engineering Chief of Staff at rapidly growing communication and productivity app Slack, has written about how every company builds products that they sell but also the culture within the company. Yet while the former is often an explicit undertaking and the result of conscious effort:

> *Culture – which we understand to mean the systems that dictate how employees relate to one another, the work to be done, and the customers – often forms without much oversight. Like any random experiment, the results of letting culture form unchecked can vary between fair to disastrous.*[4]

At Slack, culture is seen as a way to not only create the environment where people can do great work, but as a manifestation of what the company values and as way of making explicit decisions to avoid groupthink, politics and unhelpful concentrations of power.

This is reflected in how the work is done and decisions made, who they choose to hire, what they choose to reward, and encapsulated in three key values: diligence (doing the hard work to be exceptional); curiosity (not being satisfied with the status quo, considering problems from multiple angles, asking the right questions to the right people at the right time); and empathy (the ability to view things through the eyes of the customer, diversity of experience).

Similarly, social technologies company Buffer focus around nine (openly published) values that include positivity, transparency, self-improvement, listening, and being a 'no-ego' do-er. Their default to openness and transparency has seen them publish detailed monthly performance reports on their blog,[5] and even went as far as initiating an 'open salary' approach based on a formula which made remuneration for employees completely transparent.[6] Buffer CEO Joel Gascoigne has expressed why openness is so important to them: 'Transparency breeds trust, and trust is the foundation of great teamwork'.[7] While not every company might have this level of appetite for transparency, the point is that they are living their values openly and demonstrably, and that is the behaviour of a confident business.

Stories from the frontline

Joel Constable, People Development at Pinterest: Bringing agility to life at an organizational and individual level through a focus on velocity and flexibility

Figure 13.2 Bringing agility to life at an organizational and individual level through a focus on velocity and flexibility

	Velocity	Flexibility
Organization	**Remove roadblocks** Ambiguity, bottlenecks, fear	**Clarify the how** Prioritization, decision-making
Individual	**Build accountability** Ownership, accountability	**Embed reflection** Habitual reflection, what do we need to change?

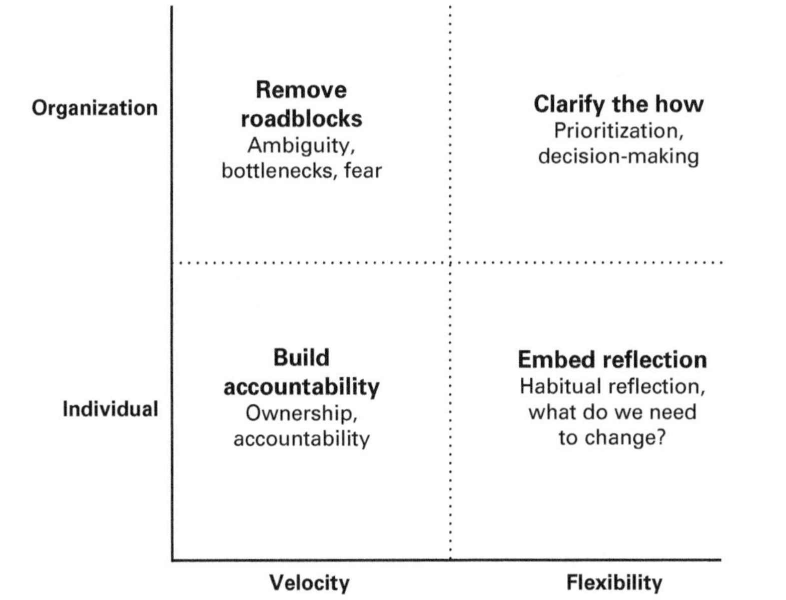

At Pinterest we bring agility to life at an organizational and individual level through a focus on velocity and flexibility (Figure 13.2). 'Organizational velocity' is about how we can create the conditions necessary to increase velocity. This primarily involves removing roadblocks. Roadblocks show up in an organization in many forms including lack of goal or role clarity, decision-making or resourcing bottlenecks, and employees' fear of taking risks and having important yet tough conversations.

We've removed these roadblocks through our semi-annual planning cycle, thoughtful cascading of critical information, and bi-weekly all company progress meetings. When every employee consistently understands our strategy and key priorities, they can make better, quicker trade-off decisions.

We also have clear owners for each of the company's major objectives who are known across the company. These individuals are accountable for key outcomes and metrics related to the goals and have the autonomy to make critical decisions.

At the organizational level, we create the conditions for flexibility through strong shared values that help guide how employees approach and complete their work. These values are built into performance reviews, enlivened through workshops, and visible in the physical work space. We use guiding principles when proposing a solution or course of action to clarify what we're optimizing for and how to think about the problem.

At the individual level, we enable velocity by helping employees feel a sense of ownership beyond their job description and accountability through performance expectations. Employees work towards clear, challenging goals and have regular discussions with their manager about their progress.

Individual flexibility is facilitated through an emphasis on embedded reflection. We've put significant investment into external coaches to work with many of our leaders (not just executives). Coaches provide our leaders with a sounding board and structured time every couple of weeks to reflect on how things are going and where they can improve or change course.

Reflection is critical for all leaders but it's been especially important for us as we've scaled quickly. As the company grows, our leaders need to frequently re-assess how best to allocate their time and invest their energy. What was the best approach six months ago will frequently not be the best approach now. I like to use two questions to help with this kind of reflection:

- Is this the most important work I can be doing right now to make the team and company successful?
- Is the process / approach / strategy we used before still the most effective approach given our current reality?

While the agile business has singular, stable, directional vision, strategy and values, it is able to adapt at speed through enabling processes, practices and culture.

Having posters on the walls with catchy slogans is the easy bit. To really bring culture to life we have to see and feel it around us, in the behaviours of those around us, in the decisions that leaders make, in the people that are hired, in the systems that make everything work, in how we judge success, in the patterns of recognition and reward. That is where real agility and competitive advantage will come from. To quote from John R Childress: 'Anyone can copy your strategy, but no one can duplicate your culture.'[8]

The right culture helps you to move fast

AirBnB co-founder Brian Chesky has described an office visit from entrepreneur Peter Thiel just after they had closed their Series C funding round in 2012 in which Thiel invested US$150 million in the fledgling business. When Chesky asked him what was the single most important piece of advice he had for them, Thiel replied 'Don't f**k up the culture'. Thiel believed that it was all too easy for the early stage culture to be destroyed as AirBnB scaled. So Chesky and his co-founders decided that culture would be one of things they focused on above all else. Not least because it helps you to move fast. The stronger the culture in a business, he says, the less process that company needs:

> *When the culture is strong, you can trust everyone to do the right thing. People can be independent and autonomous. They can be entrepreneurial. And if we have a company that is entrepreneurial in spirit, we will be able to take our next '(wo)man on the moon' leap.*[9]

Process itself is, of course, not inherently bad for business, but there is the kind that helps you to progress at pace and the kind that slows you down. Netflix, for example, delineate between good processes that help talented people to get more done (frequent release schedules, regular strategy and context updates, budgetary discipline), and bad processes that can creep in over time and often try to prevent recoverable mistakes (such as overly complex sign-off procedures, avoidable micro-management of expenditure, unnecessarily multi-level approvals).[10]

If, as Chesky defines it, culture is 'simply a shared way of doing something with passion...a thousand things, a thousand times', then organizational culture in the agile business is about enabling more intuitive decision-making and autonomy, removing unnecessary process and hierarchy, and empowering the business to move fast.

What really differentiates high-performing teams?

This feels like something of a holy-grail question for companies, and one that Google has undergone a lengthy quest to understand. Several years ago they embarked on a comprehensive study, called Project Aristotle, that studied hundreds of teams from the business in an attempt to find out what separated the exceptional from the average. Findings from a wide-ranging review of academic studies into how teams work were overlaid onto the teams inside the company to try to define which factors made a difference.

After extensive research and data analysis of many different potentially influential variable elements, there was no obvious common patterns or factors that emerged which separated teams that were high-performing from those that weren't. Surprisingly, all the elements that we might expect to be influential including team composition, longevity, degree of hierarchy, and the mix of personality, background and skills of the team members all made no difference.

Instead, further research revealed that the group norms ('the traditions, behavioural standards and unwritten rules that govern how we function when we gather')[11] that the team operated to seemed to play an important role in how successful a team was. Analysis of over a hundred groups for more than a year showed that the right norms could raise a group's collective intelligence, and the wrong ones have the opposite effect (even when individual intelligence was high).

But while team norms differed widely in character, high-performing teams all exhibited a high level of 'psychological safety'. Professor Amy Edmondson from Harvard Business School defines this as a 'shared belief held by members of a team that the team is safe for interpersonal risk-taking',[12] and also as describing a team climate that is 'characterized by interpersonal trust and mutual respect in which people are comfortable being themselves'. Feeling like you can really be yourself in the team and work environment, that you do not need to play a particular role, and that work is more than just work, really matters. Anything that detracts from this impacts not just employee happiness, but performance.

Similarly, research by Carnegie Mellon, MIT and Union College has documented the existence of a collective intelligence among teams who cooperate well that extends beyond the cognitive abilities of the group's individual members. Teams with the right kind of internal dynamics, and particularly those that exhibited higher levels of 'social sensitivity' (how well team members are able to perceive other team members emotions), and those where team members were able to speak in a more equal distribution of turn taking rather than one person in the group dominating, performed well on a wide range of assignments. Interestingly, teams containing more women demonstrated greater social sensitivity and in turn greater collective intelligence compared to teams containing fewer women. As one of the researchers noted: 'Having a bunch of smart people in a group doesn't necessarily make the group smart'.[13]

From her work, Amy Edmondson has defined three key strategies for leaders to create the environment in which psychological safety can work:

1 **Framing work as learning problems, rather than execution problems** – if leaders can depict clearly how increased uncertainty and interdependence means that each team member's input matters: 'We've never been here before; we can't know what will happen; we've got to have everybody's brains and voices in the game.'[14]
2 **Acknowledging fallibility** – simple statements or questions that acknowledge that the leader does not have all the answers, and create permission for input from others.
3 **Model curiosity by asking a lot of questions** – this creates the need to generate answers and therefore the need for voice.

Edmondson believes that the interaction between psychological safety and accountability, enabling questions and open discussion while holding people accountable, can combine to create a high performing team in an uncertain environment. Conversely, accountability without psychological safety can create anxiety and mistakes, and maintaining the open, safe culture without accountability means employees remain unchallenged and overly comfortable.

If combining psychological safety and accountability works at a group level to create high performance in uncertain climates, and a collective intelligence that is greater than the cognitive abilities of individual team members, then we need to scale this approach across the entire organization. In 1996, Rob Goffee and Gareth Jones described an approach to understanding organizational culture that plotted cultures across two axes: Sociability (emotional, non-instrumental relations, friendliness, social interaction for its own sake, 'high levels of unarticulated reciprocity'); and Solidarity (the ability to pursue shared goals effectively and quickly, regardless of personal ties, relationships based on common tasks or mutual interests).[15] This defined four main cultural types:

1 **Networked:** High sociability, low solidarity. Characterized by high trust and empathy, open door policies, loyal to social group rather than an organization.

2 **Mercenary:** Low sociability, high solidarity. Exhibited by weak social ties, encouraged competition between employees, high performance but employees stay only as long as their personal goals are met.

3 **Fragmented:** Low sociability, low solidarity. Here there is low consciousness of organizational objectives, a shut door policy, employees rarely agreeing with organization objectives.

4 **Communal:** High sociability, high solidarity. Characterized by strong team working, sharing the organizations mission, value, risk, and reward, strong friendship relations.

Goffee and Jones stress that no one of these cultures is the 'best' option, that there may well be advantages and disadvantages, and that different cultures are appropriate for different business environments.

Building on this work, and that of Amy Edmondson, we can understand that if we desire a culture that supports agility, we need to combine traits that support psychological safety at scale including sociability, openness, and risk without recrimination, while still optimizing for accountability towards a shared, common objective (Figure 13.3).

Combining both creates the culture and support systems for high-performing teams to thrive in a truly agile business.

Figure 13.3 Combining psychological safety and accountability

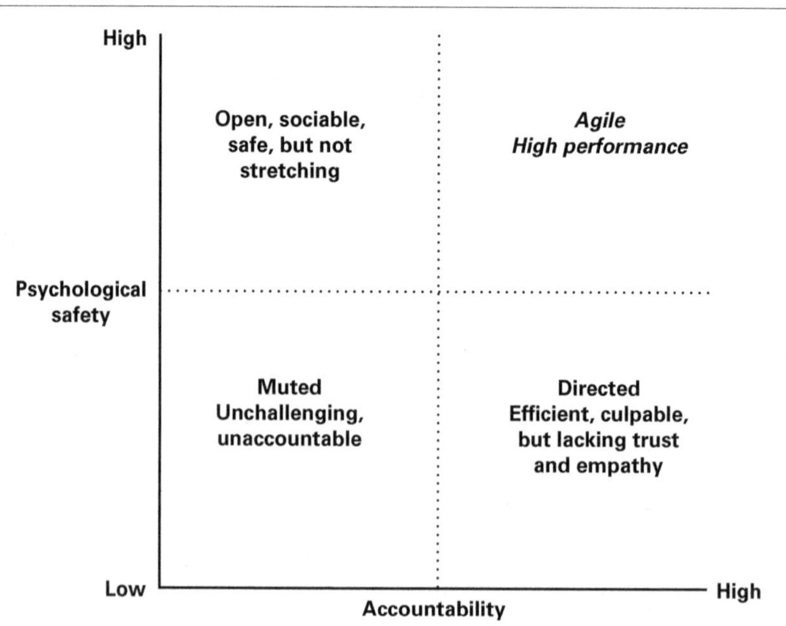

Creating the culture for real collaboration

Having established what is needed to build a culture that empowers high performance, we need to understand how at a team and intra-team level, we can empower true collaboration to enable us to move fast. It is very easy when we are trying to increase velocity as a business to over-focus on the process and under-focus on the environment that enables speed to happen. If it is a culture that is characterized by trust, which enables a greater degree of unity and autonomy then we are more likely to be able to progress at pace. There is less chance of misalignment through individual action, or micro-management, or unnecessary explanation, updates, reporting or supervision, which slows everything down.

Similarly, if it is a culture that embraces the kind of 'psychological safety' that we discussed earlier, one where staff feel like they can be their true selves in the workplace, and one that enables healthy debate, questioning and dissent, then there is less chance that we waste time with unnecessary company and team politics, which again slows everything down.

Figure 13.4 Building blocks of true collaboration

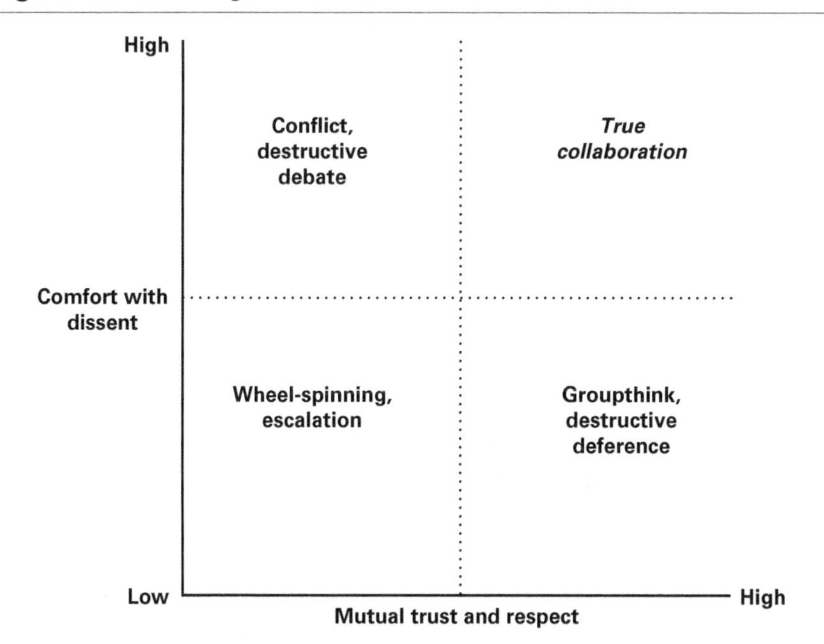

SOURCE Adapted from Ben Thompson, (July 2013) The Uncanny Valley of a Functional Organization, https://stratechery.com/2013/the-uncanny-valley-of-a-functional-organization/

Analyst Ben Thompson has described the building blocks of true collaboration as a combination of mutual trust and respect and comfort with dissent[16] (Figure 13.4). Ben makes the point that real collaboration, particularly cross-functional, is hard to achieve, and yet that is where the real value lies:

> *As much as we glorify the solitary coder or designer, the truth is that, especially in technology, breakthroughs are collaborative and iterative, borne of thousands of disagreements.*[17]

Not having the necessary cultural ingredients can lead to conflict or groupthink, so in order to truly start to break down functional silos we need to invest in enabling the kind of behaviours and cultural characteristics that empower real collaboration.

The importance of trust and 'productive informality'

When John Boyd derived his 'OODA loop' approach to military strategy, he emphasized how important trust is to the effective operation of the cycle. As his biographer, Robert Coram describes it, the commander and subordinate share a common outlook, trust being the force that binds the group together, giving the subordinate greater freedom of action:

> *They trust each other, and this trust is the glue that holds the apparently formless effort together. Trust emphasizes implicit over explicit communications. Trust is the unifying concept.*[18]

In the scenario of the battlefield, explicit communication is often simply not fast enough. In the same way, trust in the organization is essential for it to move fast. Overly formal or explicit language and behaviours can restrict, impede and slow progress. A common understanding of our direction and context combined with an environment of trust enables us to move fast.

Yet that combination needs to be actively created. Research by MIT Sloan and London Business School (based on a survey of 11,000 senior executives from more than 400 companies) demonstrates the weak link that often exists in companies between strategy and execution.[19] For the two to be aligned, a strategy must be clearly articulated and comprehensively understood. When the researchers asked people to list their company's top three to five priorities, only around half could list the same one priority (even with five tries), and only a third could list the top three. Even more surprisingly, the result was only slightly more than half for those who were *actually involved* in developing the strategy.

The research also found that execution in large organizations suffers from a lack of trust, which in turns leads to over-commitment. The findings showed that senior managers trust their colleagues to deliver all of the time less than 10 per cent of the time, the result being that senior managers end up doing the job themselves, stretching themselves and their teams too thin, letting their own commitments to other teams slip, and compounding the problem. This enduring issue results in 'passive commitments', duplication of effort, inefficiencies, and a failure to focus on or recall the firm's priorities. London Business School Teaching Fellow, Rebecca Homkes describes how it is often not ill-will that lead to cross-department commitments failing:

> *People are taking on huge volumes of work to ensure a job well done, but they also feel they cannot say 'no'. The tendency is to say 'yes', but then certain things just don't get done. That's when things start to break down.*[20]

When trust is inherent in a culture it enables not only velocity, but acceleration. Service design and innovation consultant Matt Edgar has described this as 'productive informality'.[21]

In high-performing teams, implicit rather than explicit communication is emphasized, teams are more unified in achieving a common goal, we need less forward planning, staff are collaborating as equals, and empowered with greater freedom of action. This becomes particularly important in the realm of customer-centric service design where the requirement is to tune in to potentially highly differentiated needs:

> *Productivity in service is infinitely variable. This means that optimizing for repeatable, well-known processes with narrow tolerance is actually the fastest way to leave value lying on the table... Only through continuous, informal communication can we discern and meet the full, diverse, messy, constantly shifting range of customer needs.*

The opposite scenario is characterized by non-inclusive working, late briefing or involvement, arbitrary timelines, and detailed and rigid requirements. When things go wrong the instinctive reaction is to impose a tighter rein, which simply serves to move you further away from the conditions that will most likely result in success. Instead, informality grows from trust, and trust is earned through delivery. And so there is a virtuous circle where service productivity builds trust, and that trust begets informality, which in turn enables faster, richer, continual learning that is critical for any service to be productive.

Read my user manual

Effective collaboration comes from the right environment, but also the right behaviours, and our ability to work well with diverse people. This becomes even more critical when we are working in small, multi-functional units. Whether the team is fixed or flexible, we need to understand how others like to work, not just our own preferences. When we work with people for the first time or when someone new is on-boarded it can take time to understand that person, but if we are moving at pace there is benefit in understanding that person and how they like to work as fast as possible. Ivar Kroghrud, co-founder of feedback management business Questback, advocates the idea of creating a one-page 'user-manual' to help others quickly grasp how best to work with you and to shorten the learning curve when building new teams, noting that if you want to get extraordinary results then you have to play to individual team members' strengths.[22]

Adam Bryant of *The New York Times*, built on this idea to develop a set of questions relevant to senior leaders (and others in the workplace) to help build their own user manual. These questions focus around them as individuals (such as: What are some honest, unfiltered things about you? What drives you nuts? What are your quirks? How can people earn an extra gold star with you? What qualities do you particularly value in people who work with you? What are some things that people might misunderstand about you that you should clarify?). But there are also questions relating to how you interact with others (including: How do you coach people to do their best work and develop their talents? What's the best way to communicate with you? What's the best way to convince you to do something? How do you like to give feedback? How do you like to get feedback?).[23]

It can take time to learn how best to collaborate with co-workers, but adopting simple and transparent hacks such as one-page user manuals to facilitate working at pace means that actually working at pace is far more likely to happen.

Notes

1 Michael Sahota (25 July 2012) An Agile Adoption and Transformation Survival Guide, Info Q, [Online] https://www.infoq.com/minibooks/agile-adoption-transformation [accessed 25 October 2016]

2 William E Schneider (1 March 1994) *Reengineering Alternative: A plan for making your current culture work*, Irwin Professional Publishing, ISBN-10 786301201 ISBN-13 978-0786301201

3 Jason Fried (13 May 2008) You Don't Create a Culture, Signal vs Noise, [Online] https://signalvnoise.com/posts/1022-you-dont-create-a-culture [accessed 25 October 2016]

4 Slack (13 January 2015) Building the Workplace We Want, Slack HQ.com, [Online] https://slackhq.com/building-the-workplace-we-want-31fff8d6ffe0#.bxtx8569m [accessed 25 October 2016]

5 Buffer, Buffer Monthly Reports, Buffer.com, [Online] https://open.buffer.com/category/transparency/buffer-monthly-reports/

6 Joel Gascoigne (19 December 2013) Introducing Open Salaries at Buffer: Our transparent formula and all individual salaries, [Online] https://open.buffer.com/introducing-open-salaries-at-buffer-including-our-transparent-formula-and-all-individual-salaries/ [accessed 25 October 2016]

7 Joel Gascoigne (21 September 2014) Why we have a core value of transparency at our startup, and why the reasons don't matter, [Online] http://joel.is/why-we-have-a-core-value-of-transparency-at-our-startup/ [accessed 25 October 2016]

8 John R Childress (1 December 2013) *Leverage: The CEO's guide to corporate culture*, Principia Associates, ISBN-10 957517971 ISBN-13 978-0957517974

9 Brian Chesky (20 April 2014) Don't Fuck Up the Culture, Medium, [Online] https://medium.com/@bchesky/dont-fuck-up-the-culture-597cde9ee9d4#.y9qukolei [accessed 25 October 2016]

10 Reed Hastings (1 August 2009) Netflix Culture – Freedom and Responsibility, Slideshare.net, [Online] http://www.slideshare.net/reed2001/culture-1798664 [accessed 25 October 2016]

11 Charles Duhigg (25 February 2016) What Google Learned From Its Quest to Build the Perfect Team, New York Times, [Online] http://www.nytimes.com/2016/02/28/magazine/what-google-learned-from-its-quest-to-build-the-perfect-team.html?_r=3 [accessed 25 October 2016]

12 Amy Edmondson (4 May 2014) Building a Psychologically Safe Workplace: Amy Edmondson at TEDxHGSE, YouTube, [Online] https://www.youtube.com/watch?v=LhoLuui9gX8 [accessed 25 October 2016]

13 Carnegie Mellon University (October 2010) New Study by Carnegie Mellon, MIT and Union College Shows Collective Intelligence Of Groups Exceeds Cognitive Abilities of Individual Group Members, Carnegie Mellon University, [Online] https://www.cmu.edu/news/archive/2010/October/oct1_collectiveintelligencestudy.shtml [accessed 25 October 2016]

14 Shana Lebowitz (20 November 2015) Google Considers This to Be the Most Critical Trait of Successful Teams, Business Insider, [Online] http://uk.businessinsider.com/amy-edmondson-on-psychological-safety-2015-11 [accessed 25 October 2016]

15 Rob Goffee and Gareth Jones (November 1996) What Holds the Modern Company Together?, Harvard Business Review, [Online] https://hbr.org/1996/11/what-holds-the-modern-company-together [accessed 25 October 2016]

16 Joe Turner (April 2016) The Building Blocks of Real Collaboration, Medium, [Online] https://medium.com/@joeturner/the-building-blocks-of-real-collaboration-450d1b115041#.xt7eoqk2t [accessed 25 October 2016]

17 Ben Thompson (16 July 2013) The Uncanny Valley of a Functional Organization, stratechery.com, [Online] https://stratechery.com/2013/the-uncanny-valley-of-a-functional-organization/ [accessed 25 October 2016]

18 Robert Coram (15 April 2004) *Boyd: The fighter pilot who changed the art of war,* Back Bay Books, Reprint edition, ISBN-13: 978-0316796880

19 London Business School (7 December 2015) Two Thirds of Senior Managers Can't Name Their Firms' Top Priorities, London Business School, [Online] https://www.london.edu/news-and-events/news/two-thirds-of-senior-managers-cant-name-their-firms-top-priorities [accessed 25 October 2016]

20 London Business School (7 December 2015) Two Thirds of Senior Managers Can't Name Their Firms' Top Priorities, London Business School, [Online] https://www.london.edu/news-and-events/news/two-thirds-of-senior-managers-cant-name-their-firms-top-priorities [accessed 25 October 2016]

21 Matt Edgar (July 2016) Put Down All Behaviour Hurtful to Informality!, [Online] https://blog.mattedgar.com/2016/02/07/put-down-all-behaviour-hurtful-to-informality/ [accessed 25 October 2016]

22 Adam Bryant (30 March 2013) Want to Know Me? Just Read My User Manual, New York Times, [Online] http://www.nytimes.com/2013/03/31/business/questbacks-lead-strategist-on-his-user-manual.html?_r=0 [accessed 25 October 2016]

23 Inc.com (1 January 2014) To Make Your Management Style Clear, Create a User's Manual, [Online] http://www.inc.com/the-build-network/to-make-your-management-style-clear-create-a-users-manual.html [accessed 25 October 2016]

A blueprint for flexibility: autonomy, mastery and purpose

14

Our massive employee engagement problem

One of the greatest and yet still relatively undiscussed global corporate productivity issues is the seemingly huge employee engagement problem. Gallup's 2013 State of the Global Workplace study[1] surveyed 230,000 workers from 142 countries. It found that only 13 per cent of workers feel engaged by their jobs (described as psychologically committed to their jobs, likely to be making positive contributions); 63 per cent are 'not engaged' (lack motivation, putting less effort in, especially discretionary effort towards organizational goals), and 24 per cent are 'actively disengaged' (unhappy, unproductive, liable to spread negativity). According to Gallup,[2] this translates roughly into 900 million not engaged and 340 million actively disengaged workers around the world. It is a bleak, disheartening picture.

Looking regionally, the United States and Canada have the highest proportion of engaged workers (at 29 per cent) but one of the interesting nuances to these figures was that when employee engagement is broken down by company size it reveals that a much larger proportion of employees who work in small companies (10 people or fewer) are engaged at work compared with those who work in larger companies. Gallup has estimated that actively disengaged employees cost the United States $450 billion to $550 billion in lost productivity per year.[3] Their research[4] shows that employee engagement is strongly connected to an organization's financial success, and business outcomes such as profitability, productivity and even customer engagement. Data from The State of the American Workplace report, for example, shows that:

> *... companies with 9.3 engaged employees for every actively disengaged employee in 2010–2011 experienced 147% higher earnings per share (EPS) on average in 2011–2012 compared with their competition.*[5]

The research found that over the same time period companies that had a lower average of 2.6 engaged employees for every actively disengaged employee experienced 2 per cent lower EPS compared with their competition. The exponential boost in earnings attributable to a higher engagement ratio, they conclude, is a competitive advantage that business leaders cannot afford to ignore.

Mapping strategy and culture to motivation

> *My old boss Jim Barksdale was fond of saying: 'We take care of the people, the products, and the profits – in that order'. It's a simple saying, but it's deep. 'Taking care of the people' is the most difficult of the three by far and if you don't do it, the other two won't matter. Taking care of the people means that your company is a good place to work. Most workplaces are far from good. As organizations grow large, important work can go unnoticed, the hardest workers can get passed over by the best politicians, and bureaucratic processes can choke out the creativity and remove all the joy.*
>
> Ben Horowitz[6]

Sometimes, large organizations seem almost uniquely designed to suck the motivation out of their staff. And yet, when it comes to agility and moving fast, motivation and engagement are absolutely key. In his book *Drive*,[7] Dan Pink makes a cogent, convincing and convention-challenging argument about the limitation of money in driving performance and satisfaction in the workplace, and how what really motivates us is autonomy (the ability to make decisions that can make a difference), mastery (how people can be rewarded for progress, and getting better and better at what they do), and purpose (working towards a vision or purpose that is important to us). Intuitively this makes sense, but this argument is supported by a plethora of academic studies and research.

Given how critical staff motivation is to organizational performance, it seems strange that in most companies, so few organizational constructs are focused around these principles. Yet they provide us with a compelling and effective way of framing how we can map organizational strategy, process, culture and structures to outputs in the agile business. The point being, again, that becoming more agile as an organization is not only about technology and processes, but also about the people and culture.

Autonomy

> *Knowledge workers have to manage themselves. They have to have autonomy.*
> Peter Drucker[8]

Where did it all go wrong? Data from the 2016 Edelman Trust Barometer, a global study with over 33,000 participants, demonstrates that one in three workers don't trust their employer, that trust decreases as you go down an organization's hierarchy (the proportion of staff who say they trust their organization at executive level is 64 per cent of executives, at manager level is 51 per cent of managers, and rank and file level is 48 per cent), and that for information on the company employees trust peers more than CEOs.[9] And yet, as we discussed earlier, trust is essential not only to effective collaboration but to moving fast. A true learning culture can only exist if employees are enabled with the right tools and processes, and then *trusted* to learn from their failures as well as their successes. Overly restrictive procedures and micro-management kills any chance of creating a culture of ownership and responsibility.

After flirting with a completely flat organization in 2002, Google realized that some degree of hierarchy in the company helped in prioritization, the communication of strategy, ensuring that processes were aligned with objectives, and facilitating inter and intra-team working. But they still kept that hierarchy to a minimum. Now they have only four visible, meaningful levels: individual contributor, manager, director and vice president. Rather than micro-managing, managers are focused on creating the right environment for great work and outputs. Beyond that, staff are given autonomy to fulfil objectives in the way that they believed would be most successful. A focus on outputs and results rather than inputs helps to keep teams on track and support this freedom.

When Amazon established their two-pizza team model, they structured in such a way to allow for focus through objective and direction, autonomy in prioritization and execution, and accountability through performance measures. Each one of those small teams was established with a 'fitness function', a key business metric agreed between the senior leadership and the team lead who gives the team focus. This autonomy enables greater entrepreneurialism, the opportunity for greater ownership and growth. The value in the organization is naturally oriented towards performance rather than presentation, great ideas and problem solving rather than managing upwards, expertise and capability rather than status or job title. To quote VC Ben Horowitz:

In well-run organizations people can focus on their work (as opposed to politics and bureaucratic procedures) and have confidence that if they get their work done, good things will happen both for the company and them personally. By contrast, in a poorly run organization, people spend much of their time fighting organizational boundaries and broken processes.[10]

Netflix believes that most companies naturally curtail freedom and autonomy as they scale. As organizational complexity increases, talent density decreases, heightening the need for over-burdensome process, which worsens the talent drain. In the short term the well-optimized, process-driven, efficient company may be successful but then it is unable to adapt quickly to context changes since process-adherence becomes what is valued, there are ever-fewer 'curious innovator-mavericks' introducing new thinking, and growing irrelevance ensues. CEO Reed Hastings:

Our model is to increase employee freedom as we grow, rather than to limit it, to continue to attract and nourish innovative people, so we have a better chance of long-term, continued success.[11]

Instead, Hastings advocates eliminating distracting process and rules, enabling a culture that values simplicity, and increasing talent density at a faster rate than growth in complexity. Creating an environment characterized by informal running and the freedom to make an impact but also a culture that celebrates self-discipline and high performance serves to maintain agility at scale but also attract the best talent.

This requires the right framework within which to bring autonomy alive. In Part Two we talked about how the high operational tempo that characterized *Blitzkrieg* enabled frontline commanders to have the freedom to respond quicker to shifting scenarios. *Schwerpunkt* (or the underlying goal, or intent) gave them the clarity of direction, but *Fingerspitzengefuhl* (or fingertip feel) allowed the flexibility to make rapid, intuitive decisions in the face of fluid situations. *This* is how autonomy empowers agility.

Netflix describe this as 'highly aligned' but 'loosely coupled'. The former means that the strategy and goals are clear, specific and broadly understood, but also that team interactions are focused on strategy and goals rather than just tactics. The investment in management time is in being transparent, articulate and perceptive. Being 'loosely coupled' means that cross-functional meetings are kept focused on strategy and goals. This requires a high level of trust on tactics and a low level of preview or approval between groups in order to facilitate moving fast, and leaders proactive in reaching out as needed for coordination and perspective, or doing 'post-mortems' to ensure alignment.

Frontline autonomy only works if we set the right guidelines, boundaries, direction and measures and then get out of the way. But it also needs us to be able to internalize the external. If employees (particularly digital-native talent) feel that they have out-of-work behaviour that is highly empowered by digital technologies and connections, yet conversely experience restrictive practices, technologies and expectations within the workplace they will not stick around for long. In fact they will probably leave and launch the next disruptive startup to attack your position in the market. As organizations, we need to pay attention to changes in consumer behaviour and norms around social behaviours and acceptance not only to produce better customer experiences but also better employee environments. We need to empower the people closest to the customers to make suggestions and be able to implement changes that benefit both customer and employee. Looking from the inside out means that we fall behind. It should be outside in.

Mastery

In the agile organization, mastery means empowering staff to not only learn and improve but also to visibly see the results of their learning. The role of data, in supporting data-driven decision-making but also tracking individual and team progress is central to this idea. In Part Three we looked at how using OKRs can tie execution to strategy and provide a universal framework for tracking objectives and performance. Making performance visible in real-time through dashboarding is also a powerful way to demonstrate impact and motivate improvement. As an example, the UK Government Digital Service have created public dashboards that show real-time performance across 803 services (just 541 of them account for 2.4 billion completed transactions per year at time of writing).[12]

A data-driven approach to employee performance and well-being has been championed by Laszlo Bock, long-time Head of People Operations at Google. Recognizing the paucity of data in the field of human resourcing, he initiated a long-term study involving thousands of Googlers in a bi-annual survey called 'gDNA'. Bock also established a team of people at Google, under Prasad Setty, focused on so-called 'People Analytics', who are entirely devoted to expanding a data-driven approach. Work by this team has already led Google to evolve its recruiting practices, downplaying the importance of college degrees in favour of 'intellectual humility' and other softer qualities (as discussed later in this Part).

Harvard Business School professor David Garvin has described how the People Analytics team launched a set of research questions which became Project Oxygen, another long-term research and training programme that seeks to identify, measure and improve key management behaviours.[13] Through the accumulation and analysis of multiple data points relating to management and employee effectiveness (including employee surveys, performance reviews, exit interviews, and interviews with high and low scoring managers), the team leading the programme were able to show that even small incremental improvements in manager effectiveness had significant impacts.

Google had expanded data-driven decision-making from its traditional areas of application (product development, marketing) into assessing the effectiveness of management itself. Unsurprisingly, there was a high degree of correlation between managers that scored high on quality scores, and the satisfaction of the employees in their teams. The team delved deeper into the data to identify specific traits exhibited by high-scoring managers, alighting on eight key behaviours. A good manager:

1. Is a good coach.
2. Empowers the team and does not micro-manage.
3. Expresses interest in and concern for team members' success and personal well-being.
4. Is productive and results-oriented.
5. Is a good communicator – listens and shares information.
6. Helps with career development.
7. Has a clear vision and strategy for the team.
8. Has key technical skills that help them advise the team.

These key behaviours, primarily focused on leaders of small or medium-sized teams, incorporated the kind of elements that might be thought of as classic good management techniques (including communication, team and individual development, autonomy and empowerment) but are ones that in reality are often neglected. It is also notable how softer qualities such as being a good coach, being engaged in employee well-being, and communication of team vision and strategy ranks higher than having specific technical skills.

The project has led to a quantifiable and wide-ranging improvement in management effectiveness scores over time, helped the company develop a common language and expectation around management, and impacted positively on employee perception of working at Google.

It is important that we recognize that mastery and autonomy go hand-in-hand. Laszlo Bock and his team have deliberately taken power and authority over employees at Google away from managers, meaning that decisions over recruitment, performance rating, salaries or awards are not the jurisdiction of one person, but a group of peers or a dedicated team. Younger employees (often grouped as 'millennials') increasingly desire both the freedom to make the key decisions that impact the area that they are responsible for, and the support to help them get there. One survey by Intelligence Group found that 72 per cent of 'millennials' want to be their own boss at work, and that 79 per cent wanted their superiors to act as coaches or mentors.[14] In this context, the old-style performance review, often conducted infrequently (and locked into an annual or bi-annual frequency) can do more harm than good. A succession of companies including Accenture, Deloitte, Microsoft and Adobe have moved away from these old-style reviews and replaced them with simpler, more focused evaluation processes that unfold incrementally throughout the year. When Deloitte conducted a review of their old-style performance review system it was discovered that the review cycle including administration, meetings and rating was consuming around 2 million hours a year (mostly in discussing the ratings rather than the actual performance).[15] In the context of more fluid, iterative working and embedded reflection time, there should be multiple opportunities for feedback. If there are not, you are not doing it right.

The antithesis of this is valuing upwards management over real measures of output. As Peter Thiel puts it:

> *In the most dysfunctional organizations, signaling that work is being done becomes a better strategy for career advancement than actually doing work (if this describes your company, you should quit now).*[16]

In addition to improving visibility of performance data through dashboarding, and more regular feedback, simple tools and hacks can facilitate better working in flatter, and more decentralized hierarchies. The system of 'Snippets' (originated at Google but now widely used in technology-driven and increasingly other businesses), involves staff writing down on e-mail what they have achieved in the past week, and what they are setting out to achieve in the coming one. This is compiled into a public forum and distributed as a transparent but simple way to ensure that employees take the time to reflect on progress and plans, and are more connected to their work. The 'Snippets' system (and others like it) create minimal time disruption but maximum transparency, helping to log progress and reduce internal politics.

Improved performance transparency through data, visible learning, embedded reflection, combined with the autonomy to move at pace: these are all elements that not only intuitively feel right, but drive exceptional performance.

Purpose

Much has been written about the importance of purpose to business and brands, but perhaps one of the most compelling arguments comes from Simon Sinek and his concept of the 'golden circle'. Sinek argues that people don't buy what you do, they buy *why* you do it.[17] If we consider the way in which the brain works, our neocortex deals with rational and analytical thought and language, and that aligns to the 'what'. But we ignore the 'why' at our peril since this speaks to the limbic brain, which has no capacity for language but is central to how we feel, behave and make decisions.

This is powerful not only in attracting customers but also talented employees. A compelling mission, cause or belief catalyses loyalty, alignment and motivation. People who want to make a difference in the world are attracted to organizations who themselves are setting out to achieve what no other company can do. Shared passion creates an imperative to do great work but also a great environment in which to do that work. As exceptional talent becomes more selective about where it wants to work, and employer brands become more transparent, organizations that do not have a compelling purpose will fail.

This clarity of purpose needs to run through the organization. Pixar, one of the most successful film businesses of all time, has a creative culture that relies on an interpretation of leadership firmly routed in vision and purpose. Ed Catmull, Pixar President, has said:

> *We say we are director led, which implies they make all the final decisions, [but] what it means to us is the director has to lead... and the way we can tell when they are not leading is if people say 'we are not following'.*[18]

Author Adam Grant has demonstrated why purpose is so powerful.[19] Working with employees of a university fundraising call-centre, he divided them into three groups: a control group; a group who read stories from other employees about the benefits of the job; and a group who read stories from students who had received a scholarship about how it had changed their lives. The first two groups saw no difference in performance. The third group however, grew their weekly pledges from 9 to 23 per week and their weekly fundraising by 143 per cent. Extending the study to see what would happen if another group of fundraisers actually met some recipients of scholarships, he found that the weekly fundraising for that group went up by 400 per cent. Creating a significance for the work beyond money, it seems, leads to far greater performance. Purpose brings meaning, and meaning brings connection.

Notes

1. Gallup, State of the Global Workplace, Gallup, [Online] http://www.gallup.com/services/178517/state-global-workplace.aspx [accessed 25 October 2016]
2. Gallup, Worldwide, 13% of Employees Are Engaged at Work, Gallup, [Online] http://www.gallup.com/poll/165269/worldwide-employees-engaged-work.aspx [accessed 25 October 2016]
3. Gallup, Worldwide, 13% of Employees Are Engaged at Work, Gallup, [Online] http://www.gallup.com/poll/165269/worldwide-employees-engaged-work.aspx [accessed 25 October 2016]
4. Gallup, FORTUNE 500 Employee Engagement Tools for Your Size Company, Gallup, [Online] https://q12.gallup.com/ [accessed 25 October 2016]
5. Gallup (11 June 2013) How to Tackle U.S. Employees' Stagnating Engagement, Gallup, [Online] http://www.gallup.com/businessjournal/162953/tackle-employees-stagnating-engagement.aspx [accessed 25 October 2016]
6. Ben Horowitz (24 April 2014) *The Hard Thing About Hard Things: Building a business when there are no easy answers*, Harper Business, ISBN-10 62273205 ISBN-13 978-0062273208
7. Daniel H Pink (13 January 2011) *Drive: The surprising truth about what motivates us*, Canongate Books, ISBN-10 184767769X ISBN-13 978-1847677693
8. Rick Wartzman (October 2014) What Peter Drucker Knew About 2020, Harvard Business Review, [Online] https://hbr.org/2014/10/what-peter-drucker-knew-about-2020 [accessed 25 October 2016]
9. Lydia Dishman, April 2016, Why Employees Don't Trust Their Leadership, Fast Company, [Online] https://www.fastcompany.com/3058630/why-employees-dont-trust-their-leadership [accessed 25 October 2016]

10 Ben Horowitz (24 April 2014) *The Hard Thing About Hard Things: Building a Business when there are no easy answers*, Harper Business, ISBN-10 62273205 ISBN-13 978-0062273208

11 Reed Hastings (1 August 2009) Netflix Culture – Freedom and Responsibility, Slideshare.net, [Online] http://www.slideshare.net/reed2001/culture-1798664 [accessed 25 October 2016]

12 Gov UK, https://www.gov.uk/performance

13 Harvard Business Review (December 2013) How Google Sold Its Engineers on Management, Harvard Business Review, [Online] https://hbr.org/2013/12/how-google-sold-its-engineers-on-management [accessed 25 October 2016]

14 Rob Asghar (13 January 2014) What Millennials Want in the Workplace (and Why You Should Start Giving it to Them), Forbes, [Online] http://www.forbes.com/sites/robasghar/2014/01/13/what-millennials-want-in-the-workplace-and-why-you-should-start-giving-it-to-them/#4564504f2fdf [accessed 25 October 2016]

15 Marcus Buckingham and Ashley Goodall (April 2015) Reinventing Performance Management, Harvard Business Review, [Online] https://hbr.org/2015/04/reinventing-performance-management [accessed 25 October 2016]

16 Peter Thiel and Blake Masters (16 September 2014) *Zero to One: Notes on startups, or how to build the future*, Virgin Digital, ASIN B00KHX0II4

17 Simon Sinek (September 2009) How Great Leaders Inspire Action, TED, [Online] https://www.ted.com/talks/simon_sinek_how_great_leaders_inspire_action?language=en [accessed 25 October 2016]

18 Scott Burkun (19 April 2010) Inside Pixar's Leadership, Scott Burkun, [Online] http://scottberkun.com/2010/inside-pixars-leadership/ [accessed 25 October 2016]

19 Adam Grant (April 2013) *Give and Take: A revolutionary approach to success*, Weidenfeld & Nicolson, ASIN B00CAUH7UE

Digital-native talent

15

Hiring smart

In *Good to Great*,[1] Jim Collins's research emphasized just what a difference finding the right people to fill the right positions in a company makes to that company's performance. This intuitively feels like something that should be obvious, and yet it is one of the hardest things to actually get right. Not least because of the (internal and external) pressure that often exists to fill an important position in a timely manner.

Collins found that one of the characteristics of the leaders of 'good to great' companies was that they kept searching for the right person if they were not categorically sure that the candidates in front of them were not absolutely right. They were also great at ensuring that they positioned their best employees in the optimum opportunities for growth in the business (rather than solving everyday problems). And they focused on character, ideals, values (that match those of the business), behaviour, work ethic as well as (and sometimes as a higher priority than) direct experience. In short, they valued people for who they were and not just what they could do for you, and demonstrated attributes themselves that they also looked for in others like a disciplined work ethic mixed with a sense of personal responsibility, of cultivating passion and an entrepreneurial spirit.

Earlier we discussed Eric Schmidt's concept of 'Smart Creatives', or the individuals who can combine technical knowledge, business expertise and creativity and really transform organizational capability ('when you put today's technology tools in their hands and give them lots of freedom, they can do amazing things, amazingly fast'). The empowerment of digital technologies is dramatically amplifying the potential of exceptional talent to make a difference to the business in which they work. In their research into star performers in 21st-century organizations, Herman Aguinis of the George Washington University and Ernest O'Boyle of the University of Iowa, argue that the nature of modern work has led to the emergence of a few individuals who contribute disproportionately to outputs: 'instead of a massive group of average performers dominating ... through sheer numbers, a small group of elite performers (dominate) through massive performance'.[2] Instead of following a normal distribution, individual performance follows an underlying power law distribution.

Yet the competition around exceptional digital talent is such that creating the environment in which such talent can thrive is essential, not a nice-to-have. As is taking the time and space to find them. Google front-load their people investment, spending an unusually high proportion of money and time on attracting, evaluating and cultivating new employees since they believe that talent is a major pressure ('Our greatest single constraint on growth has always, always been our ability to find great people.' Laszlo Bock).[3] Patrick Collison, founder of the (rapidly growing) payment technologies company Stripe has articulated how important it has been for them to take their time to make sure they hire the best talent. It was six months before they had hired their first two people, and another six months before they had hired the next few.[4] Peter Thiel talks about how recruitment is a core competency for any company and should never be outsourced.

When Laszlo Bock reviewed the outputs of Google's extensive employee research, he noted that school and college performance correlated poorly with predicting ultimate performance. Instead, Google have found that structured behavioural interviews involving a more consistent standard for assessing people is more useful than highly individualized interviews from different managers. Recruiting managers are encouraged to ask candidates to give examples of situations where they have solved difficult problems in the past. Such questions about direct experience enables better assessment of how candidates have reacted in a genuine situation as well as revealing good insight into what they consider to be difficult. While educational qualifications don't hurt, and while vertical or technical skills are important for a significant proportion of roles, the importance of softer skills is really emphasized:

> *For every job... the No. 1 thing we look for is general cognitive ability, and it's not I.Q. It's learning ability. It's the ability to process on the fly. It's the ability to pull together disparate bits of information.*

There is priority attributed to qualities such as ownership and humility, the latter in the context of intellectual humility, to be committed to a line or argument but then be willing to change their point of view when new data arises.

As well as intellectual humility, traditional forms of candidate selection often undervalue soft skills at the expense of direct experience. While the latter is, of course, important it is perhaps easier to quantify than softer skills such as articulation and persuasiveness and yet these latter attributes can mean the difference between an applicant who proves to be competent and one whose contribution is extraordinary. Staff who can effectively articulate complex digital concepts or ideas (particularly to non-digital specialists), and are persuasive in winning support from people (particularly those in other teams or departments) can be enormously valuable.

Culture fit, or how well a candidate's qualities align with the culture, purpose and values of the organization can be another difficult aspect to get right, and one that feels tricky to systematize. Yet it is a critical part of the hiring process for the digital-native business. As an example, Anurag Gupta, who runs data warehousing and database solutions at Amazon (Amazon Redshift and Amazon Aurora), talks about how half the interview time should focus on culture fit, and how essential it therefore is to have absolute clarity about what your company culture is, and what it is not.[5] Amazon have spent time defining their core leadership principles and have not only detailed them on their website but also thought about what those principles mean for every job at every level, and brought them to life through the language used in interviews, one-to-ones with existing staff, and in performance reviews.

The leadership principles include many qualities that we have discussed already such as customer obsession, ownership, thinking big, the ability to invent and simplify, a bias toward action, recruiting the best talent, relentlessly high standards, but also to have good instinct, and to be vocally self-critical when appropriate.[6]

The difference between good and great in talent has never been greater, nor more fundamental to organizational performance in a digitally empowered world.

Peacocks, penguins, and pie bakers

There are two kinds of people and organizations in the world: eaters and bakers. Eaters want a bigger slice of an existing pie; bakers want to make a bigger pie. Eaters think that if they win, you lose, and if you win, they lose. Bakers think that everyone can win with a bigger pie.

Guy Kawasaki[7]

We need more pie bakers in the world. To move fast we need people who can see the bigger picture, who embrace positive change as an opportunity, and are optimistic about their ability to change the world around them. But we also need to create an environment in which many different types of people can thrive. Complex problems require diversity to solve them, and solve them well. Author Scott Page has made a compelling case for how diversity supports not only better problem solving, but better predictive capability, defining four key diversity dimensions: diverse perspectives (how we represent or envision differently); diverse interpretations (how we classify); diverse heuristics (the ways in which we generate solutions); and diverse predictive models (how we extrapolate analysis or stories).[8]

Like the famed fable about *A Peacock in the Land of Penguins*,[9] we need to be able to celebrate and combine very different attributes. While the penguins are those who maintain order, and keep the system running, the peacocks are the mavericks who create the opportunity for innovative thinking and creative leaps forward. We need to celebrate non-conformism as much as we revere efficiency. We need both to flourish if we are to survive.

Redefining effective leadership for the digital age

During the research conducted for this book, one of the most interesting pieces of feedback came in the area of leadership, and notably on the value of softer skills. Traditional leadership characteristics such as having a strong commercial focus or being visionary, inspiring or clear-minded and action-oriented when it was needed were, of course, still seen as being important, but there was consistent feedback about the increasing value in 'softer' qualities such as curiosity, empathy, collaboration, creativity and adaptability.

This concurs with research from Wharton University which posits that leadership styles need to change in the context of the shift in business models, new sources of value and new types of relationship with suppliers, partners, customers that digital has enabled.[10] While more traditional 'command and control' leadership styles were still valid in some scenarios, leaders need to increasingly embrace the role of collaborator or co-creator. Where command and control assumes most of the key insights will come from the top of the organization, the modern reality is increasingly about an emphasis on ideas and insights from wherever, meaning that leaders need to draw on a wider range of leadership styles to reflect this broader set of value sources. As more business models rely on the creation of technology, or on so-called 'network orchestration' involving value being derived from more intangible assets such as relationships, leadership styles that prioritize collaboration or co-creation become more important.

IDEO founder Tim Brown has also argued that the traditional way in which we have thought about leadership as 'leading from the front' with someone at the top making all the decisions, is not the most effective way of unlocking the kind of creativity in an organization that is so crucial in an environment that dictates a need to constantly evolve. He frames the role of the leader as an explorer – someone who can set the direction but also ask the best questions. Modern, successful leadership, he says, is like a dance:

> *It's about the effective playing of a number of different leadership roles depending on the moment and the circumstances and having the skill to move between those stances as needs require.*[11]

In the digital age, effective leadership is increasingly not about telling people what to do, but more about inspiring, nurturing, persuading. It is less about directing, and more about empowerment, empathy and cultivation. It is less about control and more about setting the right context to enable great work. It is about having the determination and persistence to pursue a compelling vision, but having the humility to learn, and to know when to change direction. It is not about coercion, it is about bringing people on the journey with you.

Key takeouts

In this Part we have discussed how human-centred flexibility in culture, resourcing and behaviours can create the enabling factors and environment to catalyse real change and agility. Key takeouts include:

1. Pay attention to the balance between in-house and outsourced, central and local, and specialist and generalist resourcing, but above all maintain a heightened level of fluidity to enable responsiveness.
2. Use small multi-functional teams, working concurrently in iterative sprints, and co-located, in order to drive organizational momentum. Consider how to combine business, technical and creative skills, and utilize the power of self-organization to catalyse motivation and productivity but above all, keep the teams small.
3. Scale agility by focusing small, multi-functional units on key business or innovation challenges, and support the core team with collaborators and supporters. Recognize the need for pioneers, settlers and town planners, and pay particular attention to nurturing early stage concepts as they

come out of the innovation lab or digital team. Establish appropriate digital or change governance, perhaps through a 'digital board'.

4 Build the culture to move fast by promoting mutual trust and respect alongside comfort with dissent. Promote, recognize and exhibit behaviours that can nurture a digital-native culture. Encourage 'psychological safety' and 'productive informality' in the work environment to lead to high performance.

5 Build engagement, motivation and productivity through empowering autonomy, mastery and purpose.

6 Spend a disproportionate amount of focus and time on hiring the exceptional talent that can really make the difference.

7 Draw from a wider set of leadership qualities, and recognize the value in softer qualities in bringing people on the journey with you.

8 Celebrate the mavericks.

Notes

1 Jim Collins (4 October 2001) *Good to Great*, Random House Business, ISBN-10 712676090 ISBN-13 978-0712676090

2 Herman Aguinis and Ernest O'Boyle (May 2014) Star Performers in Twenty-First-Century Organizations, Research Gate, [Online] https://www.researchgate.net/publication/237438406_Star_Performers_in_Twenty-First-Century_Organizations [accessed 25 October 2016]

3 Laszlo Bock (7 April 2015) *Work Rules!: Insights from inside Google that will transform how you live and lead*, John Murray, ASIN B00NLHJKBE

4 Chris McCann (8 December 2015) 16 Lessons on Scaling from Eric Schmidt, Reid Hoffman, Marissa Mayer, Brian Chesky, Diane Greene, Jeff Weiner, and more, Medium, [Online] https://medium.com/cs183c-blitzscaling-class-collection/16-lessons-on-scaling-from-eric-schmidt-reid-hoffman-marissa-mayer-brian-chesky-diane-greene-3d6367e63a42#.4snhenedq [accessed 25 October 2016]

5 First Round, Mechanize Your Hiring Process to Make Better Decisions, First Round, [Online] http://firstround.com/review/Mechanize-Your-Hiring-Process-to-Make-Better-Decisions/ [accessed 25 October 2016]

6 John Rossman (2014) The Amazon Way: 14 leadership principles behind the world's most disruptive company, CreateSpace Publishing, [Online] https://pdf.k0nsl.org/C/Computer%20and%20Internet%20Collection/2015%20Computer%20and%20Internet%20Collection%20part%202/

CreateSpace%20Publishing%20The%20Amazon%20Way,%2014%20Leadership%20Principles%20Behind%20the%20World's%20Most%20Disruptive%20Company%20(2014).pdf [accessed 25 October 2016]

7 Guy Kawasaki (3 March 2011) *Enchantment: The art of changing hearts, minds and actions*, Portfolio Penguin, ASIN B004S26HB2

8 Scott E Page (11 August 2008) *The Difference: How the power of diversity creates better groups, firms, schools, and societies*, Princeton University Press, ASIN B003TFELFI

9 B J Gallagher Hateley and Warren H Schmidt (1 November 2001) *A Peacock in the Land of Penguins: A fable about creativity and courage*, Berrett-Koehler, ISBN-10 1576751732 ISBN-13 978-1576751732

10 Knowledge @ Wharton (6 February 2015) Is Your Leadership Style Right for the Digital Age?, Knowledge @ Wharton, [Online] http://knowledge.wharton.upenn.edu/article/the-right-leadership-style-for-the-digital-age/ [accessed 25 October 2016]

11 Diana Budds (May 2016) IDEO's CEO on How to Lead an Organization Creatively, Fastcompany, [Online] https://www.fastcodesign.com/3059787/ideos-ceo-on-how-to-lead-an-organization-creatively [accessed 25 October 2016]

PART FIVE
The transformation journey

True digital transformation is an enormously complex and manifold beast that is intertwined with a broad range of dependencies and factors. So there is no one definitive path to getting it right. Yet there are some useful ways of thinking about the process of transformation that we have collected here in our final Part. We are calling this Part 'The Transformation Journey' because that's exactly what it is – a journey. Change is a process, not an event.

The five dimensions of change

The journey to becoming a truly agile business is a multifaceted one involving a number of fundamental aspects. We can therefore frame this transformation in the context of five core dimensions:

1. **Personal:** the individual journey, the challenges, the ups and downs, the highs and lows.
2. **Principles:** reorienting around a new foundational organizing idea and vision, and mapping the values, behaviours and outcomes to that vision.
3. **Process:** the structure and process of change. The route into transformation, the key stages and progression of the journey.
4. **Practice:** change through behaviour, systematizing change.
5. **Pace:** the time dimension. The speed of change of component parts, and the tempo of the transformation process itself.

Dimension one: personal

The transformation leader and the 'hero's journey'

Digital transformation, like any change process, is hard. And it takes time. Potentially, a long time. Perhaps even years. Leading this change, therefore, can be a soul-crushing, thankless, morale-sapping, attritional task. But don't let us put you off. It can also be the most rewarding work you'll ever do. An unmissable opportunity to affect real change in a company. Visible change to the fundamental way in which that company works. Tangible benefits that can make the difference between whether that company prospers, or doesn't even survive.

It's an adventure. But it's not for everyone. The transformation leader needs to be optimistic, determined, and above all, resilient. People used to talk about the change management process in terms of the Kubler-Ross model for the '5 Stages of Grief' (Denial, Anger, Bargaining, Depression and Acceptance). The digital transformation leader will likely find that they need to deal with these reactions from many different sources and all at once. They may well face their own emotional 'hype cycle' (akin to the famous Gartner Hype Cycle) where initial excitement around the potential to make real, lasting change soon peaks in the face of the sheer challenge of trying to create change in the face of wearying inertia. But then, just when it seems to reach its most difficult point, a small success shows what's possible. And then another, and another. And hope, energy, momentum and motivation build until we're truly 'in the zone' (Figure P5.1).

So who are these heroes? It is critical, of course, that the impetus and support for digital transformation comes right from the very top of the organization. But more often it will be a Chief Digital Officer, Director of Transformation, or a dedicated board member who will be charged with leading the change process. These are leaders with energy, enthusiasm, a thick skin, resilience and a passion to make things better. They can keep focused on underlying needs rather than becoming distracted by the complexity and messiness that surrounds change, or the intrusive nature of the internal politics that that brings. They are the type of leader who can articulate a vision and then enthuse people to follow them on the journey to realizing it. They are not fazed by the fact that if they do their job well,

Figure P5.1 Digital transformation leader 'hype cycle'

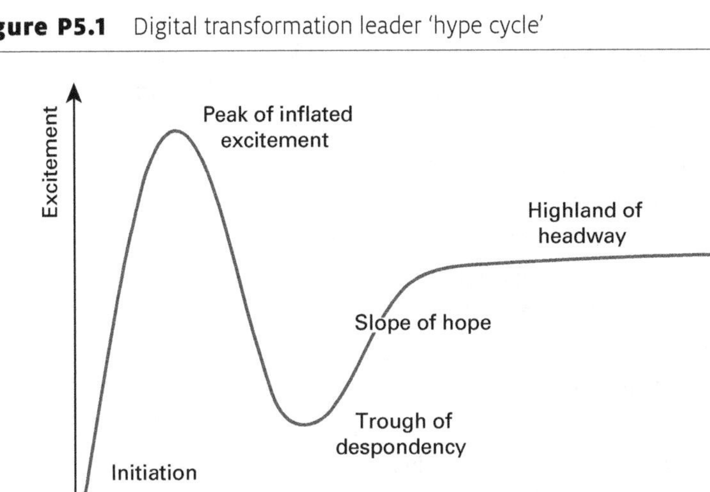

their job will eventually disappear as new practices, a new culture, a new organization takes shape and becomes the norm. Their job is essentially to make themselves redundant, but the knowledge and experience they'll gain is priceless.

Stories from the frontline

Eva Appelbaum, Partner Digital Talent @Work and former Head of Digital Marketing Transformation, BBC: The importance of resilience

Leading digital transformation is hard. It is challenging, and it is invigorating, but it is also extremely taxing. Looming over us is the fact that most transformation programmes fail. And this is the case even when the transformation entails moving from one known, fixed state to another. With digital, we have the added pressure of a future in constant flux and even the current state has not solidified enough to give us any certainties to make decisions off of.

So to lead digital transformation you either need to suspend all disbelief and jettison the organization towards a future 'you' see clearly, or, give in to the uncertainty and do your best to shepherd your businesses towards a hazy unknown. Either of these approaches require a leadership style and competencies that stretch way beyond technological know-how or commercial acumen.

Much has been said about digital leadership and the need to develop leaders who are more agile, curious, collaborative and so forth. Digital transformation in particular requires leaders who can lead with strong emotional intelligence, and who are as comfortable with uncertainty and intuition, as they are with data and process.

However, there is another side to leading transformation that is less spoken about, less acknowledged – and that is the personal resilience and strength it takes to hold these roles. Leading digital transformation means accepting a difficult, sometimes impossible mission. Stats tell you that it is unlikely you will deliver everything you set out to achieve. The business's expectations are often unrealistic to begin with. Sometimes you do not have enough resource, budget or buy-in to fully disrupt what needs to be disrupted. Other times the board has bought in too much, believing digital to be some sort of magic bullet, which will only disappoint in the end. Typically, you have no blueprint for change in your sector, as very few businesses are that far ahead of you on the journey. Your transformation vision is a mix of gut decision-making and peering into the proverbial crystal ball.

As a digital transformation leader you are simultaneously telling the story of change, running the agile programmes to drive change, leading your team, managing up, managing down, convincing some stakeholders that 'digital' IS in fact important, and convincing others that it is not going to solve everything, promoting innovation on one hand, while trying to stop too much investment in shiny but ineffective distractions on the other, all the while being seen as a potential threat to other ambitious leaders in the business.

And in the end, you will find that you have a very short life-cycle. Most transformational leaders come into a business with an aura around them, and for about six months, maybe a year, will be trusted as the champion of change with a Midas touch. It is in everyone's interest to believe in you. But by year two, the shine wears off, and by year three everyone is bored of your song and dance, and probably starts questioning what you have really delivered anyway. You start to look stale. Unfortunately, truly impactful digital transformation often takes a lot longer than three years! In order to keep the aura alive, to keep everyone on board the journey and evolve the narrative, transformational leaders have to expend a lot of their own personal energy over years keeping momentum going, telling and retelling a constantly evolving story, networking and keeping everyone on side. This can take a huge toll on the individual and it helps to have a strong balance outside of your working life to give you the reserves needed to persevere.

In the end, there is usually an in-built hard stop to your efforts. The point at which, if successful, you are able to integrate 'digital' into the businesses and effectively make yourself obsolete. And the hardest truth of all – the glory of your efforts often come after that point, and the kudos will go to others.

This is why the real differentiator for truly outstanding digital transformation leaders is personal and emotional resilience. People who thrive on this challenge and can take pleasure in the outcomes, despite the mission impossible.

Building a movement for change

How do we bring people on the journey with us? Once we have made the case for change and created the positive urgency needed to counteract the forces of inertia, we need the engagement of those who can make the change happen. There are several powerful tools we can use here:

1 **Work towards a *shared* vision.** The key word here is 'shared'. People are far more motivated to work towards a vision if they feel ownership in helping to shape what that end point is and how it is achieved. Framing the way forwards as a choice between two mutually exclusive options (perhaps as simple as the choice between doing nothing and taking decisive action) helps a broader constituency within the business feel as though they are part of a deliberate choice about where the business is going. An inclusive approach is far more likely to result in greater ownership and appropriate behaviour change than a diktat from the top. Even better if we can create a real movement for change by framing the choice as a genuine call to arms, an insurgency against the slide into irrelevance.

2 **Use the power of empathy.** This involves enabling stakeholders to see the world through the eyes of customers, to see the real pain points in current processes or approaches (customer journey mapping or other forms of immersion are excellent ways to do this). Design firm IDEO talk about 'Transformative Empathy', and how easy it is for key stakeholders in a business to become far removed from their customers, and difficult then for them to imagine how things could be different. Immersion in a

different perspective can free up thinking and gain alignment on the real problems that need to be solved.

3 **Make them look good, help them do their job better.** Everyone likes to do well, to be recognized for great work, or to find better ways to achieve objectives. Framing progress or projects in ways that enable people to understand how it will benefit them is a simple, but very powerful way to gain engagement.

4 **Use the power of advocacy.** Creating an expanding network of influencers and champions to spread new thinking through the organization helps build social proof, amplify influence and extend behaviour change. As an example of the power of wider employee digital advocacy Barclays Bank implemented a scheme called 'Digital Eagles' that created 20,000 staff champions who each volunteer their time to help explain technologies to other staff and to customers. Drawn from multiple functions, the eagles are responsible for championing the use of new technologies at a grassroots level but also running 'tea and teach' sessions designed to answer their customer's questions about digital. Hundreds of workshops have trained thousands of people over the course of the programme, creating a network of proponents for learning digital skills across the company. A partnership with the Young Rewired State organization has even seen the launch of 'tech accelerators' in over 1,500 branches in the UK. As the community has grown, so has the waiting list to become a Digital Eagle. For Barclays, they have gained not only a grassroots movement for empowering digital change, but new ways to identify talent and manage career development.

Leading a group of people who are creating real change within a much bigger organization can sometimes feel like leading an insurgency. As people, we have a strong instinct to belong to small groups defined by clear purpose and understanding, and if done in a positive way this tribalism can help build momentum. Tribe members support one another in an environment where respect and status comes from contribution value and outputs rather than job title or how many people you manage. Loyalty, shared purpose, strong bonds, and shared and individual accountability are all characteristics of belonging to a tribe. As Sebastian Junger has said:

> *Humans don't mind hardship, in fact they thrive on it; what they mind is not feeling necessary. Modern society has perfected the art of making people not feel necessary.*[1]

In his book on tribalism, Junger goes on to talk about how human beings have three basic needs to be content (with strong echoes of the autonomy, mastery and purpose that we discussed in Part Four): to feel competent at what they do; to feel authentic in their lives; and to feel connected to others. Work conducted by anthropologist Christopher Boehm has demonstrated that human groups have long been at their most productive and successful when there is an absence of arbitrary authority, and when moral behaviour stems from group pressure with good actions (like doing something for another person) being recognized and rewarded and bad behaviours (most notably a failure to share) being punished.[2] As Junger says:

> *The beauty and the tragedy of the modern world is that it eliminates many situations that require people to demonstrate a commitment to the collective good.*

We are wired to want to help one another. So organizational momentum has its foundations in a company's ability to be able to harness our fundamental need to share, feel connected, and work productively towards a common purpose with other people. Technology is the enabler.

Dealing with negativity

As we discussed earlier, leading change inevitably results in the need to face up to a not insignificant amount of negative reaction along the way. So it's as well to be prepared for what Dr John Gottman (Professor Emeritus of Psychology at the University of Washington) has identified as the 'four horsemen' – the four key reasons why work relationships fail:[3]

1. **Criticism:** while complaints focus on specific behaviour, criticism might attack the character of the person.
2. **Contempt:** open signs of disrespect, perhaps coming from an assumed or relative position of authority.
3. **Defensiveness:** often a form of self-protection.
4. **Stonewalling:** when one person closes off from the interaction.

Handled badly and in the wrong circumstances, these behaviours can serve to amplify each other, so while a degree of misunderstanding, conflict or negativity (particularly from those in the wider organization that are resistant to change) is inevitable, it's sensible to prepare strategies for dealing with it. While not necessarily feeling like the most natural thing to do, making efforts to empathize with the potential reasons for negativity can often help to diffuse conflict. We need to remove the language and behaviour of blame from situations as much as possible. Caroline Webb, in the excellent book *How To Have A Good Day: Harness the power of behavioural science to transform your working life*[4] tells how helpful it is to assume that you are a good person, but in bad circumstances or just having a bad day.

The motivation inherent in pursuing a shared vision, and the support that we can draw from the like-minded collaborators around us can go a long way to combating the negative impacts of conflict. But the work of creating a culture of appreciation, respect, constructive feedback, and healthy rather than negative dissent should never cease.

Dimension two: principles

The organizing idea

Our second dimension comes from the need in any change process to set out the vision and direction for change, and provide structure to how we can reorient the business around some foundational principles, values and behaviours. Our favourite framework for this comes from Steven Anderson (Future Kings Ltd) and Jonathan Lovatt-Young (Love Experience Ltd) who have built a one-page framework to encapsulate the key elements (the planks and the pillars) of an agile organizational strategy (Figure P5.2). The framework is useful in helping to orient the direction and activity of diverse teams working concurrently on multiple work streams, potentially across numerous initiatives and touchpoints, and motivate a tribe of change agents around a singular organizing idea and vision, providing a clear link with the strategy, execution and customer experience benefits that feed off from it.

Working from the top of the framework down:

1. **The Organizing Idea:** the overarching statement or principle which defines the fundamental orientation for the business. This is what drives the company at its most elemental level.
2. **Purpose:** a related purpose provides the reason that the company exists.
3. **Vision:** the longer-term view of the world we are building or contributing to. Although the strategy will come to life through the pillars we expand on below, it's also possible to capture an overarching strategic statement at this point.

These planks are supported by three sets of pillars that support and fulfil our vision, purpose and organizing thought. These are set out as key component blocks (captured as single words):

Figure P5.2 Organizing idea-driven experience framework

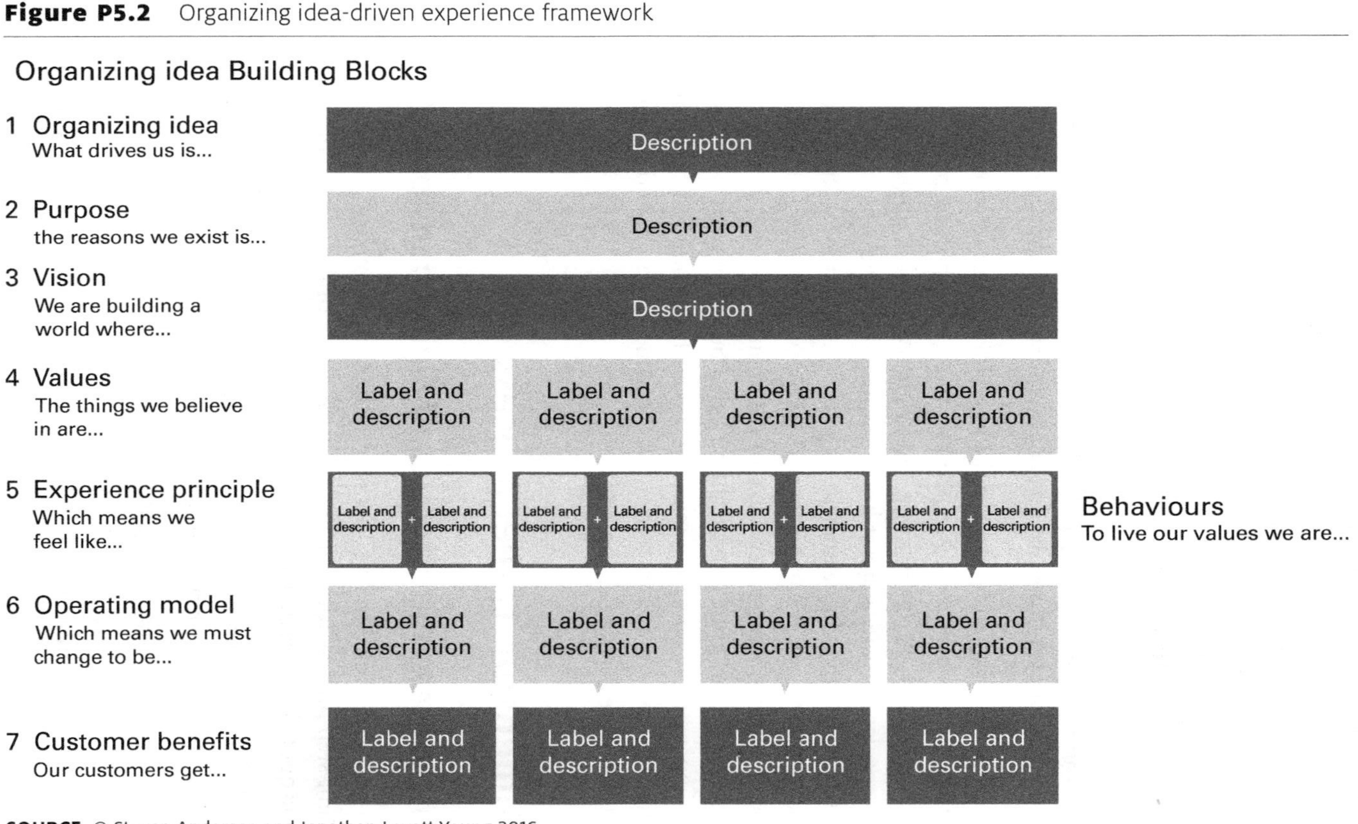

SOURCE © Steven Anderson and Jonathan Lovatt-Young 2016

4 **Values:** the things that the organization believes in.

5 **Experience principles and behaviours:** sets out what these values feel like as a customer experience and the behaviours by those in the organization who can bring these values to life (it's also possible to take these customer experience principles further to determine what functional user experience assets can really bring this to life).

6 **Operating model:** characterizes the change state that is required to fulfil these customer experience principles and related behaviours.

7 **Customer benefits:** defines the tangible benefits for the end user ensuring again that everything we do is brought back to customer need.

This framework can be used as the basis for a series of workshops that can draw out and inform the key planks and their supporting pillars.

The benefit of representing this framework on a single page is that it encapsulates in the simplest but most powerful form what the organization is setting out to achieve and the expected behaviours and customer benefits that support that. It can be circulated to new and existing employees as an uncomplicated, transparent way of communicating vision and expectation, rather than this critical information being buried in lengthy documentation or impenetrable company manuals. It can help align functional and small multi-disciplinary teams to head in the same direction, and provide a solid basis for greater ownership and autonomy.

Dimension three: process

The process and structure of digital transformation

In his 1996 book *Leading Change*,[5] John Kotter famously laid out a sensible eight-step process for change that became one of the most widely respected and quoted change management models. The eight steps were (to paraphrase):

1 Establish a sense of urgency: through analysis of market or competitive realities, major opportunities or crises and potential crises.

2 Form a powerful guiding coalition: establish a senior group who can lead the change.

3 Create a vision: to provide direction, and support that with a strategy for activation.

4 Communicate that vision: repeated communication, and setting an example via the guiding coalition.

5 Empower others to act on the vision: remove barriers, change systems and structures to prevent change being undermined.
6 Plan for and create short-term wins: recognition and reward of visible performance wins.
7 Consolidate improvements and keep the momentum for change moving: more systems change, hiring, reinvigorating with new projects.
8 Institutionalize the new approaches: visibly link new behaviours to corporate success, leadership development and succession.

In his 2014 follow-up book, *Accelerate*[6] (subtitled 'Building strategic agility for a faster-moving world'), Kotter updated the eight-step process in some key ways:

1 Where the 1996 version recommended responding to and generating episodic change in sequential and relatively rigid ways, the updated model suggested that the steps should be *run concurrently and continuously*.
2 Similarly, focusing on a linear progression characterized by doing one thing well at each stage before moving on is replaced with a *continuous search for, and activation of new opportunities*.
3 The idea of a small, guiding coalition in the old model is replaced with the idea of the engine for change coming from *a large, diverse 'volunteer army'*.
4 Where the old model recommended operating within the existing hierarchy, the new one proposed a *network-like function that could work in flexible and agile ways* in conjunction with the traditional hierarchy.

Kotter's updating of his model makes intuitive sense in the context of the fast-moving world in which we now operate. We should, after all, not take a waterfall approach to becoming more agile. But we still need a route into digital transformation, to be able to track progress against key elements of change, and there are some unique attributes to the process of digital transformation that enable us to augment existing thinking with the new.

Our framework builds on existing change management thinking to propose a more digital-native framework for change. One that utilizes much of what we have discussed so far in this book. The key to digital transformation is about generating velocity (and momentum), and combining that with the adroit application of focus (vision, strategy, execution), and the environment and culture that enables change to happen. The new reality, as Kotter's update suggests, is that this will not be a linear, waterfall process. As we work to become more agile we need to *be* agile in iterating and adapting the process to respond to ever-shifting contexts. We need to move away from a linear transition model to one where we can run multiple elements concurrently. We need to move on from the idea that this is a story with a beginning, middle and an end. It is, instead, an evolution to a new form of organization that is in a continuous state of organizational flex and flow.

Our model, the Agile Spiral (Figure P5.3) comprises three foundational components:

1 **Situation and Story:** creating the reason and impetus for change. We need to fully appreciate the new contexts that shape the world we now exist in (competitive, customer and company), where we are now and how we need to respond to these challenges. Then, we need to set out our new vision and direction, and the elemental components that can get us there. Storytelling is critical to any transformation process, not least in bringing people on the journey with us, so how we conceive, craft and tell our story is fundamental to success. The key parts to this story are therefore:

   a **Redefine:** to understand and define why the world has changed forever. Show how the new world will result in winners and losers, why fundamental change is necessary, and what happens if we do nothing.

   b **Visualize:** to visualize the promised land, frame the choice open to us, define and bring to life your organizing thought, related purpose and vision for reaching the promised land.

   c **Map:** to set out the component elements of change, define approaches to data, technology, structures, process, culture. Show how they can overcome obstacles to progress, and how the company can make the change come true. Map the dependencies that will enable success.

2 **Energize and Enable:** having crafted the vision and the story for change, we need to not just execute, but energize the drivers of change, marshal resource, remove barriers, build momentum and amplify positives. We need to prioritize and reprioritize to bring focus and give direction to the momentum. The essential ingredients here include:

   a **Communicate:** Find the most compelling way to tell the story – tell it, tell it again, never tire of telling it. Live it through behaviour, expectation and the questions you ask everyday.

   b **Lead:** Leading the insurgency – the transformation leader, the support and involvement of the senior leadership team, ongoing communication and support through the digital board, removing barriers to progress.

   c **Focus:** Gather the insurgents – centralize resource and initiatives (digital centre of excellence, innovation hub, catalyst brand) to bring focus

Figure P5.3 The Agile Spiral

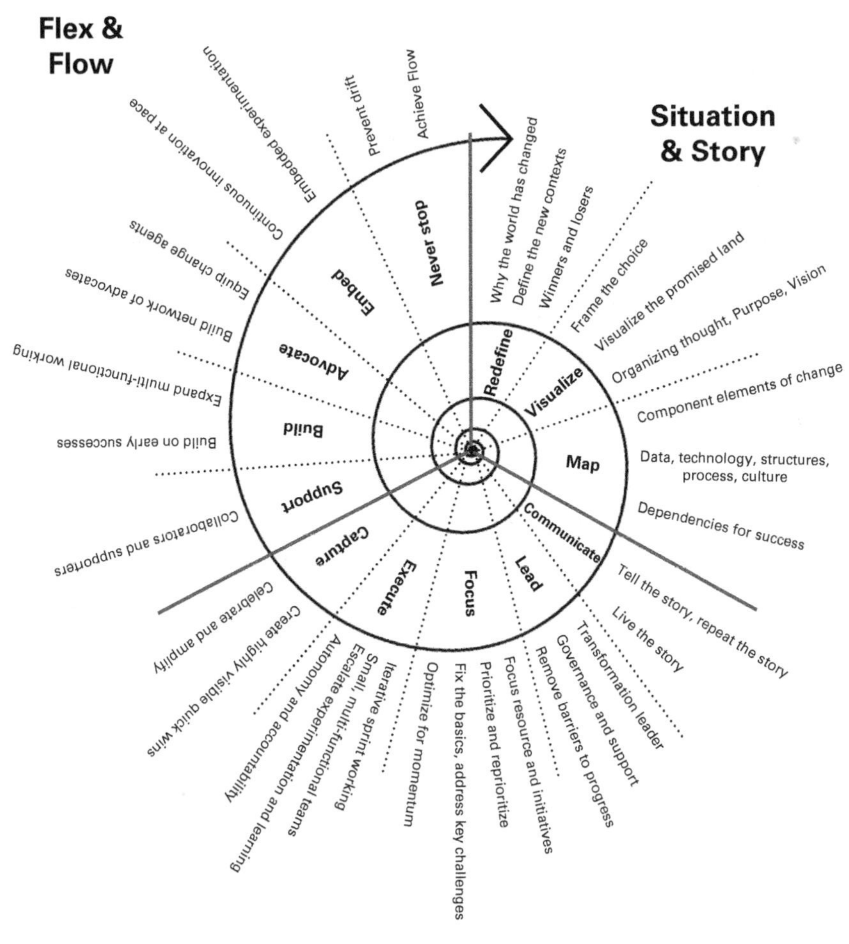

and catalyse change. Prioritize and reprioritize – fix the basics, continuously track performance and progress, but optimize for momentum (the biggest impact first) to address key business challenges and continuously search for new opportunity.

d **Execute:** Work iteratively in small, multi-functional teams to escalate experimentation and learning and build momentum. Nurture new cultures and ways of working through translator roles, by empowering autonomy and encouraging psychological safety and accountability.

e **Capture:** Create some highly visible quick wins to create the space to grow, and celebrate and amplify those wins.

3 Flex and Flow:

a **Support:** Support with a network of supporters and collaborators (agile team onions).

b **Build:** Build on early successes. Expand small, multi-functional, pod-working beyond the innovation/digital area, into functions or to address key business challenges.

c **Advocate:** Create as many advocates and champions for the new ways of working as possible – use them as an insurgent army of change agents, equip them with the tools and stories to spread change.

d **Embed:** Embed constant experimentation into resourcing.

e **Never stop:** Never stop working to resist inertia and drift, or to nourish agility and the culture of collaboration that empowers it to achieve organizational flow.

Dimension four: practice

Change through behaviour

Dr B J Fogg (founder of the Persuasive Tech Lab at Stanford University) has defined long-term behaviour change as coming from three key sources: an epiphany; a change of context; and the cumulative impact of tiny habits over time.[7] Framing the context for change, the new reality, and the new vision for addressing that reality in the ways that we discussed earlier can lead to the realization of the need to shift direction. We can change the context around decision-making, processes, structures, expectation and environment in the ways that we have also discussed at length throughout the process of change. But it is the everyday behaviours and the culture that supports and surrounds them that will ensure lasting, embedded change. Fogg also says that behaviour comes from the combination of three elements at the same time: the trigger, motivation and ability. If one of these elements is missing, then a behaviour doesn't occur.[8] This being the case, to encourage new behaviours we need to ensure that the motivation and ability to respond to triggers in a different way is present. In other words we need to create the reason for people to respond differently, and equip them with the capability to do so.

Real transformation comes from bringing a compelling long-term vision to life through everyday approaches, defaults and behaviours. In order to truly change behaviour we need a deliberate shift in the conscious choices that we make, but also shifts in the habitual behaviours, decisions and routines that shape much of corporate life.

Remaking organizational habits

All our life is but a mass of habits.

William James

Old habits die hard, or so the phrase goes. The behaviours we repeat are imprinted as patterns in our neural pathways, unconscious routines that we regularly follow. The more we repeat a process the stronger the link between the context and the action becomes, so increasing automatic behaviour. Organizations are comprised of people and so just as people develop habits over time, so might companies. These might be habits of thinking (like the kind of 'toxic assumptions' we described earlier in the book), or habits of doing. If a habit is an acquired behaviour pattern that is followed until it becomes almost involuntary or automatic, then an organizational habit is a customary practice or an inveterate response to a stimulus that is often accepted, unthinking, deep-rooted. Transforming an organization means that we not only have to be aware of what these organizational habits are, but also how powerful they can be in resisting and also enabling change.

In his book on *The Power of Habit*,[9] Charles Duhigg talks about just how powerful habits can be in shaping behaviour. A study by researchers David Neal, Wendy Wood and Jeffrey Quinn at Duke University,[10] for example, estimated that habits, rather than conscious decision-making, shape up to 45 per cent of the choices we make every day. The best way of changing a habit or ridding ourselves of a bad one, says Duhigg, is to replace it with another habit. This involves recognizing three things:

1. The cues that trigger the start of the habit.
2. The action you take.
3. The benefit you get from doing it.

Breaking it down like this helps us to understand that habits are comprised of several different elements, each of which might be challenged and changed. The cues, routines and rewards that comprise the habits that people acquire enable us to interrogate their origins and what bolsters them. Cues trigger an action, a reward reinforces it, a routine develops. Understanding this in the context of both personal habits as well as organizational habits gives a far greater opportunity to reform habits, and in the context of digital transformation, make habits our friend rather than our enemy.

With cues, says Duhigg, at the moment we feel the urge for the habit we want to change, we need to ask ourselves questions around our situation (Where are we? What just happened? Who else is involved? What did we just do? What emotion are we feeling?) that will help us identify the most commonly occurring cue.

With rewards, we need to understand the need that the habit is satisfying (for example, is it our need for status? Or ego? Or gratification or some kind?). Once the reward has been identified we can test that diagnosis by substituting another reward or experiment further with other rewards until we have found the correct one.

Having identified the cue and the reward, we can then change the habit by inserting a new routine.[11] This new activity can then still be triggered by the old cue, and deliver the same old reward. Duhigg suggests writing a plan for change along the lines of: 'When (*insert cue*), I will (*insert new routine*), because it provides me with (*insert reward*)'.

When bringing change to a company, we therefore need not only to be aware of what organizational habits have developed that support and reinforce outdated ways of working, but what the cues and rewards are that are associated with that routine. We must identify the times when old routines are no longer appropriate or are even falling apart (perhaps due to a crisis of some kind) and utilize that opportunity to bring in a new routine.

We must also focus on what Duhigg calls 'Keystone Habits', the particularly significant behaviours that can act to create a culture within a company and 'unlock all these other patterns in someone's life or in an organization'. Such keystone habits are more important than others since they can start a chain reaction, shifting other habits as they change, and starting a process that over time can transform a far wider set of behaviours. In order to identify keystone habits, Duhigg suggests focusing on the three key characteristics that they all share:

1. Keystone habits create small wins, are places from where momentum can build, and are typically characterized by giving you lots of small senses of victory.
2. They also create new platforms or a new basis from which other habits can emerge (they serve as 'the soil from which other habits can grow').
3. They change our sense of what is possible, or give us confidence, and so establish a culture where an attribute or virtue (like change, or perseverance or excellence) seemingly becomes contagious.[12]

Duhigg uses the Aluminium Company of America (Alcoa) as an example of a company that transformed through a focus on keystone habits.[13] As a newly installed CEO, Paul O'Neill was expected by analysts to focus directly on worker relations (15,000 workers had recently gone on strike), efficiency drives, margins and profits, or new markets. Instead, O'Neill surprised everyone by announcing that his top priority was going to be worker safety, and that his mission was to make Alcoa the safest company in the United States with a record of zero employee injuries.

Despite analyst scepticism, this focus on how better practices and habits could improve employee safety catalysed a whole series of improvements meaning that Alcoa became a far more efficient and profitable business. Within a year, profits had hit a record high, and over the next 13 years of O'Neill's tenure, Alcoa's market capitalization rose by US$27 billion and its net income rose to become five times larger than it was when O'Neill took over. It turns out that the focus on worker safety engendered an environment characterized by greater employee trust and more open communication of ideas, which led to significant improvements in efficiency. Focusing on worker safety as a keystone habit had catalysed a positive change to the culture of the entire company.

So, what might be the keystone habits in your organization? The answer will likely be different in different organizations, but when thinking about digital transformation the keystone habits that matter will likely be those behaviours and approaches that are fundamental to the day-to-day operations of the business, yet can also catalyse new ways of working across a broad spectrum of functions and roles. Perhaps that might be how the organization uses data in its everyday operations, or behaviours around openness and transparency, or approaches towards risk and experimentation. Whatever keystone habit is identified as sufficiently broad-based yet impactful, it is critical that the subsequent strategic focus must be brought to life in the very fabric of what the organization does every day.

Developing systematic change

As we've said earlier in this book, change is a process, not an event. That means that in order to embed long-term and impactful change, targets are not enough. Change needs to be systematic. In *How To Fail at Almost Everything and Still Win Big*[14] Scott Adams (the creator of Dilbert) defines this difference as:

> *If you do something every day, it's a system. If you're waiting to achieve it someday in the future, it's a goal.*

If a goal is a target that you set to achieve at some point in the future, a system is a change in behaviour, a way of continually looking for better options or creating the right habits to build towards success. Systems, says Adams, are ultimately more powerful than goals:

> *Goal-oriented people exist in a state of continuous pre-success failure at best, and permanent failure at worst if things never work out. Systems people succeed every time they apply their systems, in the sense that they did what they intended to do. The goals people are fighting the feeling of discouragement at each turn. The systems people are feeling good every time they apply their system. That's a big difference in terms of maintaining your personal energy in the right direction.*

This can make a significant difference in keeping energy and momentum going in the right direction. Adams gives a few examples to make his point, a simple one being setting a goal to lose weight (something that may be difficult to maintain motivation for) as compared with learning a systematic way to eat better (and substituting willpower for knowledge).

Companies love setting goals. They are nice and tangible, give a good sense of direction, and can give clarity on what targets to achieve and where activity should be directed. The classic scenario of a CEO announcing a new strategic direction, and a new set of targets to facilitate the new strategy, plays out often. What businesses are much less adept at doing, however, is developing systems that will enable change to happen. The trouble with isolated goals is that unless there is more fundamental change in behaviours, processes, skills and incentives, those goals will likely never be achieved. In this scenario, not only will the change effort fail, but also staff may well become demotivated, and even lose trust in the ability of senior management to lead change. Changing everyday behaviour, orientation and defaults are fundamental ways to systematize change and create lasting transformation. So while goals are good, finding ways to change, recognize and reward behaviours to create a new system is better.

Think, feel, know

> *The definition of insanity is doing the same thing over and over again, but expecting different results.*
>
> Albert Einstein

A key way to think about changing everyday behaviour is to consider the factors that shape it. Author Clive Hyland has written about a simple behavioural model (expanding on a coaching framework originally created by Darren Shirlaw)[15] based on three key structures of the brain, and the way in which it works in order to represent how our everyday behaviour (in relationships, team working and leadership) is shaped:[16]

1 **Think:** from the cortex (the grey outer mass of the brain). This is the domain of logic, reason and rational processing. The domain of self-awareness, sense-making, the rules of social engagement.
2 **Feel:** from the limbic region (in the middle of the brain). This is the domain of the senses, emotions, relationships, connections with others, and is most closely linked to the heart. It is about the personal, the subjective, the desire to bond and to form groups.
3 **Know:** from the basal region of the brain (just above the spinal column). This is the domain of instinct, intuition, 'gut feel'. The so-called 'reptilian brain'.

Each of these areas of the brain wields its own type of influence over our behaviour, and particular types of response may become more dominant over time, notably in response to specific circumstances. The thinking style, for example, might elicit the need for structure, logical argument and clarity of thought or method. The feeling style may make decisions based more on emotive reasons, or be influenced more by close associates. They may be more immediate, perceptive, creative. The knowing style are more intuitive, using 'gut feel' to inform decisions, and keen to get things done without distraction.

This is useful is a number of ways. It can be helpful in understanding the reasons behind certain behaviours, or empathizing with where people are coming from. It can be advantageous to consider how a great team will naturally need a combination of styles drawn from all three areas, and how different people in the team might map to different roles, and combine to greater effect. As Clive Hyland says:

> *... if people are developed in the right cultural environment they will inspire and energize one another to higher levels of achievement...*

It can also be fruitful as a way to understand how best to connect with and engage others in order to bring them on the journey with us. And it is useful as a way to understand how we might map new behaviours to particular styles, and therefore inform what levers we need to pull in order to affect behaviour change.

Dimension five: pace

Our fifth dimension draws in the key dimension of time, notably in enabling us to understand the varying tempo inherent to different elements of change, and to better manage the pace of the change process itself.

Managing the pace of transformation: pace layering

It's important to recognize that along the transformation journey, not everything changes at the same pace. Writer Stewart Brand expounded the concept of pace layering in his book *The Clock of the Long Now*.[17] Pace layering sets out six layers that function and evolve simultaneously at different speeds within society. From fastest to slowest: fashion; commerce; infrastructure; governance; culture; nature. In 2012, Gartner then used pace layering as a way to describe the different layers of an organizational technology and application strategy. From fastest to slowest: systems of innovation (characterized by experimentation); systems of differentiation (supporting processes that are different from competitors); systems of record (supporting core processes which may not be unique).[18]

In the same way, there will be layers and elements of the digital transformation process that will develop and evolve at different timescales. Broadly, from fastest to slowest: while there will be fundamental customer needs that do not change, or that develop very slowly, it is likely that we will need to respond to rapidly shifting customer interaction on a continuous basis; similarly while there will be basic approaches and procedures that will remain essential and consistent, it is also likely that we will need to adapt tactics, processes and workflow rapidly to respond to shifting requirements; as we've discussed earlier, resources need to be fluid and adaptive, so may change but will likely need to be modified at a slower pace than the practices and execution that they enable; our overarching strategy and governance is also adaptive, but changes more slowly than the tactics that they inform and oversee; our vision may adapt but should remain relatively settled and anchored; and lastly while we can take steps to begin cultural change at the earliest opportunity, this takes the longest time to transform.

A pace-layered approach to digital transformation might, therefore, look like Figure P5.4.

Figure P5.4 A pace-layered approach to digital transformation

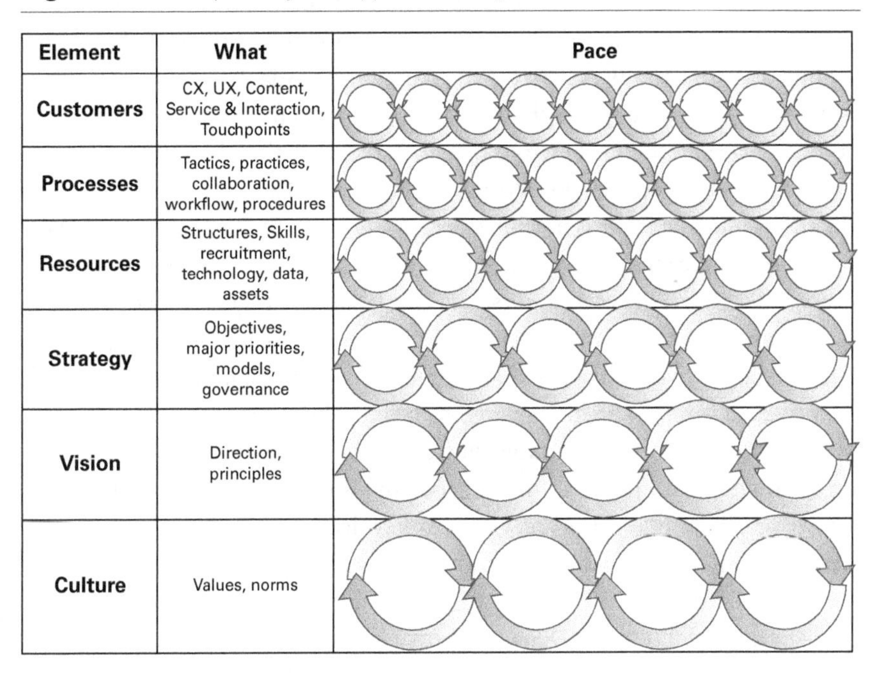

Element	What	Pace
Customers	CX, UX, Content, Service & Interaction, Touchpoints	
Processes	Tactics, practices, collaboration, workflow, procedures	
Resources	Structures, Skills, recruitment, technology, data, assets	
Strategy	Objectives, major priorities, models, governance	
Vision	Direction, principles	
Culture	Values, norms	

The productive zone: the balance between comfort and urgency

Dr Ronald Heifetz of the Center For Public Leadership at Harvard University has delineated a clear differentiation (in his book *Practice of Adaptive Leadership*)[19] between what he calls 'technical change' and 'adaptive change'. Broadly speaking, he describes technical change as the type of change that addresses more tangible things such as products, procedures or processes, whereas adaptive change is that which is more concerned with less tangible human aspects such as attitudes, thinking, beliefs, values and behavioural change.[20]

Adaptive challenges, he says, have a different timeframe to technical problems. The latter might cause a high level of disturbance that will then trigger an organizational response, but since the organization is typically already well equipped with relevant knowledge, cultural assumptions and capability to deal with such a challenge, a solution may quickly be found.

Adaptive challenges are different. Instead of being problems that might be solved rapidly with existing expertise, they require ongoing experimentation, learning, behavioural and attitudinal change from multiple parts of the organization.

Heifetz argues that we are often quite poor at distinguishing the difference between these two types of change, and yet the response required is very different. Technical change is focused on fixes to simpler problems that do not require a change to the system in which they exist. Adaptive change, however, is about more fundamental shifts to the system or environment in which the company operates, and therefore demands different thinking, the learning of new skills, and more disruptive forms of innovation. The former helps maintain the status quo, the latter is much harder to achieve since people are much more ready to embrace technical change than they are the more elemental adaptive change. Making changes to the system is something that the system itself resists.

Our argument in this book has been that businesses are increasingly facing complex, adaptive challenges that require far deeper change than the quick, easy fixes that might be more suited to technical challenges. In this scenario, staff will need to feel comfortable with a certain degree of ambiguity and have an ongoing commitment to the longer-term vision, which dictates that while clarity and communication of vision is key, leadership might well be more about asking the right questions rather than providing the final solution.

A key challenge of 'adaptive leadership', as Heifetz calls it, is to help staff to distinguish what from the past is worth building on, and what needs to be discarded. In this sense, he says, successful adaptations are 'both conservative and progressive'. As they help people to navigate through a period of potentially significant disturbance, the adaptive leader needs to be patient and persistent, determined and resilient in order to prevent the system from slipping back into its old ways.

Heifetz describes the 'productive zone of disequilibrium', whereby the focus and pressure is high enough to create forward momentum and engagement, but not so high that it creates unmanageable levels of pressure that might lead to unhappiness, chaos or the wrong kind of disruption. Building on this idea, the secret of managing effective transformation is working within these boundaries. We need to create sufficient ferment, positive restlessness and impetus to move beyond complacency and comfort zones, and to break the forces of inertia. Not reaching this threshold will mean that transformation efforts will be stifled before they have even begun. But moving beyond the limits of tolerance may result in breaking key components of the business needed to ensure positive outcomes (Figure P5.5).

Our job, in leading transformation is to stay within the 'productive transformation zone'. At the boundaries of this zone will be signals that we have either not gone far enough to create movement and momentum, or that we are starting to break things. The signs that you haven't reached the threshold for change are likely to be:

Figure P5.5 The productive zone of disequilibrium

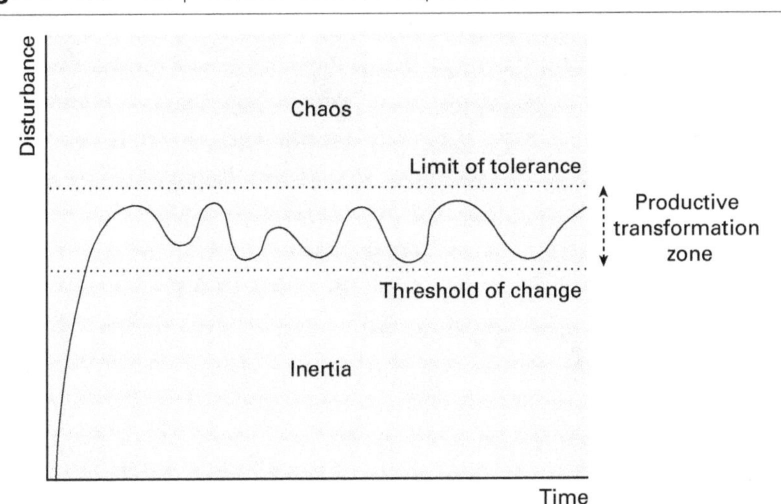

SOURCE: Adapted from: Mobilizing Adaptive Work: Beyond Visionary Leadership, Dr Ronald Heifetz with Donald L Laurie, in Jay A Conger, Gretchen M Spreitzer and Edward E Lawler III, *The Leader's Change Handbook* (San Francisco: Jossey-Bass, 1999), pp. 55-87

1. **Behaviour** – no visible changes to behaviour, no ownership for change.
2. **Inertia** – change too slow, old relationship capital still dominates.
3. **Drift** – the business starts to drift immediately back to the old ways of doing things.
4. **Innovation** – marginal improvements rather than breakthrough innovation, no change to rate of innovation/experimentation.
5. **Complacency** – people still within their comfort zone, not exhibiting changed behaviour or priorities.

The signs that you're exceeding the limit of tolerance are likely to be:

1. **Morale** – dispirited workforce, lack of belief in leadership.
2. **Performance** – lack of attention to the core business, outputs suffer, performance declines rapidly.
3. **Behaviour** – becomes overly pressured, unpredictable, or characterized by unwanted shortcuts.
4. **Talent** – the most talented people start to leave, challenges in retaining the best staff.
5. **Focus and governance** – unfocused or poorly thought through innovation initiatives, disjointed focus, breakdown in governance processes and structures.

The workings of an organization, says Heifetz, can be like dancing on a dance floor. When you're busy dancing you only really notice what is immediately around you, but the adaptive leader needs to periodically 'get on the balcony' to see the wider picture of what's happening, and gain a true perspective in order to avoid applying technical solutions to adaptive challenges. This is also true of digital transformation. Every now and then we need to take a step back to look for the signals that can tell us whether we are still in the productive zone of transformation or not.

Staying agile

The danger of drift

Once we have begun to create real momentum for change the work, of course, does not stop there. A company that does not keep pushing the drivers for change will lose momentum in the same way that a car that runs out of petrol will coast to a stop. As we mentioned in Part One of this book, this is not a transformation with a beginning, middle and an end, it is journey to becoming a new type of organization that is characterized itself by continuous change, fluidity and rapid adaptation. Losing momentum in the renewal process means losing performance, position and advantage.

Analysis by Boston Consulting Group found that 75 per cent of transformation efforts ultimately fail (only 25 per cent having outperformed in the long term).[21] Their research indicated two common trajectories whereby a period of short-term recovery (typically following an initial streamlining process to reduce inefficiencies) was followed either by long-term slow decline or less commonly by long-term reinvigoration of growth and performance. Which 'chapter two' trajectory (following the 'chapter one' efficiency drive) a company followed was determined by their commitment to creating lasting change, deploy, grow and innovate around a new vision, model and/or strategy and then refine it over a multiyear period.

Success was dependent on many of the factors that we've discussed already in the book: a conscious decision to move beyond efficiency and refocus on growth and innovation; the creation of room for experimentation and separation of new business models from legacy operations, coupled with a new and clear shift in strategy; an appetite to challenge the old assumptions, ask the big questions and reinvent business models; multi-dimensional innovation; determination in taking the long view, sticking to the vision over a long period of time, and persisting through internal resistance and setbacks;

evolving transformation through test and learn, deploying a portfolio of initiatives to drive growth, and constant adaptation of a flexible plan.

Interestingly, the research also revealed a number of key traps from those that attempted transformation but ultimately failed. To paraphrase:

- **The early-wins trap:** calling victory too early, after initial gains in efficiency, and failing to move to 'chapter two' and create lasting change.
- **The efficiency trap:** over-lengthy and enthusiastic cost-cutting and efficiency drives.
- **The legacy trap:** not moving on from legacy assumptions and ways of working.
- **The proportionality trap:** dabbling in change (eg a small-scale series of pilots) rather than properly addressing the scale of the challenge with a fundamental and scaled response.
- **The false certainty trap:** sticking to a rigid transformation plan instead of iterating and adapting continually in response to new knowledge or contexts.
- **The proximity trap:** keeping the new business too close to the legacy business, and thereby undermining its chances of survival.
- **The persistency trap:** giving up too soon and underestimating the amount of time needed to realize results.

Avoiding these traps requires long-term commitment to a vision, and to continuous adaptation, and the right approaches to implementing and embedding lasting change. Irresolute or lackluster executions do not work. Bringing in new ways of working and implementing agile, for example, half-heartedly simply leads to doing waterfall in an agile way, which will not work. Underpinning these traps is the fundamental risk of how easy it is for large organizations to succumb to what Russell Davies (former Director of Strategy at the UK Government Digital Service) has called 'principle drift'. It's always possible, he says, to make the internet fit the business model you understand:

> *... the biggest challenge in Digital Transformation is not in the initial refocusing on a new organizing principle, it's in resisting the steady drift back to the old one... Or, worse, to something that looks like the new one but is, in fact, the old one.*[22]

Digital transformation is not a quick fix. Becoming an agile organization is a fundamental, long-term shift, and so we need to be resolute in our determination, stamina *and* in pursuing our vision.

Minimum viable bureaucracy

Once we have established a growing momentum behind new ways of working, one of the key ways to kill them is to allow a drift back to legacy practices that are unnecessarily additive to bureaucracy and serve only to slow things down. We need to be single-minded in maintaining the focus to stay fast. One of the key battles to wage is against low value time-suck and, in particular, meeting creep.

There are two types of meetings: those that result in action and those that result in a loss of very valuable time. Paul Graham (Silicon Valley startup incubator founder) has drawn a distinction between what he calls a 'maker's schedule' and a 'manager's schedule'. Makers (creative types, writers, programmers, do-ers) prefer to use time in units of at least half a day since you can't complete a project or write or program well in anything less. Managers use time in a different way, typically segmenting time into one-hour slots. Several hours can be blocked off to complete a specific task, but the default is that you change what you do every hour. For those on a manager's schedule, a meeting is simply a matter of finding an open slot and booking it in. But when you're operating on the maker's schedule meetings can be a disaster, since one meeting can blow the whole afternoon by breaking it up into chunks too small to do anything truly productive with. The different types of schedule can work in isolation but problems arise, says Paul, when they meet. And since most bosses operate on the manager's schedule 'they're in a position to make everyone resonate at their frequency if they want to'.[23] Protecting blocks of time for key staff to make progress on initiatives is essential.

Yet meetings are a necessary part of corporate life. People need to get together in order to give and receive updates, make decisions, move projects on so when we do need to have them we should run them in the right way and question the defaults we have. It is, after all, very easy for a growing internally focused, meeting-driven culture to permeate. Noah Brier (co-founder of innovative marketing technology platform Percolate, based in New York) describes how the slow growth and normalization of this behaviour can slow everything down:

> *In the case of meetings what starts as a one-off meeting to discuss something, becomes a weekly meeting for 15 minutes, eventually with more people involved, and eventually you have 15 people spending an hour together without any real sense for what they're talking about or why.*

Add in a layer of creeping formalization, which manifests in the form of evermore convoluted preprepared reports which eventually create a mountain of pre-meeting reading, and you have created a serious brake on agility and actually getting things done. Noah's company has introduced six rules for meetings:[24]

- Do you really need a meeting?
- Meetings should be 15 minutes by default.
- No spectators.
- Have a purpose, state it upfront.
- Make tasks, assign them to people.
- Don't bring computers or phones.

The questioning about whether you need a meeting at all should always happen. Setting a time default that pushes teams to make decisions or to update quickly resets the norms away from the one-hour blocks of time that typically characterize the manager's schedule (and meetings have a habit of growing to fit the time allocated even if that is not needed). Clarity about objectives and outputs seems obvious but can often slip. And screens distract from the task at hand. Sensible, but important.

At LinkedIn they begin by defining the success criteria for the meeting, apply the RAPID framework (making sure the key people are in the room – the recommender (R), where necessary key people who agree with recommendation (A), the performer who executes the decision (P), if appropriate those with key input (I), and the decision-maker (D)), always begin with a silent read through, rely on as few slides as possible, poll the room, and then afterwards distribute and cascade actions, and follow up.[25] These might sound like obvious best practice, but meetings are often run in multiple, unstructured ways in a business (dependent on who is chairing it) which, when the majority of management time may well be spent in this way, can lead to a significant drain on resources.

Amazon have a no PowerPoint rule for meetings. Says Jeff Bezos:

> *The traditional kind of corporate meeting starts with a presentation. Somebody gets up in front of the room and presents with a PowerPoint presentation, some type of slide show. In our view you get very little information, you get bullet points. This is easy for the presenter, but difficult for the audience.*[26]

Instead, a six-page narrative memo is created and attendees sit and read it in silence at the beginning of the meeting. This forces greater clarity, better presentation of data and reasoning, it removes unnecessary questioning, and ensures better decisioning.

It's important to find your own rules and norms for maintaining time efficiency but establishing better defaults and common expectations is a good place to start.

The ultimate goal: achieving organizational 'flow'

When we talk about being 'in the zone', we're usually describing what psychologist Mihály Csíkszentmihályi has termed 'flow', the mental state where we are completely immersed and absorbed, with deeply focused motivation, on a singular task or activity.[27] The concept has been applied to a broad range of contexts including work, education, music, art, sports and gaming.

If becoming a truly agile organization is about transitioning to a highly manoeuvrable state of continuous adaptation and renewal, then we might also say that it is about achieving a state of 'organizational flow'. Csíkszentmihályi has described how achieving flow in the workplace requires clear goals that are combined with more immediate feedback and the right balance between opportunity and capacity.[28]

The ultimate goal of the agile organization is to achieve a highly productive state of organizational flow, the characteristics of which can be described as:

- Complete focus on achieving clearly defined goals, with no distraction.
- Tight feedback loops that enable constant feedback and action.
- Seamless adaptation to continually accommodate improved ways of achieving objectives.
- Exceptional manoeuvrability and fluidity in response to rapidly shifting contexts.
- Restless, constant innovation and experimentation in search of opportunity.
- Deeply ingrained learning culture.
- An energizing, absorbing, invigorating environment in which to work.
- Propelled by a self-perpetuating momentum that never slows.
- The personification of a singular, bold, confident business.

Only when we have achieved a state of organizational flow, can we really say that we have created a truly agile business.

What now?

Go do it!

Notes

1. Sebastian Junger (24 May 2016) *Tribe: On homecoming and belonging*, Twelve, ISBN-10 1455566381 ISBN-13 978-1455566389
2. Christopher Boehm (July 2008) Conscience Origins, Sanctioning Selection, and the Evolution of Altruism in Homo Sapiens, [Online] https://view.officeapps.live.com/op/view.aspx?src=https://media.eurekalert.org/aaasnewsroom/2009/FIL_000000000621/BBS%20FINAL%20July%2019%2008%20FOR%20COLLEAGUES.doc [accessed 25 October 2016]
3. Ellie Lisitsa (24 April 2013) The Four Horsemen: Criticism, Contempt, Defensiveness, and Stonewalling, The Gottman Institute, [Online] https://www.gottman.com/blog/the-four-horsemen-recognizing-criticism-contempt-defensiveness-and-stonewalling/ [accessed 25 October 2016]
4. Caroline Webb (14 January 2016) *How To Have A Good Day: Harness the power of behavioural science to transform your working life*, Macmillan, ASIN B00ZCCX55I
5. John P Kotter (13 November 2012) *Leading Change*, Harvard Business Review Press, ISBN-10 1422186431 ISBN-13 978-1422186435
6. John P Kotter (25 February 2014) *Accelerate: Building strategic agility for a faster-moving world*, Harvard Business Review Press, ISBN-10 1625271743 ISBN-13 978-1625271747
7. B J Fogg (18 June 2016) Tiny Habits Method, tinyhabits.com, [Online] http://tinyhabits.com/ [accessed 25 October 2016]
8. B J Fogg (2016) Behaviour Model, [Online] http://behaviormodel.org/ [accessed 25 October 2016]
9. Charles Duhigg (7 January 2014) *The Power of Habit: Why we do what we do in life and business*, Random House Trade Paperbacks, ISBN-10 081298160X ISBN-13 978-0812981605
10. David T Neal, Wendy Wood and Jeffrey M Quinn (August 2006) Habits – A Repeat Performance, Research Gate, [Online] http://www.researchgate.net/publication/252798940_HabitsA_Repeat_Performance [accessed 25 October 2016]
11. Charles Duhigg, Need to Break a Bad Habit?, charlesduhigg.com, [Online] http://charlesduhigg.com/need-to-break-a-bad-habit/ [accessed 25 October 2016]

12 Charles Duhigg, April 2012, The Right Habits, Lifehacker.com http://lifehacker.com/5896846/the-right-habits [accessed 25 October 2016]

13 Charles Duhigg (28 April 2012) How 'Keystone Habits' Transformed a Corporation, Huffington Post, [Online] http://www.huffingtonpost.com/charles-duhigg/the-power-of-habit_b_1304550.html [accessed 25 October 2016]

14 Scott Adams (8 April 2014) *How To Fail at Almost Everything and Still Win Big: Kind of the story of my life*, Brilliance Audio, ISBN-10 1491518855 ISBN-13 978-1491518854

15 Shirlaws, TFK FAQ: Compass from Shirlaws, Shirlaws, [Online] http://www.shirlawscompass.com/tfkfaq [accessed 25 October 2016]

16 Clive Hyland (27 February 2013) *Connect: Through THINK FEEL KNOW*, Anoma Press Ltd, ASIN B00BMJTTJG

17 Stewart Brand (16 March 2000) *Clock of the Long Now: Time and responsibility – the ideas behind the world's slowest computer*, Basic Books, ISBN-10 465007805 ISBN-13 978-0465007806

18 Gartner newsroom (14 February 2012) Gartner Says Adopting a Pace-Layered Application Strategy Can Accelerate Innovation, Gartner, [Online] http://www.gartner.com/newsroom/id/1923014 [accessed 25 October 2016]

19 Ronald A Heifetz, Martin Linsky and Alexander Grashow (1 April 2009) *Practice of Adaptive Leadership: Tools and tactics for changing your organization and the world: A fieldbook for practitioners*, Harvard Business School Press, ISBN-10 1422105768 ISBN-13 978-1422105764

20 Dr Ronald Heifetz (14 August 2011) Adaptive vs Technical – Dr. Ronald Heifetz, YouTube, [Online] https://www.youtube.com/watch?v=UwWylIUIvmo [accessed 25 October 2016]

21 B Martin Reeves, Kaelin Goulet, Gideon Walter and Michael Shanahan (21 October 2013) Why Transformation Needs a Second Chapter Lean, but Not Yet Mean, Boston Consulting Group, Perspectives, [Online] https://www.bcgperspectives.com/content/articles/transformation_growth_why_transformation_needs_second_chapter_lean_not_yet_mean/ [accessed 25 October 2016]

22 Russell Davies, January 2015 Principle Drift, Russell Davies http://russell-davies.typepad.com/planning/2015/01/principledrift.html [accessed 25 October 2016]

23 Paul Graham (July 2009) Maker's Schedule, Manager's Schedule, Paul Graham.com, [Online] http://www.paulgraham.com/makersschedule.html [accessed 25 October 2016]

24 Noah Brier (9 June 2014) CULTURE The 6 Meeting Rules of Percolate, Percolate, [Online] https://blog.percolate.com/2014/06/6-meeting-rules-of-percolate/ [accessed 25 October 2016]

25 Brian Rumao (9 March 2015) How LinkedIn Execs Run Meetings, Linkedin.com, [Online] https://www.linkedin.com/pulse/how-linkedin-execs-run-meetings-brian-rumao [accessed 25 October 2016]

26 Brad Porter, September 22, 2015, The Beauty of Amazon's 6-Pager, Linkedin.com, [Online] https://www.linkedin.com/pulse/beauty-amazons-6-pager-brad-porter [accessed 25 October 2016]

27 Mihály Csíkszentmihályi (1 August 2002) *Flow: The psychology of happiness: The classic work on how to achieve happiness*, Rider, ISBN-10 712657592 ISBN-13 978-0712657594

28 Mihály Csíkszentmihályi (5 January 2004) *Good Business: Leadership, flow and the making of meaning*, Hodder Paperbacks, ISBN-10 340739738 ISBN-13 978-0340739730

INDEX

Note: Chapter notes and 'stories from the frontline' are indexed as such. Page numbers in *italics* indicate Figures or Tables.

CPSIA information can be obtained
at www.ICGtesting.com
Printed in the USA
BVHW04s0734100818
524034BV00026B/107/P

9 780749 480394